Northwest Vista College
Learning Resource Center
3535 North Ellison Drive
San Antonio, Texas 78251

HQ
75.12
.C67

NORTHWEST VISTA COLLEGE

Are we thinking straight?

34009001166660

New Approaches in Sociology
Studies in Social Inequality, Social Change, and Social Justice

Edited by
Nancy A. Naples
University of Connecticut

A Routledge Series

New Approaches in Sociology
Studies in Social Inequality, Social Change, and Social Justice
Nancy A. Naples, *General Editor*

The Social Organization of Policy
An Institutional Ethnography of UN Forest Deliberations
Lauren E. Eastwood

The Struggle over Gay, Lesbian, and Bisexual Rights
Facing Off in Cincinnati
Kimberly B. Dugan

Parenting for the State
An Ethnographic Analysis of Non-Profit Foster Care
Teresa Toguchi Swartz

Talking Back to Psychiatry
The Psychiatric Consumer/Survivor/Ex-Patient Movement
Linda J. Morrison

Contextualizing Homelessness
Critical Theory, Homelessness, and Federal Policy Addressing the Homeless
Ken Kyle

Linking Activism
Ecology, Social Justice, and Education for Social Change
Morgan Gardner

The Everyday Lives of Sex Workers in the Netherlands
Katherine Gregory

Striving and Surviving
A Daily Life Analysis of Honduran Transnational Families
Leah Schmalzbauer

Unequal Partnerships
Beyond the Rhetoric of Philanthropic Collaboration
Ira Silver

Domestic Democracy
At Home in South Africa
Jennifer Natalie Fish

Praxis and Politics
Knowledge Production in Social Movements
Janet M. Conway

The Suppression of Dissent
How the State and Mass Media Squelch USAmerican Social Movements
Jules Boykoff

Are We Thinking Straight?
The Politics of Straightness in a Lesbian and Gay Social Movement Organization
Daniel K. Cortese

Are We Thinking Straight?
The Politics of Straightness in a Lesbian and Gay Social Movement Organization

Daniel K. Cortese

Routledge
New York & London

Published in 2006 by
Routledge
Taylor & Francis Group
270 Madison Avenue
New York, NY 10016

Published in Great Britain by
Routledge
Taylor & Francis Group
2 Park Square
Milton Park, Abingdon
Oxon OX14 4RN

© 2006 by Taylor & Francis Group, LLC
Routledge is an imprint of Taylor & Francis Group

Printed in the United States of America on acid-free paper
10 9 8 7 6 5 4 3 2 1

International Standard Book Number-10: 0-415-97701-0 (Hardcover)
International Standard Book Number-13: 978-0-415-97701-2 (Hardcover)
Library of Congress Card Number 2005029589

No part of this book may be reprinted, reproduced, transmitted, or utilized in any form by any electronic, mechanical, or other means, now known or hereafter invented, including photocopying, microfilming, and recording, or in any information storage or retrieval system, without written permission from the publishers.

Trademark Notice: Product or corporate names may be trademarks or registered trademarks, and are used only for identification and explanation without intent to infringe.

Library of Congress Cataloging-in-Publication Data

Cortese, Daniel K.
   Are we thinking straight? : the politics of straightness in a lesbian and gay social movement organization / Daniel K. Cortese.
      p. cm. -- (New approaches in sociology)
   ISBN 0-415-97701-0
   1. Straight and Gay Alliance. 2. Homosexuality--United States--Societies, etc. 3. Gay-straight alliances in schools--United States. 4. Social action--United States. 5. Gays--United States--Identity. 6. Gay rights--United States. 7. Organizational sociology. I. Title. II. Series.

HQ75.12.C67 2006
306.76'60973--dc22
                                                  2005029589

Taylor & Francis Group
is the Academic Division of Informa plc.

Visit the Taylor & Francis Web site at
http://www.taylorandfrancis.com

and the Routledge Web site at
http://www.routledge-ny.com

This book is dedicated to those who selflessly commit their lives to serve others, particularly the SAGA activists who shared with me their time and their knowledge.

And to Judith Cortese, who waited twenty-nine years to say four little words:
"My son, the Doctor!"
I did it, ma!

Contents

List of Figures — ix

List of Tables — xi

Acknowledgments — xiii

Chapter One
Introduction — 1

Chapter Two
Theory and Research Methods — 15

Chapter Three
Organizational Diversity in SAGA — 57

Chapter Four
God Is on Our Side: The Mission of SAGA — 87

Chapter Five
No Joking About the "S" in SAGA: "Straight" Strategy — 115

Chapter Six
Political Environments Shape Identity Deployment — 141

Chapter Seven
Straight Ahead and Moving Forward — 173

Appendix A — 183

Appendix B	187
Appendix C	189
Appendix D	191
Notes	193
References	195
Index	203

List of Figures

Figure 1:	Location of SAGA in Social Movement Industries	31
Figure 2:	SAGA-Based Sociopolitical Regions of the United States	37
Figure 3:	Breakdown of Sexual Identity of Research Participants	47
Figure 4:	SAGA National Board of Directors; By Race, Gender, and Sexuality	59
Figure 5:	SAGA National Staff Members; By Race, Gender, and Sexuality	59

List of Tables

Table 1:	Interview Sample Demographics	44
Table 2:	Participant Demographics by Years a SAGA Board Member	46
Table 3:	Participant Demographics by Age	46
Table 4:	Participant Demographics by Gender	46
Table 5:	Participant Demographics by Sexuality	46
Table 6:	Participant Demographics by Race	47
Table 7:	Participant Demographics by Income Level	48
Table 8:	Participant Demographics by Political Party Affiliation	48
Table 9:	Participant Demographics by Political Ideology	49
Table 10:	Organizational Diversity of SAGA National	58

Acknowledgments

There are so many people who helped make this book possible by helping me see my lifelong goal through to the end. I wish I could thank them all by name, but it is impossible to list them all in this limited space. To those who I am unable to individually thank in these pages, including those who are with us only in spirit, know that you are dear to my heart!

I first thank *la mia famiglia* for their love, support, and most of all, patience through this arduous journey. I adoringly thank my life-partner Abelardo González for his unwavering love and support throughout the entire research and writing process. He saw me through the project from start to finish, and lovingly nurtured me throughout the laughter and the tears. I thank him for helping care for my twenty-year-old cat Lemon as I traveled extensively for this research, which allowed her to be with us against all the odds. I also wish to thank my mother Judy who continues to give me the strength and love to see my goals through. I love and appreciate my godmother Barbara Colao for opening up her home during my research process and excitedly joining me in Austin for my graduation. I also extend love to my sister Kerryann Billman, her husband Jeffrey, my nephew and godson Stephen Caputo, my nephew Justin, and my niece Crystal for their blessings. I hope this book is a testament to my family that through the love of God shining through *la nostra famiglia*, and a lot of dedicated work, all things are possible and all dreams are attainable.

I thank my dissertation co-chairs Anne Kane and Michael Young who guided me from the project's inception to its completion, as well as thank my committee members Christopher Ellison, Sharmila Rudrappa, Yolanda Padilla, and Gloria González-López for their helpful feedback. Included in my gratitude is this series editor Nancy Naples who, along with my colleagues outside of the University of Texas such as Joshua Gamson, Julie Dowling, Mary Bernstein, Arlene Stein, and Jodi O'Brien helped me shape my thoughts into cogent arguments and provided valuable feedback in the revision process.

I am also indebted to the entire Parma family who are my "extended" Texas-sized family. Throughout my graduate training, Bob and Sue Parma welcomed me into their home with so much love, especially when I was alone and unable to visit my mom and sister in New York during the holidays. I also thank Pam Parma and her husband Jeff Kelly who invited me into their home during my dissertation revision process and lovingly made sure that I was well taken care of during my stay. And, who can forget my dearest friend Christine Parma who met me fresh out of high school and grew with me throughout my college career? Christine always knew the right ways to break me away from Austin and my work. Christine, I love you so much!

I thank Fr. Rick Wilkinson and Sr. Ann Francis Monedero for being my spiritual mentors through the final stages of research and writing. As tremendous allies, they helped Abelardo and I develop a closer relationship with God as both a couple and individuals. Their prayers helped us both garner the spiritual strength to finish this project with grace and love.

And, most of all, I thank the Holy Trinity (God, Jesus Christ, and the Holy Spirit) for blessing me with many gifts and talents, and for sending down angels to surround me with love. I pray that my sacrifices and hard work here on Earth pleases You in Heaven.

Chapter One
Introduction

It seems that this book topic elicits quite a bit of interest because it explores how a particular lesbian and gay organization uses *heterosexuality* as a social movement tool in order to garner political successes. At functions, I am often asked the question, "So, what is your research about?" I nonchalantly respond: "Oh, I study straight people in gay and lesbian organizations." Very rarely does the conversation end there. Quizzical faces, pensive stares, or polite nods of agreement typically force me to explain myself further: "Straight people sometimes join gay and lesbian organizations. They identify with the cause, but are not gay themselves. And, in the organization that I am studying, they actually *use* a visible straight identity to reach their goals. So, what I wanted to know was, what are the benefits, and the potential costs, to following this strategy? But I also wondered, is this strategy applied similarly throughout the organization in the United States?" Before long, social scientists discuss how my research adds to theory of how organizations and movements interact. And, activists are fascinated as to why the organization does not self-destruct because of competing identities, or how an ally can be a useful social movement tool. Relishing the opportunity to discuss my work, I begin my explanation by challenging many of the common assumptions that many of us hold regarding sexuality, as well as gay and lesbian movement organizing.

First, Western culture and its social structure enforce and reinforce heterosexuality as the expected social norm (i.e., heteronormative). People that see themselves as sharing the common social experience of transgressing the heteronormative social boundaries (i.e., queer people, gay, lesbian, etc.) will typically consider themselves as distinct (at least in terms of sexuality) from heterosexual people. And, if non-heterosexual people attend organizations whose goals are to challenge the heteronormative social institutions (queer political organizations), they will most likely expect members to also be non-heterosexual. And, they likewise, might expect that these organizations will reflect the socially defined identity boundaries between non-heterosexual and heterosexual, or else they run the risk of losing their organizational identity. In other words, lesbian and gay people expect the organizations that they created to reflect their shared identity.

Many gay activists, such as myself, almost take it for granted that our organizations will reflect the coalition of non-normative sexual and gender expressions, which are, in common parlance, referred to as lesbian, gay, bisexual, and transgender (LGBT). We, almost unconsciously, believe that our movement will be "queer" like us. We assume that all of the participants in our movement will understand our unique issues, needs, and desires through the experiences from the "first person." And, many of us presuppose that the strategies we devise will build upon our shared history of gay liberation, which in some way or another will embrace the idea that "we're here, we're queer," and the straight people in this world must eventually "get used to it." But what happens when the obvious assumptions no longer ring true? What happens when straight people identify with the LGBT movement and join it in order to challenge the heteronormative social institutions that, as straight people, will ultimately benefit from? Would our queer organizations and possibly our collective identity as queer self-destruct because of the inclusion of straight people into our group? Would our organizations and identities become meaningless?

Straight and Gay Alliance[1] (SAGA) is an organization that creates a nexus of the lesbian, gay, bisexual, and transgender (LGBT) and the safe schools social movements. Unlike other organizations working specifically on LGBT issues, SAGA proudly includes straight people in both the name of the organization, as well as the general leadership and membership. At almost every opportunity, SAGA accentuates the fact that straight people share in the organizational mission to protect LGBT youth from harassment in schools as a political strategy to successfully achieve its mission. SAGA has had remarkable success in achieving its political goals considering that only ten years ago, discussing issues of sexuality outside of the realm of heterosexual biological sexual necessities was the "third-rail" of politics. If any open discussion with policymakers about LGBT issues in school could be considered an organizational success, then SAGA has found at the end of the (LGBT) rainbow, a (straight) pot of gold.

This book explores the strategies of this success, and addresses two specific research questions: First, why would an LGBT organization use a straight identity as a tool by which to effectively achieve their political goals? Second, would the local politics of particular regions of the United States affect the deployment of a straight identity?

Introduction

I learned from a collection of over sixty hours of interviews with thirty SAGA activists in five United States cities, and analyzing over nine hundred pages of interview transcripts, that the benefits of deploying a straight identity in the safe schools movement outweigh the political costs of "putting on" a straight face to the public. The LGBT SAGA activists I spoke with overwhelmingly agreed that, at times, it was necessary to openly demonstrate to school administrators, policy makers, and the public at large that straight people can be intimate allies with the LGBT movement and must work together in one organization to achieve their shared goals. Furthermore, I learned that these strategies vary according to geography. In more conservative areas of the United States, the SAGA activists rely more on the visibility of straight people for political legitimacy than in more liberal areas, where they focus more on the straight allies in the organization as a way to help broaden their fundraising networks.

BRINGING THEM IN: ARE WE THINKING STRAIGHT?

The main title phrase of my book, *Are We Thinking Straight,* is an intentional pun meant to evoke several possible meanings. The Merriam-Webster Dictionary On-Line[2] defines the word "straight" extensively; in the play on words in my title, I refer specifically to a subset of the Merriam-Webster definition:

> . . . **2a**: lying along or holding to a direct or proper course or method [a *straight* thinker] . . . **3b**: properly ordered or arranged . . . [set us *straight* on that issue]; *also: Correct* [get the facts *straight*] . . . **3g**: exhibiting no deviation from what is established or accepted as usual, normal, or proper: *Conventional* . . . **5h** *Heterosexual*

SAGA both is and is not thinking "straight." By including straight people in their LGBT organization, SAGA activists are significantly deviating in strategy from what is accepted as usual, normal, or even proper for LGBT movements. However, SAGA is not really thinking as if they were straight (heterosexual) rather than queer; these sexual identity boundaries remain visible in both the organization and the identity strategies employed by SAGA.

How could an LGBT organization use a straight identity as one tool by which to effectively achieve their political goals? In order to address this question, I look to the concept of "identity deployment" in social movement theory as developed by sociologist Mary Bernstein (1997). In her study on the historical study of identity and LGBT movement strategies, Bernstein (1997) finds that lesbians and gays in the United States have, in their challenge to the heteronormative social structure, strategically deployed identity to either accentuate their difference from or similarities to straight people.

Although only inferred in her 1997 study, the identity strategies employed continue to use an "us-versus-them" definition of identity boundaries, where the LGBT people are deploying identities to a nebulous "other" comprised of heterosexuals, as well as to the normative expectations of heterosexuality. In other words, the strategies that the organizations fighting for LGBT rights use are conceptualized as one entity with a shared (although "tenuous," as she notes in her 2002 research) collective identity of "lesbian-and-gay" which is juxtaposed to the normative "straight" identity, regardless of the different political interests that may exist amongst lesbians and gays. In her theory of identity deployment, straight people are conceptualized as having no place in the organizations that queer people create, and certainly do not identify with the LGBT identity.

SAGA operates within the broader LGBT movement, and yet includes straight people as active and vital members of the organization. Furthermore, SAGA deploys sexualized identities strategically in a similar process as Bernstein (1997) finds in her study of the lesbian and gay movement. But there is one major difference between the identity strategies of SAGA and what Bernstein finds in her research: SAGA is strategically deploying a *straight* identity, rather than queer identities, in order to achieve its political goals. Why *this* strategy in particular? And, does it work reasonably well? Are there any potential pitfalls? These perplexing questions cannot be answered by the current literature on identity and social movements, and therefore are at the foundation of my research project.

But, if straight people join an LGBT organization, would it not be true that the organization and its members would lose their "queer" identity because its boundaries are blurred? Joshua Gamson (1995, 1997a, 1997b) explored the issue of identity boundary maintenance in LGBT movements. In his research on queer movements, Joshua Gamson (1995) answers why queer movements, whose goal was to eradicate identity boundaries, did not "self-destruct" in the process of deconstructing identity boundaries. Even as queer activists sought to weaken the boundaries based on gender, sexuality, or race by rejecting identity labels, they ended up re-creating new boundaries of "us" and "them" in the movement by excluding some as queer and not others. Gamson's theory does not specifically address the issue of identity particular to SAGA. However, we can use his theory on identity deconstruction and boundary maintenance to explain why SAGA does not self-destruct with the inclusion of straight people into the movement. This is despite the fact that these two identities were created in opposition to each other in order to challenge the normative expectations of being straight.

As members of SAGA, LGBT and straight activists continue to maintain the sexual identity boundaries within the organization by calling the straight members "allies," as opposed to more inclusionary terms like "honorary gay people" and the like. Colloquially, queer people consider straight people an "ally" because they, by definition, can never truly become a part of the "queer" identity. Straight people take on this "ally" identity while simultaneously existing within an LGBT organization as a member. This is also an important reconceptualization of the sociological term "ally" because it suggests that in SAGA's case, an "ally" can not only be a member of the organization furthering LGBT interests and goals, but also a supporter of LGBT causes who may or may not be members of the organization. Furthermore, even though the activists maintain that the message of school safety for LGBT youth transcends sexuality differences, they continue to profess that their sexual identities are obviously different in how they are perceived by U.S. society. To my knowledge, no research on LGBT movements has yet to consider the political benefits and possible ramifications of this strategic deployment of a straight identity. To that end, this book directly fills this lacuna in the research on identity and social movements.

Would the local politics of particular regions of the United States have an effect on whether or not activists rely upon the deployment of a straight identity? As the research on political ecology as explored by Debra Minkoff (1993, 1997, 1999) posits, the sociopolitical environments in which social movement organizations operate have an effect on movement trajectories. In Minkoff's studies, she measures organizational success primarily on whether or not it remains in existence, and not on its ability to achieve its stated goals while it existed. Likewise, Bernstein's (1997) research on United States LGBT movements specifically, demonstrates that the deployment of identity strategies also vary based on political region. In order to fully understand these important issues, my findings build upon the concepts and theories introduced in both Minkoff's and Bernstein's research.

In vast swaths of the United States—"Red" and "Blue" states alike—SAGA's mission to bring about an open and educated discussion about LGBT safety in schools remains a deadly political "third rail" that administrators and the public at large will not touch without serious trepidation about the repercussions. However, this is especially true in the more conservative regions of the United States. Yet, in the more liberal areas, SAGA finds less of a need to accentuate a straight identity for political legitimacy, but use straight allies as a source of building fundraising and membership networks. The theories developed from previous research cannot explain the different strategies that vary by region. Therefore, I address this lacuna in the political sociological research on social movement organizations by building on identity deployment and political ecology theories in my study of straight people in LGBT movement organizations.

What makes this research project different from other studies on the inclusion of political "allies," such as whites in the black civil rights movements or men in the feminist movements, into their specific organizations? Some scholars might argue that the identity deployment strategy of SAGA has historical precedent; white people helped found the NAACP (Morris 1984) and were active in the 1960s civil rights movement (McAdam 1988), and men assisted women achieve suffrage and other equal rights (Buechler 1990), and so on. My book is different from other social movement and political sociology research in a number of ways, one of which is specific to the research on LGBT movements. As I argued earlier in the chapter, it conceptualizes the inclusion of identities that are *different* from the collective identity of the organizational members, and uses it as a particular identity deployment strategy.

A second difference from other studies on the inclusion of allies in movements is in regards to the LGBT identity itself. For example, let us consider the social identity category of "woman." Although Patricia Hill Collins (1990) notes that black women and white women experience gender differently based on their race, I argue that the identity category of "woman" is still a relatively stable and culturally understood concept. Women, regardless of race, class, nationality, or other categories share a common base identity of "woman." All women can potentially unite as being a woman, so long as all members of the identity recognize differences based on other identity categories. We, for the most part, can agree on what the cultural meaning of "woman" is, and so all women have the potential to unite under this shared cultural meaning.

However, the identity of "LGBT" or "queer" is actually a coalition of separate identities that also vary based on differences from other social categories, specifically gender. There is no unified cultural understanding of LGBT, or even queer, because its members are really separate identities with very different histories of what it means to be "queer." For example, lesbians have different social experiences than gay men. In the 1980s and 1990s, AIDS affected gays and lesbians differently. (Rom 2000; Schroedel and Fiber 2000) Gay men and their sexual partners died in large numbers, while lesbians did not similarly contract HIV in as great a percentage (Schroedel and Fiber 2000). Lesbians joined AIDS movement organizations, but some experienced ambivalence in their participation in reaction to the sexism experienced from gay men, and the relevance to AIDS in the lives and health of lesbians (Rom 2000; Schroedel and Fiber 2000; Whittier 1995). Another difference in political issues between lesbians and gays is the issue of breast cancer (Plumb 2000; Schroedel and Fiber 2000). This issue, although salient to the lives of lesbians, has almost no direct effect on the health lives of gay men.

The lesbian and gay movement is a quintessential identity-based movement (Melucci 1989) that is really comprised of separate sexualized gender identities of lesbian and gay united under one "tenuous coalition of identities" (Bernstein 2002) that have different social meanings and histories. This fragile coalition is held together by a boundary that defines itself as different from what is socially acceptable as normative; in this instance, heterosexuality. However, this definition also would include bisexuals and transgenders under a uniting category of "queer" or LGBT. Although who may self-identify (or, even be identified by others) as "homosexual" may not always be the same across time periods (Chauncey 1989, 1994) or nationality (Cantú 1999), the boundary of the LGBT identity in the West today is defined as distinct from the normative definition of sexuality, that being heterosexuality.

Lesbians and gay men may be able to unify under the identity of being queer, but there is evidence of boundary negotiation and the exclusion of bisexuals in the identity who are seen by lesbians and gays as fence-sitting (Rust 1995). Transgenders are sometimes viewed by lesbian and gay people as not exhibiting a same-sex desire, and therefore do not belong in the fight for lesbian and gay equality (J. Gamson 1997a). So, the LGBT identity is a tenuous coalition of identities that, although similar to other identity categories based on gender or race, are still relatively unique to be conceptualized differently from the formation of other identity categories. Therefore, the inclusion of straight allies within a movement might have historical similarities, but is significantly different from other research because of the tenuous and fragile coalition of identities themselves. Including straight people into the identity fold makes this union all the more unusual and important to study.

A third reason why my book is different from other research that conceptualizes the inclusion of allies in social movements is specific to the social assumptions of homosexuality as a choice. As I learned by speaking with the straight activists, particularly the men, their heterosexuality is questioned upon joining SAGA. It is assumed that if they join SAGA, they must really be gay themselves. However, as one example, the research on the American civil rights movement (e.g., Morris 1984, McAdam 1988) have not remarked that the race of white people who join the African

American civil rights movement organization is assumed to be black; they are recognized as white. Likewise, if a man joins a feminist organization, his biological sex is not going to be questioned as really female. However, as a demonstration of the interconnection between sexism and homophobia, the feminist men often experiences questions of his sexuality and his masculinity (Kimmel 1996). Although there may be some similarities with regards to the feminist movement, the experiences of the straight people in SAGA to consistently defend their straight sexual identity to the public make this project different from previous research.

THE ORIGINS OF SAGA

Very few major organizations originated so late in the LGBT equal rights movement, or work on both the national and local levels in order to effect social change. This makes SAGA even more unusual in comparison to other LGBT social movement organizations. The seeds of SAGA began in the late 1980s in the northeastern United States as a support group for gay and lesbian teachers in private schools. Originally called GLAT[3] (Gay and Lesbian Association of Teachers), the group's goals were two-fold: 1) provide support for gay and lesbian teachers, and 2) transform the culture of the education system positively for gay and lesbian teachers and youth. Although the organizational mission always welcomed the assistance of straight people in achieving the political goals, in its earliest stages, the organization was primarily an LGBT support group for teachers who sought school safety from homophobia for themselves, as well as their students.

In the mid-1990s, the organization moved its headquarters closer to the political epicenter of Washington, D.C. in order to support the number of local-level GLAT organizations (called chapters) springing up across the country. Also at this time, GLAT changed its name to Straight and Gay Alliance (SAGA), a move that now included straight people within the mission, and the name, in what was hitherto an avowedly LGBT organization. No longer was the organization to be an LGBT support group for teachers; its mission was to actively include straight people, who were primarily teachers and parents of LGBT students, into the mission and activate social changes in the school system to protect students and teachers from violence and homophobia. This transformation from GLAT to SAGA, and its inclusion of straight people, makes SAGA a unique organization within the LGBT social movement, and one of the first LGBT organizations to recognize the potential of including straight people for strategic purposes.

Shortly after this name change, a professional board of directors was created to manage the future growth and stability of SAGA, and a skeletal staff was hired to perform the administrative tasks. Joshua David, one of the original founders of SAGA and one of the primary leaders of SAGA, elucidated further the structure of the board. In early 2003, shortly before my research began, the structure of the national board changed again from its original representative model (where one or two representatives from different regions sat on the executive board) into a business model (where members are elected to the board based on their particular movement expertise). In this model, diversity is ensured structurally, as a certain number of youth, straight people, and racial/ethnic minorities must be represented on the board (Interview with Joshua David, SAGA National).

During my interview with Joshua David, I asked him about these name and structural changes and what they meant to the mission of SAGA. In his response, Joshua stressed, "SAGA's mission has *never* changed. We've always been about seeking change in schools." The mission always centered on school safety, but the methods to achieve this goal had transformed, as explained earlier. Joshua continues on, explaining the rationale for the name change:

> We found the name was scaring away a lot of people who cared a lot about what we were doing. So, we decided to come up with a name that spoke about more of what we do . . . We grew out of teachers like me, but we never saw ourselves as a group *just* for teachers. We saw ourselves as a group that is about changing the schools.

In this quote, it is clear that changing the name from GLAT to SAGA was a strategic decision to garner more supporters who shared in the mission of SAGA, but were frightened away by the word "teacher." Joshua suggests that people were scared away because the activists interested in the organization may not have been involved in the education system and, therefore, felt that they were not necessarily welcomed as members. The name change, therefore, was less of a philosophic change, but a strategy to help broaden the membership base (Interview with Joshua David, SAGA National).

In its earliest forms, SAGA did not include highly visible straight people into its strategy or name, but welcomed straight teachers into the fold as support. This move would eventually evolve the organization into including more and more straight people into the organization to assist chapters and the national organization to make inroads into the conservative institution of public education. Although in 2003 the organization was comprised mostly of LGBT people, approximately thirteen percent of the National board comprises of straight people. This makes SAGA unique in both the safe schools and the LGBT movement organizations (see Figure 1 and Figure 4 in Chapter Two).

THE ORGANIZATIONAL STRUCTURE OF SAGA

SAGA is modeled along what sociologists call a federated organizational structure (McCarthy and Zald 1977; Rohlinger 2002). SAGA has a "parent" organization (heretofore referred as SAGA National) headquartered near Washington, D.C. that creates and amends, if necessary, the general organizational mission of SAGA. Under the guidance and name of SAGA National, there are local-level chapter affiliations that implement this mission in a specified geographical jurisdiction (i.e., a state, county, city, or municipality). These chapters are semi-autonomous, meaning that as long as the chapter continues to adequately meet the goals of the organizational mission, National does not have the authority to oust its local leadership, sanction the local organization for decisions it feels may be poorly executed, or regulate the implementation of SAGA's mission on local levels. However, if a chapter strays too far from the mission statement of SAGA, such as fighting for gay marriage instead of school safety, the organizational rules state that National can prohibit the chapter from using SAGA's name. But, even in cases of publicized scandals regarding a chapter, which have happened in the past, the structure of SAGA prohibits SAGA National from overriding the actions of the local chapters as long as the chapter did not stray from the organizational mission at the time of the issue.

SAGA typically starts a chapter when at least three people within a particular geographical area express an interest in founding a chapter. Chapter names are derived from combining the name of the parent organization and the geographic region in which it is formed and/or responsible. An example would be SAGA Tallahassee[4], where the national organization's name is positioned first in the name as evidence of its chapter affiliation, and then followed by the name of the specific geographical territory where the chapter will focus all of its efforts of fulfilling the national organization's mission statement (the city of Tallahassee). With the assistance of SAGA National, each chapter decides the boundaries of the particular geographical region for which it will be responsible. Under the guidance of SAGA National, the chapter conducts a "needs assessment" survey of the local school system to define the tangible political goals of the organization over the next several years. Once a group forms, defines the boundary of the chapter, and conducts a needs assessment, it is deemed an "official chartered chapter of SAGA" in a process called "accreditation" (SAGA 1997). Currently, chapters must be approved for re-accreditation every three years.

THE STRAIGHT AND NARROW

Many readers of this book will read the words of the activists and recognize that there are gendered, racial, or class notions subsumed under the "straight identity." Analyzing this was not the framework of this research project. Although I proposed a study that would explicate this phenomenon further, and applied to monetary granting agencies that support sexuality and social scientific research, my proposals were ultimately passed over for whatever reasons. Given these financial and organizational limitations, I cannot elucidate these issues in great detail here in this book. Perhaps in the near future I, or other scholars, will secure the necessary financial and institutional support to conduct the critical research and draw meaningful analyses and conclusions of the gendered, racial, and class semiotics in creating a particular straight identity in order to maximize political success.

When conducting qualitative or feminist methodologies, it is important to note that the discourse between interviewer and participant requires a mutual and shared understanding of symbols and meanings (See, for example, Naples 2003 and Ezzy 2002). In other words, when I asked activists about the benefits and weaknesses of straight people in an organization in order to answer my research question on identity deployment strategies, we must agree on how to define "straight." This is typically done in the context of a dialogue and not explicitly stated. However, in our interviews there are shared agreements on what is defined as "straight" and what is "gay," which often become obvious as our discussions develop. I learn quickly that they identify as gay or straight based on the anatomical sex of the person or persons with whom they have intimate sexual relations and/or feelings. Only a few activists were vague on these definitions as first noted in the interview questionnaire. An example is Edit Aloo, who states that she "lives in a sexual ocean & swims where I please." No matter what the answer given in the questionnaire, we discussed their answers on the audiotape to ensure that we were in agreement on definitions.

Scholars who study sexuality, such as Lionel Cantú (1999), may find that study participants do not identify with the cultural construction and meanings attributed to sexual behavior. So, men who have sex with men may identify as "straight," even though scholars using the sexuality rubric of Kinsey, Pomeroy, and Martin (1948) would say these men are gay or bisexual. Modern scholars may choose other terminology, such as "men who have sex with men" (MSM), to rectify the difference in cultural definitions of sexual activity in relationship to identity (Cantú 1999). In SAGA, this was not a major issue for the study participants.

The goal of this book is not to engage in semiotic debates of heterosexuality, as this was not an objective in the research questions or methodological framework. However, it should be noted that the "straight identity" appears constructed around a heteronormative conceptualization of sexuality, as well as particular notions of gender, race, and class. Since part of the role of the qualitative sociologist is to also analyze and interpret the meanings of what *isn't* being said in the interviews, much of how activists construct the ideal "straight" is also found in what they say implicitly as well.

For example, in Chapter Five, I explore how SAGA activists envision the strengths and weaknesses of straight people in the organization. When activists from the area of Piedmont in the Northeast talk about the benefits of a straight member, their words tend to echo the characteristics of Judy Eberhardt, a straight mother and co-chair of SAGA Piedmont. As they discuss the strengths of a "parent," many of the SAGA Piedmont activists allude to the idea that their construction of what a successful activist parent is based on how well they perceive Judy Eberhardt. Similarly, when Adam Lieberman talks about how Greg Adler can use his straightness as an asset, the conceptualization is gendered in that he is not necessarily characterized by his status of "parent" as much as him being a straight male and, perhaps, his status of "school teacher."

Clearly there are both tacit and overt gendered assumptions of straightness in play here, which merit further investigation by social science scholars and activists. What I note is that by and large, this was a tacit assumption that is beyond the scope of this book due to data limitations, and it is impossible to comment very deeply on this gendered construction. Doing so would be unscientific conjecture and a disservice to the reader. However, the clearer examples of gendered patterns are addressed to the best of my abilities when appropriate.

ORGANIZATION OF THE BOOK

This book is organized so that the data explained in each chapter build upon each other until the final conclusion in Chapter Seven. I begin Chapter Two introducing the pertinent social movement literatures in political science, sociology, and queer studies that consider identity strategies in social movements. I then discuss my research methodology and the demographics of the activists, followed by a brief explanation of some of the more memorable problems that arose during my fieldwork.

In Chapter Three, I discuss the organizational diversity of SAGA. I find that although the organization builds its mission on inclusiveness and diversity, middle-class white gay men dominate the SAGA chapters. I describe the ways in which the activists I spoke with tried to address this issue of diversity, and the solutions they have implemented with very little success. I also explore how straight activists understand their heterosexual privilege by analyzing the ways in which they attempt to shed their privilege when joining SAGA, while simultaneously expected by the organization to deploy it as an identity strategy. I find that the shedding of heterosexual privilege helps the collective identity of the LGBT organization avoid the potential pitfall of self-destructing due to the inclusion of straight people into the LGBT identity coalition.

Chapter Four delves deeper into the history of SAGA by exploring the SAGA's organizational mission in depth. I find that SAGA's mission is perhaps shaped by the Christian beliefs of one of the founders, Joshua David. With the data I collected, I question the theoretical conceptualization of framing strategies as diametrically opposed in the "culture war" debates, where moral frames primarily utilized by religious right movements, and a more secular injustice frame used by liberal left movements. I find that SAGA situates the mission in both moral *and* injustice frames, which makes SAGA unique in the LGBT social movement industry that typically relies heavily on an injustice frame in its political challenges (see Cain 2000).

Chapter Five explores the benefits and costs of deploying straight identities in an LGBT organization. I find that SAGA activists generally believe straight people are a political necessity in order for SAGA to achieve its political goals, but that their greatest strength of *not* being gay or lesbian is also their greatest weakness because they do not share the experiences by members of an LGBT identity. I also find that despite the ambivalence expressed by LGBT activists of straight people joining SAGA, the participants continue to use the privileges that straight people have in our society to the benefit of the organization. The access that straight people have into the power networks of our society is a benefit that SAGA activists believe LGBT people cannot achieve on their own without the assistance of straight allies.

Chapter Six explores the theory of identity deployment by considering how the local environments affect how a straight identity is deployed at the grassroots level. What I learned from my interviews is that in highly conservative areas, successful SAGA chapters rely heavily on straight people as a form of political legitimacy to their message, in an attempt to secure tangible political goals. However, in the more liberal areas I studied, I found that chapters rely less on straight people as a legitimization of their message, but more as an access point to the social networks of straight people in order to secure resources and broaden their effectiveness.

Chapter Seven concludes the book by highlighting the important findings of my research endeavor in relation to the prevalent sociological theories of identity and social movement strategy. I summarize how these findings require us to re-engage with identity deployment, political ecology, and "culture war" theories in order to incorporate the unique strategies of SAGA. I conclude the chapter with a discussion on the ways in which these unique strategies of SAGA have practical applications and limitations in social activism as well, particularly with regards to the same-sex marriage debate. Likewise, I explore the potential pitfalls, of including straight people in an LGBT movement, and how SAGA has mitigated the costs of this inclusion.

Chapter Two
Theory and Research Methods

In the sociological debates concerning LGBT social movements, straight people are rarely mentioned as an integral part to the movement's successes, but rather as the source of LGBT challenges and oppression. Over the past decade, sociologists have written about the role of identities with regard to political strategy in social movements (Bernstein 1997, 2002, 2003; J. Gamson 1995; 1997a; 1997b; Gould 2001; Phelan 1993; Raeburn 2000; Seidman 1993). Few, if any, considered the ways in which *straight* identities become important tools in achieving the goals of an LGBT social movement. If straight people are the primary source of oppression, then why do activists in SAGA, an LGBT organization, consider vocal and visible straight people as a benefit to social movement outcomes? Although sociologists have written about coalitions of identities within social movement organizations (Bernstein 2002; Gamson 1995; Otis 2001; Scott 1998), the question of how SAGA can use a straight identity *within* an organization, instead of outside the organization, remains unanswered in the literature. I address this dearth specifically in this book.

In the literature review, I first address how allies are theorized in social movement theory by looking at what political scientists and sociologists have said about this topic. Included in this literature, I explain how the particular circumstance of SAGA, by including straight people into an LGBT organization, requires a reconceptualization of the concept of "allies" and "alliances." Following this discussion, I review the research on collective identity, and explain the ways in which allies are conceptualized in these literatures. In addition, I connect the insights of organizational theory drawn from the area of political sociology to hypothesize about the ways in which identities may be strategically deployed differently in various political environments in order to reach different movement objectives. And, lastly, following the literature review, I discuss the research methodology of this project and highlight some of the more significant methodological issues that arose during my fieldwork.

STRAIGHT ALLIES AND IDENTITY DEPLOYMENT

This chapter includes a review of the important literature that illuminates the understanding of the strategy of identity deployment in social movements. In the first part of the chapter, I focus on the concept of "ally" because of the way that the "straight" identity is created in relationship to an LGBT (or queer) identity. As I stated in Chapter One, members of SAGA, queer and straight alike, create and maintain an identity boundary of "us versus them." LGBT and straight activists maintain this boundary by differentiating between those who are "LGBT" and "straight" through the use of identity labels. One of the labels used is "ally" to describe straight people who support LGBT people and/or many of their issues. The straight activists with whom I spoke with also referred to themselves throughout the interviews as both straight and an ally because, colloquially at least, these terms are interchangeable in the LGBT community. In other words, all allies are straight (or else they would be LGBT); however, not all straight people are allies. By using the term "ally," activists understand that one is not referring to someone in the coalition of queer identities, but rather a straight supporter of LGBT people and/or their struggle for many of their equal rights.

This conflation of terms by activists involved in the LGBT community may pose a conceptualization issue with readers familiar with the sociological and political definition of "ally." A review of my interview schedules (Appendices C and D) reveals that I asked activists what they thought were the strengths and weaknesses that straight *people* bring to SAGA. In nearly every interview activists referred to straight people as "straight *allies*," being more specific than I in how one was to conceptualize straight people in SAGA. The activists, by and large, used the term "straight" and "ally" interchangeably. This colloquial interchangeable use can be perplexing and downright bothersome to the readers who are familiar with the political scientific and sociological term of "ally."

The idea of "ally" must be reconceptualized to fit the circumstances of identity coalitions and identity deployment in the LGBT organization SAGA. Overwhelmingly in the political science, sociological, and queer studies literatures we find that researchers almost always consider movement allies as existing *outside* of the movement organization, and certainly not sharing in the collective identity of movement actors. But, in the case of SAGA, straight people not only join the movement, but are an integral part of the collective identity in the organization, often relinquishing their heterosexual privilege in the society at large to join an avowedly LGBT organization in order to advocate the safety of children from homophobia.

In order to understand the importance of allies within a social movement, I first must highlight the literature that discusses the general role of allies in movements and their movement organizations. I then follow this discussion with understanding identity in social movements, referring to how straight allies can actually operate within an LGBT organization, rather than support the cause from the outside. This provides the theoretical foundation for answering my research questions of how an LGBT social movement can strategically deploy a straight identity to achieve its political goals, and how the strategy may vary according to geography.

Political science research typically considers allies at a macro-level, such as international political alliances amongst allied states as a positive function of nation-building or national security (Morrow 1991). Others have conceptualized allies as nebulous entities, such as "communities" that have assisted political actors within the power elite, such as winning elections or strengthening union gains (Craft 1990; Wilhite and Theilmann 1986). When political science (political sociology included) considers the effects of collective identity on allied groups, the social actors vie for power *within* the political structures (Drummond 2001; Eyal 2000). This conceptualization is in contrast to social movement actors who are situated outside of the power structure. Taken together, political science tends to take much too macro-level view of alliances to understand the processes of SAGA's unique inclusion of straight people. To this end, we look to the social movement literature to illuminate our understanding of allies, both the kinds among social movement organizations and social movement actors.

Within the social movement theories, particularly within resource mobilization theory, gaining allies who are members of the elite are rational decisions by activists to gain monetary resources and expand their social networks. Among the earliest writers in this paradigm were John McCarthy and Mayer Zald who posited that social movement actors were *rational* and made strategic decisions to mobilize activists and resources to maximize the potential of social movement impacts (McCarthy and Zald 1977). Supporters, the term McCarthy and Zald used, provide money, facilities, and even labor, but do not share in the commitment to the values that underlie specific movements (McCarthy and Zald 1977). The resource mobilization framework includes an additional category of movement "sympathizers," who were typically people outside of the social movement organization that are drawn from the polity or elite publics (McCarthy and Zald 1977; Morris 1984). It is assumed that this conceptualization of allies can be applied to either national social movement organizations or grassroots levels.

But, in the case of SAGA, supporters and sympathizers *become* members of the movement organization who share in the mission of SAGA on both the national and grassroots level. In the specific circumstances of SAGA, resource mobilization theories tantalize, but do not explicitly conceptualize about allies being integral to a movement organization, despite the robust description of the ways in which allies are integral to a movement's success. To explain my findings from my research on both the national and local levels of SAGA, it is important to reconceptualize resource mobilization theory by addressing the special circumstances of SAGA's interest in gaining allies and achieving its political goals.

With regard to SAGA, I find that the methods by which activists try to gain allies differ by geography; in the more conservative political environments, SAGA requires straight people as allies within the organization in order to provide political legitimacy for the organization. Allies, in this instance, do not provide overwhelming monetary resources to the local chapters because the bulk of the money that these organizations gather tend to be through membership dues and small fundraising functions. However, in the more liberal areas included in this research project, organizations had very large budgets, most of which came from organizational grants and donations from allies outside of the organization. These chapters were able to provide community services like conferences for LGBT youth and educators. However, I still find that to a lesser extent in liberal areas, a straight identity is still presented as a form of a political legitimacy, but is relied on less because their opposition tends to be either less vocal or, in some instances, even weaker.

In light of these findings, it is important to build upon the tenet of ally support in resource mobilization theory by stating that when a national organization exists in the form of local chapters as well, the theory must be revised by considering the local sociopolitical environment. This is particularly true in the case of SAGA where some allies of the LGBT movement *join* the organization, rather than supporting the movement from the outside, and whose identities are used strategically in order to achieve the political goals of the organization.

Political opportunity, another social movement paradigm, has as a central tenet that events and structures in the political environment affect what movements do (Kowalchuk 2003). In this dominant theoretical paradigm in "American" social movement studies (McDonald 2002), rational choice is assumed on the part of protesters, who assess the political environment and make calculations about the likely impact of collective action or inaction (Jenkins and Jacobs 2003; McAdam 1988). Most political opportunity scholars concur that mobilization is strongest when the political system is in the process of fragmentation, making it open to movement demands, rather than when access is denied or all the movement's demands have been met by the power elite (Gamson 1975; Kowalchuk 2003; McAdam 1982; McAdam, Tarrow, and Tilly 2001; Tarrow 1998). This fragmentation leads to political opportunities, which activists recognize and make strategic choices on when and how to best proceed to maximize success. This is an important theoretical foundation in order to understand the rational strategies SAGA activists make when including straight allies in the organization, and present a straight identity openly to the public in order to obtain its movement goals.

In political opportunity theory, the mobilized actors in the movement do not include those who are in the power structure or members of the power elite. Similar to resource mobilization theory, allies are the elite "who sympathize with or support the goals of movements, and that possess resources and/or political influence that movements lack" (Kowalchuk 2003: 314). Social movements benefit from these allies as they typically have the resources and bargaining leverage to compel the state to make concessions to movements (Burstein, Einhower, and Hollander 1995). In addition, allies may benefit mobilization as they can serve as intermediaries in negotiations with state actors (Tarrow 1998), thereby broadening or sustaining the movement's access to the political system (Kowalchuk 2003; McAdam 1988). And, in cases of extremely oppressed people, allies can even strengthen the ability to mobilize (Brockett 1991; Kowalchuk 2003). But, like the resource mobilization models, allies in the political opportunity models are not movement actors themselves (A notable exception is McAdam 1988), and are typically theorized to only exist outside of the movement organization within the power structure (della Porta and Diani 1999; Jenkins and Jacobs 2003; McAdam 1982; McAdam, Tarrow, and Tilly 2001; Piven and Cloward 1977). However, as previously explained in the introduction, SAGA has uncommon circumstances that make the inclusion of allies significantly different from other organizations that, at times, may have also included allies.

As currently theorized, resource mobilization and political opportunity theories cannot adequately explain the particular circumstances of including straight allies in SAGA, nor the methods or reasons why using that identity can be a social movement tool. One of the most helpful theories to explain this concept, though, is the theory of identity deployment as posited by Mary Bernstein (1997). In her study on the historical study of identity and LGBT movement strategies, Bernstein builds upon resource mobilization and political opportunity theories, as well as incorporates the major contributions of new social movement theory—identity—to develop a theory called "identity deployment." She finds that lesbians and gays in the United States have, in their challenge to the heteronormative social structure, strategically deployed a lesbian-and-gay identity to either accentuate their difference from or similarities to straight people. At times when lesbian and gay activists were working towards winning anti-discrimination policies, faced organized opposition, and led by organizations uninterested in building coalitions, the activists would deploy an "identity for critique," meaning they confronted the "values, categories, and practices of the dominant culture" (Bernstein 1997: 537).

The identity for critique strategy that Bernstein (1997) discusses would create a favorable environment for the inclusion of straight allies in the movement, although her research does not directly include this in her findings. Because the lesbian and gay movement is built upon a tenuous coalition of socially constructed, essentialist identities (Bernstein 2002), one would expect that the development of a collective identity to successfully include allies within an organization to be a complex and difficult task. This model, I argue, cannot completely explain the identity deployment model under SAGA's circumstances of inclusion of allies within the organization, and deploying a straight identity strategically.

Movements with a strong organizational infrastructure or had access to political elites suppressed their differences from the mainstream values and practices of the dominant culture to gain legitimacy in what Bernstein calls "identity for education" (Bernstein 1997). She argues that activists outside of LGBT organizations can employ these strategies; she suggests that in the women's movement, too, there is evidence of "identity for critique" (see also Evans 1979), as well as "identity for education" (see also Mansbridge 1986) in the strategies of activists (Bernstein 1997; 2005). Again, the problem here for understanding my findings from SAGA lay in the inclusion of straight allies in an LGBT organization, and the methods of which activists deploy a straight identity.

Bernstein argues that, at times, LGBT activists have utilized what she calls a "mixed model" of identity deployment that exhibits characteristics from both types of identity deployment. It is this particular aspect of Bernstein's identity deployment model that is most helpful in understanding SAGA's inclusion and deployment of straight identities. In SAGA, the identity deployment strategy of straightness varies by the distinct political environments contingent upon its geographical location in the United States. Therefore, I find it helpful to build upon the identity deployment model by exploring ecological models of organizations as understood by political sociologists.

The sociopolitical environments in which organizations operate have an effect on movement trajectories and organizational existence (Bernstein 1997; Minkoff 1993; 1997). However, as I addressed earlier, the identity deployment strategies of "straightness" vary by geography. Specifically, I consider the ways in which activists in SAGA rely more on a straight identity for political validation in more conservative political areas of the United States. And, although activists in more liberal areas continue to deploy a straight identity as well, they rely less on this as a form of political legitimacy and more on gaining broader access into "straight" social networks.

As political opportunity theory suggests, activists will gauge the possibilities of success based on how they perceive these sociopolitical environments. Sometimes, in sociopolitical environments that are less amenable for success, activists will seek other movement impacts besides political success, such as cultural or mobilization impacts (Bernstein 2003; Staggenborg 1995). For example, in Oregon during the "No-On-Nine" campaign to challenge the anti-gay rights proposition in the early and mid 1990s, local LGBT activists who lived in the rural village of Timbertown[1] worked to transform the local culture toward inclusivity while mobilizing allies (and other LGBT people) in the fight to defeat the ballot measure (Stein 2001).

The federalist structure of the United States government can dampen the overall level of social mobilization when compared to decentralized governments, especially for state-oriented challengers (Amenta and Young 1999). To compensate for these difficulties, some organizations have opted for a federalist structure of organizing to organize constituents into small local units. Organizations such as the NAACP, NOW, and CWA are organized in this manner (Morris 1984; Rohlinger 2002). Social movement organizations that develop a federated structure may deal with constituents directly, or through chapters (McCarthy and Zald 1977). According to Rohlinger, a federated social movement organization:

> . . . that is located near or in political epicenters, with a centralized leadership, a professionalized staff, and a clear division of labor will be able to respond to political happenings . . . better than an informal grassroots organization that relies on volunteers, lacks, clear leadership, and has more limited resources. (Rohlinger 2002: 481).

SAGA is also a federated structure headquartered near a political epicenter, and implements its mission through local chapters. These chapters must contend with even smaller political environments than states: local school districts. Policies must be fought on all levels at once. Joshua David of SAGA National summarized this idea beautifully:

> We're trying to change this entire nation's education system with virtually no resources. HRC (Human Rights Campaign) has seven times as much money as we do, and they only have 535 people they're looking at: 100 Senators, 435 Congresspeople. We have 15,000 school boards, but with over [hundreds of thousands of] members as a group that we're trying to effect with a lot less resources.

Doing so requires a lot of resources, which small organizations cannot have without organizational, as well as individual, allies. This is how and why straight people become a tremendous advantage. Allies included into the organization bring legitimacy to the message in conservative political environments, while also uniting networks of people and organizations that have typically been out of easy reach by the LGBT movement. For example, the American church has historically been a source of civil rights movement activity, such as antislavery and suffragist movements (Morris 1984; Young 2002). But, the Christian religious institutions and followers today for the most part have been cool to the idea of assisting LGBT social movements in their fight for social justice (Adam 1987; Herman 2000; Linneman 2003; Stein 2001). Judeo-Christian, church- or synagogue- going allies, like the ones I found in SAGA, explain how they bridge together the LGBT and religious communities. They find their religious communities an asset, especially in certain conservative regions where broad-base support for LGBT causes is difficult to garner without the assistance of straight allies.

In these varied political environments, straight allies may make the difference in success and failure. Excluding them from the organization would only be to the detriment of SAGA. Likewise, in some places where chapters are located, the political environment is so hostile that straight people led the student-run gay/straight alliances (GSAs) in high schools because many LGBT students are too afraid to come out without the security of straight people to speak out for them (see Lee 2002 for one of the few published research on the impact of GSAs). And, interestingly, a member of SAGA National stated that the board in a chapter in Alaska[2] is comprised entirely of straight people because of the difficulty with being "out" as LGBT or queer in the political climate. In this book, I argue that the strategy of using straight people is particularly important in varied sociopolitical environments, which is why I chose a sample of organizations throughout the United States to be included in this study (explained further in the methodology section of this chapter).

FRAMING IDENTITY DEPLOYMENT STRATEGY AND THE CULTURE WAR

Framing analysis, as employed by social movements theorists, can help explain the process by which SAGA activists utilize identity deployment in achieving their political goals at the national and local levels of organizing, as well as in distinct sociopolitical environments. In addition, the literature on framing debates is helpful in understanding what social scientists call a "culture war" amongst liberal people who seek to expand equal rights and conservative people who wish to revert society to a Christian moral one by limiting personal freedoms. What are typically presented today as two opposing frames used by the sides of the culture war, the data I find in SAGA suggest that these frames are not oppositional but, in SAGA's case, ever-so-gently infused together.

Framing analysis informs the collective behavior debates by incorporating the interpretation of cultural symbols with movement strategy. Building on the work of Goffman (1974), frame alignment theorists consider both social psychological and the structural/organizational factors in movement mobilization and participation (Snow, Rochford, Worden, and Benford 1986). According to Rohlinger, "frames are a central organizing idea that tells an audience what is at issue and outlines the boundaries of a debate" (Rohlinger 2002: 480). In this paradigm, organizational leaders present frames to define situations as problematic, call people to action, and articulate reasonable solutions to the public, power holders, and fellow activists (Rohlinger 2002; Snow and Benford 1992; Snow, Rochford, Worden, and Benford 1986). Social movement actors hope that certain frames, especially master frames created by other successful movements, will resonate with audiences to gain sympathizers and achieve its results (Snow and Benford 1992). This permits a greater realm in which movement actors can gain allies and, in the instance of SAGA, include straight allies into the organization and then deploy a straight identity strategically.

Frame analysis is built upon the "tool-kit" model of organizational strategies and its use of cultural symbols (Clemens 1993; Swidler 1986). From my observations of SAGA, I noted that the activists strategically deploy the cultural meanings of what "straightness" is, as well as a straight identity in a "tool-kit" fashion. This framing of what straightness means in society and, therefore, what the cultural message must mean to witness straight people joining the mission is also contingent upon the sociopolitical environment in which each chapter exists. For example, in Chapter Four, I explain the process by which SAGA activists frame the organizational message of school safety for LGBT youth to the public at large and policymakers through comments like, " . . . In terms of the work that we do, the heterosexual allies are the ones that make it sellable to a greater audience. It no longer becomes 'the gay agenda.' It becomes a human agenda" (Personal interview with Adam Lieberman). If straight allies are willing to join a gay organization, SAGA activists argue, then the policymakers will notice that SAGA's message carries greater weight than if only LGBT people spoke on the issue of school safety. This helps frame the debate of why straight people who are unfamiliar with, or perhaps uninterested in, LGBT issues should listen to SAGA's message. Furthermore, as we will see as well, this strategic framing of the organizational message assists activists with identity deployment of a straight identity.

Activists were not always cognizant of certain cultural symbols as a possible social movement strategy. One notable example from my research on SAGA regards Christian moral symbolism in the message of SAGA. As I note in Chapter Four, some of the SAGA activists are personally religious, and participate in SAGA because of what they consider a moral necessity. Although they may openly express their Judeo-Christian faith as a member of the organization, they do not *strategically* use moral symbolism as a means to a particular social movement goal. Rather, in SAGA, some activists ever-so-delicately infuse a Christian moral frame with an injustice frame in order to achieve the organizational mission.

Other research demonstrates that this is not unusual for movements in general (For example, see McAdam 1988; Young 2001, 2002), but in many of the recent theories on the culture war movements, it is understood that identity-based "liberal" organizations, such as the feminist or queer movements, typically rely upon the injustice frame, and their political opposition (religious right movements), primarily utilize a moral frame (For example, see Rohlinger 2002; see also Stein 2001).

Using the abortion debate as an example, I take a closer look at how the current theories of "culture war" in sociology conceptualizes the use of moral and injustice frames as distinctly different paradigms in organizing. In her analysis of the different media strategies in a movement-countermovement dynamic, Rohlinger (2002) finds that organizations such as National Organization for Women (NOW) assessed the political climate, public attitudes, and countermovement claims toward abortion and adjusted frames in the media accordingly. She finds that NOW successfully sharpened their frames when the sociopolitical climate warranted (Rohlinger 2002), which was based almost exclusively on a frame of "equality" and "injustice." This is a complex and double-edged frame, particularly in the media, because the strategy can backfire on the movement actors (W. A. Gamson 1997). But in the instance of NOW in Rohlinger's research, the frame was successful. Furthermore, NOW found allies within the media through this successful framework.

However, the organization Concerned Women for America (CWA) saw the abortion issue an unchanging moral absolute, and in turn, framed the abortion debate differently in the media by packaging it in terms of "morality" (Rohlinger 2002). In the face of what the CWA perceived as a biased depiction of them in the media (who Rohlinger finds are allies of NOW), the CWA adjusted their frames accordingly to accommodate the sociopolitical realities over the course of only a few years to only moderate success. Rohlinger notes that even though the frame presentations were adjusted by CWA to find more success (and allies) within the media, the frames continued to be distinctly based on morality.

In political science, these two opposing bases of organizing are typically referred to as deriving from a "culture war" where the moralists and secularists are engaged in a battle for what one of the SAGA activists (and political televangelist Pat Robertson in the 1988 Republican National Convention) referred to as "the spirit of America" (For further elaboration on the culture war theory, see Hunter 1994; see also Linneman 2003; Stein 2001). My findings from my interviews with a number of SAGA activists directly challenge the conceptualization that these frames are always diametrically opposed. I find that SAGA bridges together these two frames (moral and injustice), and permit the inclusion of straight people into the organization. By doing so, straight people who join SAGA may, in their personal lives and through their social networks, bridge together the straight and gay communities in their shared quest to fulfill the mission of SAGA. Without the unification of the moral and injustice frames in the organizational message, the deployment of a straight identity by SAGA may not be possible because it would end up alienating many straight activists interested in SAGA's mission, some of who are drawn into the organization because of what they saw was a moral necessity derived from their Judeo-Christian beliefs.

Framing theories elucidate our understanding of allies in relationship to social movements. Similar to resource mobilization and political opportunity theories, frame analysis conceptualizes allies as a strategic addition to a movement organization, although they typically are not members of the organization in any formal way. When we further consider the ways in which the interplay of contending movements, it becomes clearer how important allies can be. As in the example above on the abortion debate, allies are a benefit to movement organizations if activists can get allies to sympathize with their concerns, even if they exist outside of the institutionalized power structure. This is especially true during the formation of a countermovement. When there is strong contention toward a particular movement, a countermovement may emerge (Meyer and Staggenborg 1996; Mottl 1997; Rohlinger 2002). In these instances, movement organizations must compete with countermovements in order to gain political allies and, hopefully, an advantage over the opposing movement organization (Meyer and Staggenborg 1996).

In the earlier example, NOW and its countermovement CWA assessed the ability to get and accurate media coverage, then framed and adjusted their messages accordingly. In the case of gaining allies, one of the advantages for NOW during this countermovement activity was that they considered sympathetic news reporters "strong allies" of NOW (Rohlinger 2002: 479). By and large in framing theory, allies play a minor role in movements; in theatrical terms, allies would be of little importance to the plot or the climax, relegated to being on the list of minor characters in the credits. However, in SAGA, the allies *are* the main characters, and when used strategically, play in integral role in the success of the movement. My research on SAGA fills a void in the literature on allies, as there are few, if any, research endeavors that consider the importance of allies, and this strategic deployment of their identities, *within* a social movement organization.

One of the few times social movement theory has done so is regarding celebrities' participation in social movements. In the face of adverse political environments, David Meyer and Joshua Gamson (1995) suggest that cultural elites, such as celebrities, can be beneficial to movement success. As long as celebrities could claim a legitimate standing and gain credible attention in, they were most likely to engage or redefine the movements in which they participate (Meyer and Gamson 1995). Yet, Meyer and Gamson never go so far as to address them as *allies,* and in their conceptualization of celebrities, they are neither fully inside nor completely outside of the movement. Their unique status as members of the cultural elite brings to question whether or not they can be conceptualized as movement allies, or just "prime time" activists (Meyer and Gamson 1995; Ryan 1991). By defining celebrities in this way, celebrities could speak *for* a movement, without participating in the movement organization in any substantive way.

In the case of SAGA, the "celebrities" can be considered on one level the straight allies who join the organization and speak for a movement cause[3]. But, as I note in Chapter Three, the straight and LGBT activists often mention in my discussions with them that straight members should, on one level, relinquish their heterosexual privilege by speaking *with* their fellow LGBT activists, rather than *for* them. And yet, paradoxically, part of the identity deployment strategy is for the straight activists to utilize their heterosexual privileges in order to achieve the goals of garnering political legitimacy and, eventually, broaden the social networks from which the organization gains resources. The understanding is that celebrities, of which SAGA activists will most likely have little direct contact with, are expected to speak *for* activists, while the straight allies with whom LGBT activists have day-to-day contact within the organization must not replicate heterosexual privilege and instead, speak *with* LGBT people in a collective voice.

COLLECTIVE IDENTITIES AND THE ISSUE OF LGBT MOVEMENTS

Although the resource mobilization, political opportunity, and frame theories are a solid foundation upon which I build upon in understanding the strategies of using allies in a social movement, it is important to understand how identity construction processes affect strategies, especially in political environments. In this section, I discuss these processes within the social movement literature.

As I mentioned in the beginning of this chapter, in the sociological debates concerning social movements, sociologists have written about using identities strategically in social movements based on a "collective identity" (Bernstein 1997, 2002; J. Gamson 1997a, 1997b), but few—if any—have considered the ways in which *ally* identities become important tools in achieving the goals of a social movement. This omission in the research on social movements is directly addressed by my findings written in this book. In order to fully understand the role of straight allies with assisting a social movement organization, I discuss the concept of collective identity in social movements by addressing the insights of new social movement theory. Lastly, I explore how identity interplays in social movement organizations.

Notably absent in the dominant works of both resource mobilization and political opportunity theories is the concept of collective identity as a mobilizing and unifying factor of social movements (Polletta and Jasper 2001). In these rational-actor (resource mobilization) and structuralist (political opportunity) models, collective identity has been relegated to a residual category to describe what happens outside rational actions and structures, rather than identifying the "circumstances in which different relations between interest and identity, strategy and identity, and politics and identity operate" (Polletta and Jasper 2001: 285). In this book, I include the insights of identity from new social movement theory into the conceptualization of strategy in resource mobilization, political process, and framing theories.

The insights of new social movement theorists fleshed out the importance of collective identity in movements, as they posited that participation in movements after 1960 could not be predicted by class location and that actors sought recognition for new identities and lifestyles (Best and Kellner 1998; Duyvendak and Giugni 1995; Johnson, Larana, and Gusfield 1997; Melucci 1989; Polletta and Jasper 2001; Touraine 1981). But what is collective identity? I use Polletta and Jasper's definition as "an individual's cognitive, moral, and emotional connection with a broader community, category, practice, or institution . . . and carries with it positive feelings for other members of the group" (Polletta and Jasper 2001: 285). Although some social movement theorists question the "newness" of modern social movements (Cohen 1996; Gould 1993; Pichardo 1997), most collective behavior scholars now agree that in order for a movement to exist, there must be a collective sense of "we" that actors continuously develop and reshape, before and during mobilization.

Most of the current research on the collective identities of ethnicity, race, and/or nationalism "rests upon a model of ethnicity as a set of socially constructed boundaries in political, economic, cultural, social, and moral time and space" (Nagel 2000: 110). According to Mary Waters (1990), white people have a wide array of "ethnic options" to choose from as an identity, suggesting that identity hinges upon cultural meanings of a particular category. However, in Waters study, the identity categories of whites carried very little meaning; people identifying as Irish really only saw their heritage as celebrating in a St. Patrick's Day parade, and not shaping their everyday lives with meaning, such as those identities that are oppressed through the social norms. For queer people, their shared identity carries cultural meanings, and through it they can forge a collective identity, even if it is a tenuous coalition of at least four (lesbian, gay, bisexual, and transgender) distinct identities. From this we can explain the process by which LGBT people develop identity boundaries about who is (or is not) considered similar to them.

When we consider the vast permutations of identities in social movements, we recognize that there must be boundary-construction in the creation of politicized identities (Taylor and Whittier 1992). These boundary constructions in social movements become more complex when we consider how multiple identities co-exist within an identity community, defined as "a shared definition of a group that derives from its members' common interests, experiences, and solidarity" (Taylor and Whittier 1992: 105). In pan-ethnic movements of the United States, people coming from diverse cultures such as Indian, Chinese, or Vietnamese are included in pan-ethnic alliances with other Asians because of the consequences of their common racialization by the dominant culture (Bloul 1999; Espiritu 1992; 1994). These pan-ethnic alliances can be difficult to negotiate within organizations and movements (Espiritu 1994).

The dominant research on sexuality posits that sexuality is socially constructed in similar processes as ethnicity (Nagel 2000). The understanding of the social construction of homosexuality, as well as its relationship to the construction of heterosexuality is well-documented (Chauncey 1989; D'Emilio 1992; Epstein 1994; Foucault 1978; Gagnon and Simon 1973; Katz 1997; Nagel 2000; Sedgwick 1993). Sexuality construction processes are interconnected with gender concepts as well; Herdt (1997) demonstrates this developmental relationship using cross-cultural data, while Vicinus (1992) and Chauncey (1994) investigated the historical constructions of sexuality in relation to cultural concepts of gender in the late 19th and early 20th centuries. These processes influence identities of "lesbian" and "gay" differently because of the cross-cutting of gender and class (see Valocchi 1999) in these identity constructions.

Recently, Gamson (1997a; 1997b) explored the developmental relationship of lesbian and gay identity with regards to identity construction within current lesbian and gay organizations. In order to secure political gains and achieve successful resistance, lesbians and gays created a "minority" identity that is conceptualized as fixed, or "essentialist" (Bernstein 2002; Gamson 1995; Seidman 1993). Lesbians and gays have created common political and cultural institutions, much like an ethnicity—even having its own flag as a symbol of a collective "we" (Cortese and Dowling 2003; D'Emilio 1992; Gamson 1995). However, the coalition of identities can be considered a quasi-ethnic because it is not based on a shared nationality *heritage* of members, but notions of a shared fixed cultural *construction* of sexuality. In the lesbian and gay movement, their "quasi-ethnic" status poses difficulties in organizing and forging a common identity (Bernstein 2002; J. Gamson 1995). A tenuous coalition of identities, lesbians and gays are caught in a quagmire of differences based on their dissimilar experiences of patriarchy (see Adam 1987, Ch. 5), which they must resolve by creating a politics of commonality based on fixed or essentialist notions of sexuality (Bernstein 2002; Phelan 1993; Seidman 1993).

By being lumped into one pluralistic identity that is imposed onto members first by the dominant culture, it can make for tenuous coalitions that might not have existed had they not been forced together in response to oppression. According to sociologist Eileen Otis, alliances within the pan-Asian ethnic movement organization "are not guaranteed—they require time and painstaking efforts to foster . . . [but] continue to be critical to avoid a complete fragmentation between groups as well as possible political paralysis" (Otis 2001: 350). Race and ethnicity pose similar concerns in developing alliances within feminist organizations, as Ellen Scott finds that white and Latina women struggled with maintaining political alliances while constructing identities within these organizations (Scott 1998). Similarly, lesbians and gay organizations now give deference to bisexuals and transgenders who historically have battled over their inclusion into their collective identity (J. Gamson 1997a; Rust 1995).

SAGA is similar to other organizations today that try to interconnect a wide array of identities into one pan-organizational alliance. As we see in Chapter Three, SAGA's mission is intimately tied with the goal of diversity and inclusion within the organization. And yet, SAGA is not very diverse in its activist, board, and staff composition. By and large, the SAGA activists I spoke with saw the LGBT movement *in general* addressed and pursued issues that were male-dominated, white, and with middle-class concerns. Interestingly, most of the activists who said this concluded that SAGA was different. Most of the activists stated that organizational mission of SAGA is built around inclusivity; they believe that the goal of SAGA is to promote safe schools for LGBT students, teachers, and staff, which means that the mission in itself is *not* a middle-class, white, or male issue.

Although collective identity construction may have at its foundation a rational-actor dynamic, activists do not live on rationality alone in their struggle to forge collective identity. Key movement processes, such as mobilization, building solidarity, forging alliances and/or gaining allies, and identity construction "is as emotional as it is cognitive and strategic" (Kane 2001: 256). The emotions involved with creating, forging, and framing to the public an identity requires strategy and finesse. In the gay community, scholars have found that this process may be subject to the ambivalence of the movement actors (Gould 2001). Many of the SAGA activists are similarly ambivalent about these alliances on some level (see Chapter Five). However, contrary to Gould's findings, the activists overwhelmingly claim that there are benefits to the inclusion of straight people that, by far, outweigh any concerns they may have about their inclusion and the identity deployment of straight allies.

When we consider SAGA, movement actors who are deploying a straight identity, managing emotions to be considered a "moderate voice" in the hostile debates between the LGBT and the Religious Right movement organizations is a difficult task for SAGA. Being perceived as "too gay" by the opposition may close the doors and windows of opportunity for the activists. And yet, being perceived as "too moderate" may risk being called a political "sell out" and shunned from LGBT organizations with a liberationist slant. Walking this fine "Goldilocks" line requires continuous reframing to traverse these difficult emotional paths with impeccable strategies not to offend either movement. For SAGA, the "us-versus-them" of LGBT identity politics has no place when they deploy an

Theory and Research Methods

"identity for education," particularly since some of the "them" (straight people) in SAGA are a visible and vocal part of the "us" (the LGBT people). How can they do it? How has SAGA managed to include allies within the organization for over ten years without fragmenting?

Part of the answer may be in which particular *social movement industry*[4] the organization belongs. I borrow this term from McCarthy and Zald (1977) in their resource mobilization model to explain SAGA's unique identity strategy. In hostile political environments and conditions, such as those seen within many school systems, SAGA members believe is advantageous for the organization to deploy a collective identity as education and situate itself out of the broader LGBT movement. When dealing with sexuality in schools, it is bound to prompt ardor and rancor based on the irrational myths of the homosexual predator. Outside of the myriad of LGBT organizations within the LGBT social movement industry, SAGA positions itself as an "education organization that is working on LGBT issues"[5] that situates it within both the safe schools and the LGBT movements. If SAGA does not identify itself as an LGBT organization, then one might say that the basis of the arguments in this book is moot. But, SAGA cannot be excluded from either social movement industry because, as is noted in Figure 1, their organizational identities and interests overlap.

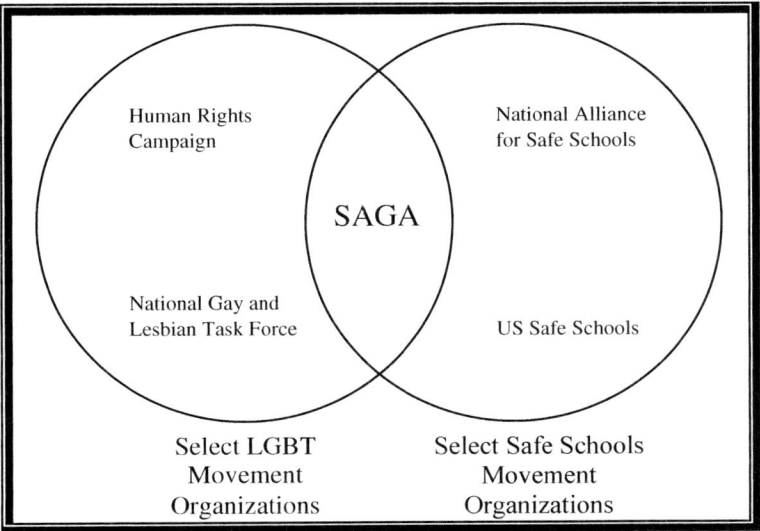

Figure 1. Location of SAGA in Social Movement Industries

This unique position of SAGA as being an LGBT organization outside of the dominant LGBT movement is a definite strategy of the organization. If SAGA convinces policymakers that it is *outside* of the LGBT movement (which frames their fight in an injustice frame), and presents public images of straight people (who are clearly *not* gay) as people who believe in the mission of the organization, then they have won half the battle. In SAGA, it is not an LGBT identity they are constructing, but rather, an identity of youth advocate. The frames are not spoken as "injustice" against lesbian and gays, but that it is unjust to fail at "protecting innocent children." Without this strategic shift, it is unlikely that allies could mobilize *within* the organization.

An overwhelming majority of the activists I interviewed identify as lesbian, gay, bisexual, transgender, or "queer," which is further confirmed by the demographic data that SAGA National collects in the accreditation process. Their shared identity and their shared mission in the safe schools movement situates them clearly within *both* movements, regardless of the protests by the SAGA activists that they are outside of the LGBT movement (see Chapter Four for an elaboration on this point). Furthermore, the interorganizational alliances that it creates are typically with other organizations in the LGBT movement. For all intents and purposes, SAGA can be conceptualized as an LGBT organization for the reasons stated above.

In conclusion, SAGA is an intriguing LGBT organization that embraces the inclusion of straight allies in order to deploy a straight identity so that it can achieve its political goals. Although social movement theories on resource mobilization, political process, and framing analysis provide us with a solid theoretical foundation to understand the particular circumstances of SAGA's deployment of a straight identity, it requires a reconceptualization of the sociological term "ally." Likewise, in this section, I utilize Mary Bernstein's (1997) concept of "identity deployment" to explain the methods by which SAGA activists deploy a straight identity. In understanding the unique circumstances of SAGA in the active inclusion of differently-identified allies within an identity-based movement, it is important to consider the sociopolitical environments in which organizations must operate. Lastly, I discussed the issue of collective identity and LGBT movement organizing, and explained the processes by which SAGA seeks to overcome this problem when including straight allies into the organization. To this end, I will discuss my research methodology in the next section.

RESEARCH METHODOLOGY

On more than one occasion, participants asked me, "Why are you studying SAGA?" Perhaps no other person was as forthright as Casey Lina from the Pacific Northwestern United States. At the end of the interview in her house, I asked Casey if she had any questions for me. Without hesitation, she seamlessly became the interviewer. Hinting to me that she wanted an explanation more candid than the jargon found on the informed consent form, Casey queried: "Why did you choose SAGA, honestly? Was it just because something that hadn't been done? A sweet little organization that makes everybody smile and is about kids and teaching?" With the tape recorder still pointed at Casey Lina, I responded frankly with a brief explanation of my research project besides it being "something that hadn't been done" before.

Although I discuss the organizational structure of SAGA in Chapter One, SAGA has a very specific organizational mission. They define themselves, as Joshua David from SAGA National states, as "an education organization that works on LGBT issues. We don't define ourselves as an LGBT rights group." In many ways, SAGA parallels the development of the NAACP at the turn of the century in that it was established with a strong centralized national organization that oversaw local grassroots chapters that were established using the parent organization's name (see Morris 1984).

Another similarity to the development of the NAACP is the inclusion of elites in its leadership. According to Morris, African-American and White educated elites who helped found the organization saw it necessary to include elites in order to successfully mobilize resources and achieve their political goals. However, SAGA differs from other studies because of the fact that SAGA is situated in a quintessential identity movement, making the inclusion of its oppositional reference category more intriguing

Let us again consider my research questions, which ask the following: Why would an LGBT organization use a straight identity as one tool by which to effectively achieve their political goals? And, would the local politics of particular regions of the United States affect the deployment of a straight identity? SAGA is a prime organization to consider for answering my research questions since it works on both the national and local levels on a very specific issue within LGBT communities, and created itself intentionally to include straight people into its leadership in order to use straight allies as an identity deployment strategy.

In the next sub-sections, I discuss the research methods for this book project, including why I selected SAGA as the unit of analysis for this study, why I chose these particular SAGA chapters, and how I selected activists for inclusion in my research project. In addition, I also discuss the demographics of the activists[6] and touch upon how these demographics shape the organizational culture and mission. Lastly, I discuss some of the issues and problems that arose during my fieldwork regarding the collection of data and interaction with activists as an "insider," meaning that the researcher is a self-identified gay male activist.

Fieldwork, Sampling, and Data Collection

Before beginning the interview, I provided respondents the opportunity to answer a demographic questionnaire (see Appendices A and B). I did this at the beginning of each interview to provide activists a moment to relax and talk so that we could build rapport before diving into the questions. While they completed the questionnaire, I turned on the tape recorder and provided an opportunity for conversation about any questions they may have. Some interesting information came from participants while reading through the questionnaire, such as how they define their sexuality, SAGA's relationship with organization, diversity in the board members of SAGA, and the like. The fact that this unstructured part of the interview remained on audiotape record proved to be very helpful in the data analysis and in the writing of this book.

In this questionnaire, which provides only a tape number and contains no personal identifying information, participants answered a series of questions that asked for certain demographic information such as self-identified gender, sexuality, income range, occupation, and political party affiliation. In addition, the questionnaire included queries about their knowledge of their chapter's history and organizational alliances in order to develop a clearer picture of each chapter (see Appendix A). I provided a similar questionnaire to the National organization with only minor changes, such as changing "board member" to "staff member" in Question 17 (see Appendix B) and eliminating questions that were specific only to local grassroots chapters, such as the date of founding and board diversity. Upon my first visit to SAGA National, one of the staff members provided me with a spreadsheet of the board and staff diversity of National, so this question became unnecessary to ask on the questionnaire.

In planning this research endeavor, I followed a feminist methodological approach to my interviews, which sought to empower the activists, as well as enlighten me on their knowledge (Richardson, Taylor, and Whittier 2001). Rather than relying exclusively on telephone interviews, I would meet with activists on a personal level and conduct one-on-one interviews. On average, I interviewed between three and five activists from every region between March 2003 and September 2003. Interviews varied in time between thirty-five minutes and three hours, but most interviews were around ninety minutes long. Interview questions were semi-structured and divided into the

Theory and Research Methods

following three themes: 1) Social movement experience, 2) Identities in the organization, and 3) Thoughts of the future (See Appendices C and D). Similar to the demographic questionnaire, some questions were changed for the interviews with the staff of SAGA National (See Appendix D).

Within my in-depth, open-ended question interview schedule, I incorporated the approach of what Gloria González-López (2000) calls "story telling." As González-López states, "story telling . . . triggers past life events which are recollected by the informants in the present in a particular context" (2000: 17). In addition, González-López cites Ken Plummer's (1995) success in utilizing this type of approach in his sexuality research because, as she states, "he demonstrates how reconstructing past stories while going through a process of story telling becomes a sociological phenomenon (González-López 2000: 17). Likewise, Jerome Bruner (1990) argues that narrative is the ideal vehicle to express and shape one's personal experiences. Much of my interview included activists recalling what they perceived as successful or unsuccessful strategies, and reconstructing the circumstances surrounding these incidents. Information gathered from these stories provided additional support for the concept that activists deploy a straight identity strategically.

This research method provided me with a beautiful example of how the researcher who enters the field can bring the result of empowering the participants who share their stories with me. One of the activists, Adam Lieberman, sent me a moving email several weeks after we met in April of 2003. As a young gay Jewish male co-chair of a chapter in the Southwest, he shared with me his frustrations and concerns over the chapter's inability to fully recover from some very hostile meetings surrounding anti-LGBT situations at local school board meetings. In this email, he tells me how my interviews with the SAGA activists prompted reflective discussions on the future of SAGA El Reto County:

> . . . My chapter found the [interview] experience to actually be very helpful in shaping some of our current activities and future goals. . . . Your interview gave me a chance to reflect on my own journey with SAGA and where the organization as a whole is going. . . . Many of my board members have approached me in the time after the interview to both thank me for the opportunity but also have continued the conversations you started with them.

My research project was conducted in accordance with the human subjects protocol as specified by the Institutional Review Board (IRB) at the University of Texas at Austin, which was approved in October of 2002. According to the guidelines specified under the IRB approval, I contacted the executive director of SAGA, specifying in a brief email the goals of my research project, and ask permission to visit local chapters of SAGA, as well as SAGA National, in order to interview activists for this project. Unfortunately, because SAGA addresses only one very specific issue of youth education, the executive director of SAGA responded that I could not interview activists without, "in good faith," assuring the confidentiality of both the organization and the activists. This meant changing the name of organization, as well as the names of the participants. Included in the executive director's requirement was for me to mask the names of the cities in which chapters exist, in order to ensure confidentiality. Furthermore, I could only meet with SAGA National staff members on their personal time.

After garnering written permission from the national leadership of SAGA, I contacted ten local chapters in four broad regions based on SAGA's local level organizational design, where each region had a "Chapter Director" to assist local chapters with their concerns. These regions were: South, West, Midwest, and East. I selected chapters based on organizational size, activity, and agreement to participate in the study. In the summer of 2002, I contacted the co-chairs of ten chapters in each of the four regions via mail that briefly introduced my research question, asking their permission to include their chapter in my study, and specifying exactly what their agreement to participate would entail. Included in these letters was my business card with my telephone number and email address, a self-addressed, stamped envelope for them to return a signed pre-printed sheet that I enclosed in the letter, and specified that they wished to be included in this research project.

Only one chapter, SAGA Sunntach, contacted me immediately. After three months, I followed up with letters similarly written to the first batch, and included two more chapters in the West. I waited three months for responses knowing that many of the chapters do not hold meetings during the summer months. I wanted to give chapters the time to discuss their interest with the board members and reply at their convenience. After one follow-up letter, I received only one negative response via email from the co-chair of a Colorado chapter in the Mountain states, which specified that the local economy would give me skewed results, so she did not want their chapter to participate. I emailed the co-chair back that their situation may be of interest to my research question anyway, but I never received another response.

Theory and Research Methods 37

By December of 2002, I received permission from five chapters: two in the West, one in the South, one in the Northeast, and one in the Midwest. In the interest of equal representation, I altered the boundaries of the regions included in the study. To accommodate the positive response from the western states, I divided the West into two sociopolitical parts: The Pacific Northwest and the Southwest. These two regions are distinguishable both culturally and politically (Linneman 2003; Stein 2001), so these cultural distinctions are appropriate for this project. As seen in Figure 2, The Pacific Northwest includes the states of Alaska, California (North), Oregon, and Washington. The Southwest includes the states of California (South), Nevada, Arizona, and New Mexico.

There are only a few active chapters in the Mountain region because the sparse population and the conservative local politics are a hindrance to sustaining chapter development (Personal interview with Cameron Fine, SAGA National). In this region, chapters did not respond to my repeated requests for interviews or they declined participation, attributing it to decreased interest in participation because of the economic downturn in their area. This region is unfortunately left out of my analysis at this time. However, as "luck" would have it, two chapters agreed to participate in the study from the West.

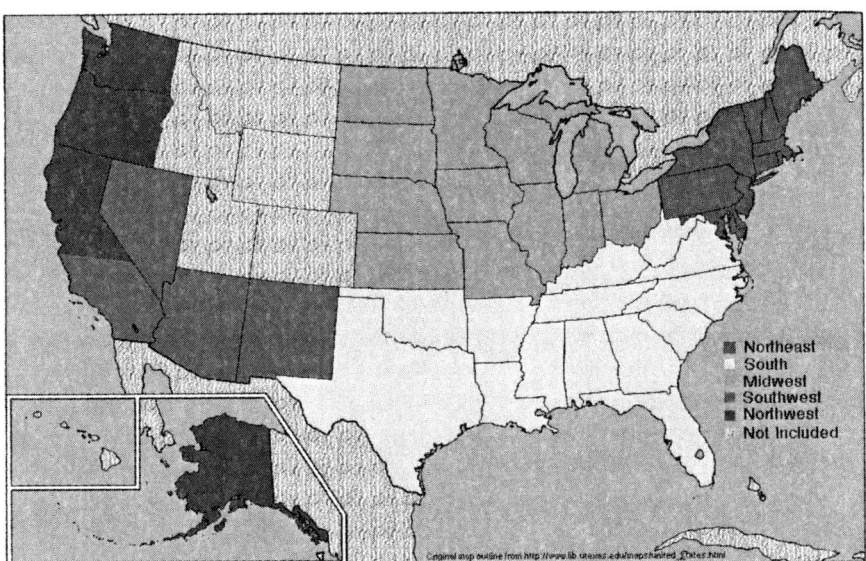

Figure 2. SAGA-Based Sociopolitical Regions of the United States

Although fully supported by colleagues in my applications for dissertation grant money that focused on either sexuality or social science research, this broad project covering six cities across the United States was self-funded through student loans and airline miles. In January and February of 2003, I contacted via email the chapters which agreed to participate in the study and asked them if we could coordinate our schedules for me to fly in for five days at a time between March and June of 2003. Since I was teaching a class at 8:00 am on Tuesdays and Thursdays during the semester, I scheduled my flights so that I could leave at 11:00 am on Thursday, and arrive on the latest flight on Monday night. I attempted to coordinate my flights as efficiently as possible in order to coordinate the schedules of activists, many of whom are teachers. In late May and early June of 2003, between the Spring and Summer semesters, I utilized an "open jaw" flight, where I would leave Austin, travel to the Midwest for nine days, then fly to the Northeast for six days, and then return back to Austin.

This scheduling strategy worked well for the activists, since many would meet with me at night or weekends. Unfortunately, because of my teaching responsibilities and short flights during the semester, I could conduct only two interviews a day in the brief time after I arrived or before I prepared to leave the city. Interviews sometimes lasted three hours, so this schedule proved difficult to write extensive field and interview debriefing notes at convenient times. Many times I would multitask and write my field notes from interviews in a local Starbucks or restaurant so that I could eat between scheduled meetings. Likewise, I would listen to my recently conducted interviews while driving in the rental car to the next interview, or at night after I wrote my debriefing notes of the interview or interviews over the day.

I met with activists at locations of their choosing, such as their office or a coffeehouse. I asked all respondents to sign an informed consent form before our interview. I obtained their permission to tape record the interviews, informing them that the tapes would be stored in my locked file cabinet for later analyses and would be heard only by me and/or my associates (i.e., transcriptionists). Audiotapes were sealed and opened in front of the activists, and assigned a number that corresponded to their questionnaire. These assigned numbers were written in front of the activists so that they would have visual confirmation that there was no identifying information visible. I informed respondents of their right to refuse answering any questions, and could end the interview at any time without any penalty. Although my interviews generally went well, there were several setbacks, some of which I discuss later in this section. By the end

Theory and Research Methods 39

of the interview process, I completed a total of thirty interviews with current and former local SAGA board members and SAGA National staff members.

Following this compressed travel schedule meant, of course, that in larger chapters I could not interview everyone in one visit. In order to accommodate their interest and schedules, I opted on telephone interviews with activists at their convenience. I interviewed five activists utilizing this method. In these instances, I faxed or emailed copies of the demographic questionnaire and consent forms to participants, and then we conducted tape-recorded telephone interviews on a later date.

As mentioned earlier, the geographical names in the nomenclature of SAGA chapters are pseudonyms in accordance with IRB requirements. In some regions, I use actual place names found within the region. This is because of the vast number of locations mentioned within the interviews made it almost impossible to come up with original location names. In the Pacific Northwest, I renamed the SAGA organization that I studied SAGA Victoria, named after the Canadian city found in the British Columbia. It is a name that is familiar in the area, but unique and general enough not to immediately lead to the real name of the city. Likewise, in the Northeast, the SAGA organization is renamed Piedmont, which in French means "foot of the mountain," because the organization is located in the vast plateau region of the eastern United States between the Appalachian Mountains and the Atlantic coast.

In the other three regions (the South, the Southwest, and the Midwest), I named locations based on my observations and impressions drawn from the interviews. In the South, I renamed the SAGA organization after the fictitious place "Davis City," which reflects the conservative politics of the state that is located in the "Deep South." Davis City, although somewhat liberal in its politics, still espouses public debates on whether or not to display monuments with the confederate flag as a tribute to its heritage on public lands. In the Southwest, I chose to rename the SAGA organization that I studied to SAGA El Reto County to reflect the region's Mexican heritage before its annexation by the United States in the Mexican War. In Spanish, "el reto" means "the challenge," and as we see later in the book, SAGA El Reto County endured many challenges from both LGBT organizations and the religious right as they sought to be the moderate voice in the midst of a local "culture war." And lastly, the SAGA organization in the Midwest was renamed SAGA Sunntach. Since the heritage of many residents in the region can be traced to Northern and Eastern Europe, I chose a Gaelic (the indigenous language of Ireland) word, "sunntach," which means "joyful." In the interviews with local activists, they expressed as sense of joy and pride in their work, saying that they felt like a family unit working toward a common good. Hence, my name for the location reflected this positive attitude.

Data Analysis

Working closely with one of my mentors Dr. Gloria González-López, we devised a data analysis plan during the research process. My analytical methods focused on one progressive stage of my qualitative data analysis. These stages were a continuous series as it began during the interview process, and continued on until after I completed the transcription of the interviews[7], and printed a total of over 900 single-spaced pages containing my interview data.

These stages consisted of seven steps:

1) I reviewed my field and interview debriefing notes, which consisted of my personal observations, comments, and reactions from the interviews, shortly after my interviews for the particular day in order to identify significant themes.

2) As I listened to the interviews shortly after transcribing them (or, for ten, when the completed transcripts were returned to me), I carefully listened to the words and audible reactions of the study participants, and noted them in the transcripts.

3) In an intermediary step between the transcribed interview and the data analysis, I created, identified, and saved separate Microsoft Word files for each theme in order to classify the information that I copied-and-pasted directly from the interview data. This provided me the opportunity to generate broad themes which would give shape to the eventual book chapters. Examples of such themes were: diversity and identity, emotions, race/class/gender issues, straight identity, thoughts of the future, and time constraints, among others. Each quote began with the pseudonym of the participant, followed by the line numbers of the beginning and end of the quote for easy reference.

4) It was necessary to transform the theme files into analyzable data and generate more specific themes for deeper analysis. From the data gathered in the Microsoft Word file, I individually numbered a row in a column of a Microsoft Excel sheet, and next to each numbered row, I copied-and-pasted the activists' quotes. Each file

of copied quotes fit into each one of these specific themes, e.g., diversity and identity, political environments, race/class/gender references, straight identity, definition of an activist, and thoughts of the future, among others. Every row of quotes began with the pseudonym of the participant, followed by the line numbers of the beginning and end of the quote for easy reference.

5) I printed each Microsoft Excel sheet and I cut the paper along the line separating each numbered row.

6) I read each sheet for each different theme category, and I placed them in piles on the floor around me. Each pile was called a "master theme." For those quotes I could not easily categorize into an obvious theme, I temporarily placed in a pile titled "miscellaneous." After developing more specific themes from the other piles, I then re-assigned their location in relation to these honed themes.

7) On one side of a sheet of yellow legal pad paper, I wrote the name in pencil of the activist, along with its corresponding numbered row, and a general synopsis of the quote for every master theme. I repeated this process for each quote in a master theme. From there, I placed the yellow sheet of paper into a clear plastic pouch with the written side visible, and placed the paper clippings from the Excel spreadsheet (Step 5) for each quote on the obverse side so that I could easily see both the contents and the synopses. These sheaths were stored in an inexpensive plastic briefcase, which I carried around with me at all times. I used these master files to develop the major chapters and sub-themes with the chapters.

I used this seven-step method to organize, code, and analyze the over 900 pages of interview data. As I continued to classify my data, I selectively chose only master files that I would use for this book. For example, although interesting, I did not include an analysis of how the participants defined the term "activist," and how they see themselves in relation to this definition. This information proves not directly relevant to my analysis of the strategic deployment of a straight identity. However, I kept this information to possibly be used for subsequent publications.

During the seven-step process of data analysis, I often experienced moments when the data "spoke" to me in innovative ways. I would notice some of the comments from the participants that would comport with other theories or concepts that I had not thought would be relevant to this study. Immediately, I would cease what I was doing, whether it was transcription, data analysis, or developing master files, and would write down my thoughts or ideas in a memo file. This process is based on the qualitative research methods used by Kathy Charmaz (1983), where one writes down their thoughts in a memo format. This is similar to the ethnographic field note process I utilized as discussed by Robert Emerson, et al. (1995). In this method, I would quickly jot down my thoughts, ideas, theoretical connections to other research, or additional questions for participants that came to mind during each interview. While I began to write my findings, I would reference these memos and field notes to assist me with some of the more complex themes derived from the master files.

In addition to this qualitative data used as the bulk of the data from the book, I included a quantitative analysis to provide descriptive data used mostly in this chapter and again in Chapter Six, which focuses on political environments. In this next paragraph, I describe the five stages of this analytical process:

1) I created a Microsoft Excel file named "Activist Demographics" and I made individual tabs for each one of these specific themes, e.g., basic demographic data that was self-reported by the activist, demographics of each SAGA board as reported by each participant, the organizational alliances as reported by the participant, as well as an organized table of the interview sample to be included in the book as Table 1.

2) I created an additional tab titled "Data Analysis" to systematically compute demographic tables, which were later inserted into the book where appropriate.

3) From the data in the "Data Analysis" tab, I directed Microsoft Excel to create pie charts to graphically represent the percentages of race, gender, and sexuality on the SAGA National Board of Directors, SAGA National staff members, as well as the sexuality of the participants included in this study. These figures were formatted to fit correctly into the book.

4) I went to the United States Census webpage to American FactFinder, and using Summary File 3 (Census 2000), I created tables that provided the square mileage of the geographic boundaries of

which each SAGA chapter is responsible, and computed the racial composition for each territory. I downloaded the data into a separate Microsoft Excel sheet.

5) Similarly, I used Summary File 3 from American FactFinder and computed the number of unmarried same-sex partner households for all the census tracts in the territory for each SAGA chapter. This method is done because there are no direct questions asking for a person's sexual identity on the census and is the only way that I could ascertain an approximation of the lesbian or gay population[8] within each geographical boundary.

Demographics of SAGA Activists

In this section, I explore the general demographics of SAGA activists I interviewed. Table 1 below is a listing of the interview sample's demographics. Following the table is a more descriptive analysis of SAGA's demographics. As seen in Table 2 and Table 3, most of the SAGA activists interviewed were relatively young and on the board for less than two years. The mean age of the activists I interviewed is 34.5 years, but the median age is 32 years. Generally, most of the activists with whom I interviewed were younger middle-class, professional gay males. Although I made every attempt to include a diverse sample, this was not always possible given the lack of board diversity from which my participants were drawn. Also, a broader sample was difficult because participation was voluntary. Since I had no control over these realities, maximizing the diversity of the sample was difficult.

I made an attempt to interview a diverse group of activists. However, this was a difficult task mainly because the organizations I visited tended to be dominated by gay males. About two-thirds of my respondents were male (see Table 4), and sixty percent of activists I interviewed self-identified as gay males, with only 10% self-identifying as lesbian or bisexual women (see Figure 3 and Table 5).

This leads to a conundrum; SAGA National works toward inclusivity in chapters as an ideal, but despite all attempts to build diversity within the structure, the local chapters continue to be dominated by gay males. El Reto County is the notable exception with two straight males on the board. However, for the most part, the straight activists tended to be women. Xavier and Adam were concerned that the arrangement of gay men and straight women only replicates the stereotype of the "gay man with fag hag" where the "fag hag" is the straight woman who nurtures and protects gay men from homophobia (see Chapter Three).

Table 1. Interview Sample Demographics

Name (Pseudonym)	Age (2003)	Gender Identity	Race / Ethnicity	Sexual Identity	Class Background	Occupation
Amanda Candor	26	Female	White	Bisexual	Working	Customer Service
Ruth Huerta	46	Female	Latina	Straight	Working	Professor
Paul Freeman	64	Male	Black	Straight	Working	Principal, Retired
Adam Lieberman	23	Male	White	Gay	Middle	Technology
Greg Adler	32	Male	White	Straight	Middle	Teacher
Grant Daniels	28	Male	White	Gay	Working	Management, Non-profit
Vincent Pasquarelli	33	Male	White	Gay	Middle	Principal
Gloria Wentworth	56	Female	White	Straight	Middle	Education, Retired
Trey McIntyre	20	Male	White	Gay	Upper	Student
Taylor Lynde	52	Male	White	Gay	Working	Teacher, Retired
Chrissy Williams	27	Female	White	Queer	Middle	Middle Management, Non-profit
Casey Lina	34	Female	White	Bisexual	Upper	Unemployed
Brooks Shepperd	30	Male	White	Gay	Working	Teacher
Don Sotheby	28	Male	White	Gay	Working	Teacher
Marc Andersen	24	Male	White	Gay	Upper	Executive Management, Non-profit
Anson Meyers	58	Male	White	Gay	Working	College Faculty

(continued)

Table 1.—*(continued)*

Name (Pseudonym)	Age (2003)	Gender Identity	Race / Ethnicity	Sexual Identity	Class Background	Occupation
Edit Aloo	35	Trans	Other	Queer	Working	Management, Non-profit
Reid Roberts	55	Male	White	Gay	Middle	Teacher, Retired
Dixon Harrington	33	Male	White	Gay	Working	Management, Non-profit
Joshua David	40	Male	White	Gay	Working	Management, Non-profit
Judy Eberhardt	58	Female	White	Straight	Middle	Social Work
Justin Petrov	19	Male	White	Gay	Upper	Student
Raul Gomez	32	Male	Latino	Gay	Working	Social Work
Sebastian St. James	32	Male	White	Gay	Upper	Teacher
Melissa Eggert	25	Female	White	Lesbian	Upper	Editor
C.J. Fleischer	35	Male	White	Gay	Middle	Management, Private sector
Chase O'Donnell	18	Male	White	Gay	Upper	Self-Employed
Janet Sfaldato	25	Female	White	Queer	Middle	Teacher
Xavier Lucas	23	Male	White	Gay	Upper	Management, Non-profit
Cameron Fine	23	Trans	White	Queer	Middle	Management, Non-profit

Table 2. Participant Demographics by Years a SAGA Board Member

Board Since?	n	%
1 year or less	11	36.67%
2 years	5	16.67%
3 years	3	10.00%
4 years	6	20.00%
5 or more years	5	16.67%

Table 3. Participant Demographics by Age

Age	n
Mean	34.5
Median	32
Mode	23

Table 4. Participant Demographics by Gender

Gender	n	%
Female	8	26.67%
Male	20	66.67%
Transgender	2	6.67%

Table 5. Participant Demographics by Sexuality

Sexuality	n	%
Gay (Male)	18	60.00%
Lesbian	1	3.33%
Bisexual	2	6.67%
Straight	5	16.67%
"Queer"	4	13.33%

Theory and Research Methods

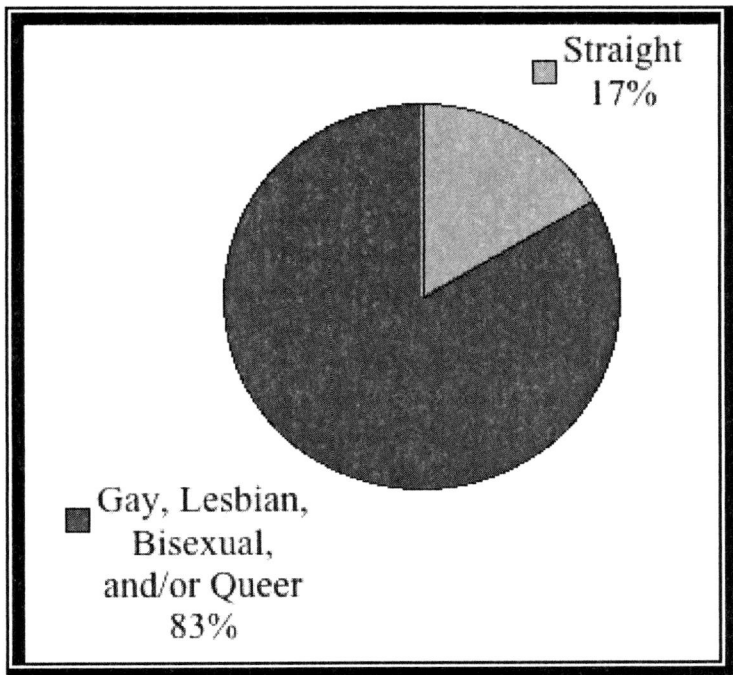

Figure 3. Breakdown of Sexual Identity of Research Participants

The activists in the organization are also mostly white, middle-class, and come from middle-class families. Only four activists self-identified as a racial or ethnic minority (see Table 6), and over one half of participants had a yearly household income greater than $55,000 a year (see Table 7).

Table 6. Participant Demographics by Race

Race	n	%
Asian	0	0.00%
Black	1	3.33%
Latino/a	2	6.67%
White	26	86.67%
Other	1	3.33%

Table 7. Participant Demographics by Income Level

Yearly Household Income	n	%
Under $10,000	0	0.00%
$10,000–$25,000	0	0.00%
$25,001–$40,000	12	40.00%
$40,001–$55,000	3	10.00%
$55,001–$70,000	5	16.67%
$70,001–$85,000	1	3.33%
$85,001–$100,000	3	10.00%
Over $100,000	6	20.00%

Only after beginning my data analysis did I realize some problems with the question about income. Some of the younger students had little to no income, but since they lived at home, they wrote down their family's income. In addition, the partnered households where both worked combined their income, which skewed the data higher than if they were single. But, from my question asking about their or of their parents' careers, I learned that many of the activists' parents had bachelor's degrees or higher, and were professionals.

Not surprisingly, as we see in Table 8, most of the activists registered their political party affiliation as Democrats considering the Party's inclusion of gay rights issues in the party's platform since the 1980 Democratic National Convention (O'Leary 2000). One notable exception is one

Table 8. Participant Demographics by Political Party Affiliation

Party Affiliation	n	%
Democrat	22	73.33%
Republican	1	3.33%
Libertarian	0	0.00%
Green	1	3.33%
Independent	6	20.00%

Republican, Melissa Eggert from El Reto County and Green Party member Trey McIntyre. Others chose to be politically independent. Xavier Lucas needed to be because, as an employee at a non-partisan lobbyist firm, it was expected for him to demonstrate this non-partisan slant.

Twenty percent of activists identified as political independents, and each of the independents self-identified with a more liberal political ideology. All of the activists self-identify with a liberal political ideology, and over half of the activists identified as a "Strong Liberal" (see Table 9).

A third of all respondents self-identified as "Liberal," and only four out of thirty respondents that I interviewed thought that they "Lean Liberal" in political ideology. Melissa Eggert is an activist from El Reto County in the Southwest, and although she identifies with a "liberal" political ideology, Melissa is registered as a Republican. As seen below, Melissa explains this situation by connecting her political ideology to working for change "from the inside." This is definitely a characteristic of SAGA, since it relies upon straight people to work "from the inside" where LGBT people often find it difficult to enter, as we see in Chapter Five.

> . . . [E]veryone that meets me are like, "You cannot be a registered Republican! What the hell is wrong with you?" I am probably by society's standards I know I'm very liberal, but at the same time I'm very fiscally conservative. I come from a family of registered Republicans who are all very liberal, ironically. . . . We were always raised to believe in civil rights and social movements and fighting for the underdog and making sure that everyone was equal. So, in that way I'm extremely liberal, I guess.

Table 9. Participant Demographics by Political Ideology

Political Ideology	n	%
Not Political	0	0.00%
Strong Liberal	16	53.33%
Liberal	10	33.33%
Lean Liberal	4	13.33%
Lean Conservative	0	0.00%
Conservative	0	0.00%
Strong Conservative	0	0.00%

However, finding a registered self-identified liberal Republican is a rare instance in the demographic data I collected from the activists. Although it is an interesting finding, it is further evidence of the complexities in the sociological understanding of identity construction in an LGBT political organization.

Methodological Issues

Although I am not a chronic sufferer of "Murphy's Law," there were occasions when my sanity was tested when everything that could go wrong inevitably did. One example is when SAGA Sunntach declined to participate in the study two days after my arrival to the city. Since my stay in Sunntach was pre-paid, and I would be in the city for longer than any other time (9 days), I contacted another SAGA organization about three hours away to participate. The SAGA chapter is in a rural area of the state and has three board members and only one person, Anson Ross, agreed to participate.

Unable to draw any regional conclusions from one interview, I persuaded two former co-chairs (Marc Andersen and Sebastian St. James) and the current co-chair of Sunntach (C.J., a self-identified gay man in his mid-thirties) to participate but only after agreeing to an unusual request from C.J., the new co-chair. C.J. reluctantly agreed to participate only if I was able to furnish him with testimonials from other activists who were interviewed previously. I quickly emailed activists Adam and Paul from El Reto County, and Casey and Taylor from Victoria if they would mind sending an email to C.J. explaining the benefits of participating in the research. The activists from El Reto County and Victoria wrote beautiful responses explaining how they personally and the organizations have benefited from the interviews because it allowed them to reflect back on their successes and roles in shaping these successes and failures. An example of one of these emails is found earlier in this chapter in the methodology section. I was thrilled that they did not let me down and was touched by their warm responses.

After receiving these emails, C.J. permitted SAGA Sunntach to be included in my study, but only if the activists contacted *me* first. However, it was unclear who knew about my research project and who did not. One activist curtly wrote me a one-sentence email in response to my previous requests: "Please don't contact me again." The two former co-chairs, Sebastian and Marc, did email me to be included in the study. Marc apologetically agreed to an interview in-person because of what he called "guilt." This is because the primary reason why SAGA Sunntach declined after agreeing to participate is that a week prior to my arrival, both co-chairs who agreed to participate were no longer in charge. In essence, the new leadership headed by C.J. Fleischer overruled the decision of the previous co-chairs.

From what I learned through my interview with Marc (and from an anonymous informant in SAGA National), the female co-chair hastily resigned her position the week prior to my arrival after experiencing a dispute with chapter members over the direction of the organization. This could not have come at a worse time for me because Marc's term as co-chair also expired, and he was the other co-chair who agreed to include SAGA Sunntach in the project. But, I also learned that another reason may be due to a mistrust of SAGA National. From what I gathered via my interviews in SAGA Sunntach is that many activists feared that I really was working for the president of SAGA and was masking my snooping under 'academic pursuit.'

Another issue that arose during my fieldwork also stemmed from a mistrust of academics. Gloria Wentworth, a self-identified straight woman activist from SAGA Victoria in her late 50s, was aware of the problems with confidentiality that stem from academic research. She exhibited caution in divulging too much during our interview. Through personal connections, she knew activists that were interviewed by Arlene Stein in her book *The Stranger Next Door* (2001). Although Stein was careful to change the name of the city and names of the people she interviewed, Gloria confided in me that her friends felt somewhat betrayed because people in the small town renamed "Timbertown" knew who said what because the population in the area was so small. Throughout the interview, Gloria was cautious with her words to be sure that her identity, and the identity of others, would remain confidential in my dissemination of the data. At the close of the interview, Gloria expressed her concerns more clearly, still unsure what my "true" motives were, even after reading the informed consent form.

> I think you're conscientious and responsible, but no matter what there's a measure of risk with confidentiality, and . . . I'm just very sensitive to being confidential.

Gloria expressed further concerns about the confidentiality of the study, primarily because of the nature of SAGA chapters:

> And I think your motives are to study and learn and identify what's going on, and that you do care about success for the GLBT community, and inherently success for SAGA. But that's still the most uncomfortable issue to deal with . . . I guess, you know it's a volunteer organization . . . [*Why as a volunteer organization is it more difficult to answer?*] Well, I think it's a more—any volunteer organization, it's a more fragile structure, and I guess I feel a little more protective maybe.

As we see in the quote above, Gloria repeats to me that she assumes my motives are pure, but there is still that protectiveness of a "fragile" organizational structure, just in case she is incorrect in her assessment of my academic intentions. And yet, once I divulged that I was a gay activist at the close of the interview, Gloria hugged me goodbye and wished me luck on my travels.

Although trepidation was a rare occurrence in my fieldwork, I still experienced interviews where I knew that the activists did not quite trust my intent, despite providing activists the opportunity for questions about my research. As I discussed above in the story about SAGA Sunntach, C.J. was also very reluctant to meet with me, and instead requested that we conduct a brief telephone interview at his convenience. Our telephone interview occurred nearly two months after arriving in Sunntach. In my field notes, I noted that he paused unusually long after every question that I posed. In one instance, he commented that he was still there on the phone, even though there was a long silence after my question. C.J. also accentuated the positives in every response—so much so that there were no negative references to grassroots organizing at all. Although I could confirm through analyzing my interviews with Marc and Sebastian many of the positive accounts C.J. provided, I increasingly wondered if he was being completely forthright with me as a researcher on the positives and negatives of grassroots organizing, or if he was treating me as he would the press with everything having a positive "spin."

One last issue arose during a SAGA Victoria meeting. I was unexpectedly drawn into a dispute amongst board members regarding a scholarship fund. Like many of the activists I spoke with, I personally liked Taylor Lynde, who is a retired schoolteacher in his early 50s and believed that he truly wanted what was the best for SAGA. But, Taylor demonstrated on a number of occasions that he was unaware of the social or political ramifications to some of his decisions. In the SAGA Victoria meeting, Taylor drew me into a board dispute over money, which forced me to step out of my role of sociologist. During our interview, Taylor mentions a new idea that he probably thought up in the middle of our interview when he was talking about retiring: a scholarship fund for SAGA youth. Its implementation has nepotism concerns:

> Now this year, my stretch—and I just kind of realized this because my niece who is turning eighteen. She's going to [a community college]. She wants to be a teacher. And I'm retiring this year. So, I am asking all the faculty and all the people that instead of buying me a retiring gift if they will donate that other money they were going to give to me for my

retirement gift to a scholarship fund for SAGA. And I am going to talk to [my niece]. I am going to set up a foundation for SAGA. My stretch is that I'm going to try to take that five-hundred dollars that SAGA is talking about and I'm going to put that into a foundation, a scholarship, and this very first year, it's my retirement money that's going into it. It's my five hundred dollars.

To summarize Taylor's thoughts, he believed that since this was his retirement money, he had the right to determine to whom and how it should be spent. The devil, though, is in the details; by giving it to SAGA, the money no longer belongs to him but to the organization.

Taylor's interview was the most difficult to conduct because it lasted three-and-a-half hours long and I rarely had the opportunity to ask him a question. The interview mostly centered on his stream of consciousness, rather than a semi-structured interview format. To be honest, my field notes from his interview did not even mention this scholarship plan. Given that it was said in passing during the last half-hour of the interview, I probably looked at him affirmatively or nodded in agreement as I waited for the opportunity to interject with a question that was more in line with the research agenda. Little did I realize that my body language was probably misread as agreement to his plan, which would later come back to haunt me in the context of the SAGA meeting.

Members of SAGA Victoria repeatedly stated that meetings are very similar to my experience with Taylor. The meeting does not follow an agenda, and consists of a relatively uninterrupted stream of consciousness by Taylor in a top-down format that discourages open dialogue and discussion. In this meeting, Taylor mentions this scholarship idea to the entire group. He provides no details to the plan; there is no specification to how much money the scholarship would be, or what the criteria are for receiving the grant (other than the financial need of his niece). And, similar to what I learned from the activists, Taylor asked that the board vote that evening agreeing that this was a good plan. What is worse is that he tells the group that he got the idea "from Danny in the interview." Although the tape recorded interviews sometimes notes "mm-hmms" and other audible agreements as said by me, the recording of Taylor's interview does not indicate any audible agreement to his comment. Simply put, I cannot imagine what I did that would have indicated my agreement with Taylor's proposal, but whatever he thought was agreement was clearly misinterpreted.

In light of his comment, I struggled to remain silent in the meeting. But, as I expected, the scholarship caused a heated disagreement among those present, citing concerns of nepotism and improper accounting. At that point, Taylor kept asking why his plan was such a bad idea. My observations were that he did not listen to the concerns of the board, and other activists whom I spoke with after the meeting confirmed my impressions. Hastily, I broke my silence as an impartial observer and addressed Taylor, as well as the group, emphatically stating that I did not believe that SAGA National would approve of any chapter setting up a scholarship in SAGA's name to only give it to a relative of the chair, or without an objective selection process. Taylor then agreed, saying, "Oh, yeah, I didn't think of that." I continued on, stressing the fact that I did not agree with his proposal in the interview, and that my decision not to comment on it during our interview should not have been interpreted as a tacit approval of his plan.

After my comments, Taylor kept repeating that he wanted to donate his retirement gift funds in SAGA's name to his niece, but would do it under his name. When Casey suggested that it be a Taylor Lynde Scholarship Fund, he declined that he did not want it named after him, but he wanted it to be SAGA, and that is why he kept pressing for it to be to his niece under SAGA's name. But other activists began to pointedly question Taylor, asking him what his niece has done to further SAGA's mission, or even more generally for LGBT youth (being that she, herself, was not LGBT). At this moment, unable to answer these questions, Taylor backed down. At that point, another activist, Casey, nominated herself to be on a committee to figure this out, table it for next month, and tell Taylor what they came up with as far as criteria for choosing recipients. Recognizing that I perhaps stepped out of line, I remained quiet observing the group for the remainder of the meeting.

I do not know if board members were convinced by my adamant denial of suggesting Taylor's nepotistic plan or not, but after that meeting, no one from Victoria ever contacted me again regarding the project. I also was unable to schedule interviews with other participants other than Don Sotheby, with whom I had already scheduled before the commencement of the SAGA meeting. I do not know whether this instance affected the likelihood of garnering additional interviews or not. My feeling is that it may have frightened away possible participants, but that most of the activists I already interviewed believed that I would adhere to objective methodology and not have advised Taylor to go ahead with his scholarship plan.

STRAIGHT AHEAD OR MOVING FORWARD?

In the next chapter, I analyze the organizational diversity of SAGA by exploring the ways in which activists conceptualize diversity. Is the prevalence of middle class gay white males and white heterosexual women a result of geography, organizational structure, or a replication of the patriarchal biases of Western culture? Although important in understanding identity deployment in this particular LGBT organization, many of the findings I present are from the activists' own words in response to a particular question asking for them to comment on whether or not they viewed the LGBT movement as middle-class gay white male dominated. Sometimes in the interview, activists note contradictions in how they conceptualize diversity. Other times I find activists seek strict adherence to the goal of maximizing diverse opinions in the organization. However, it is important to note that these findings are not derived from a substantial part of the project rubric or methodology, and so further research on SAGA is necessary to explicate these findings beyond the findings discussed in the following chapter.

Chapter Three
Organizational Diversity in SAGA

LGBT activists have become more vocal in asserting that nearly all of the most politically influential gay rights organizations in the United States are white male-dominated, even if there are visible lesbians in positions of power (see Chasin 2000; Vaid 1995). But, is SAGA similar to the others? Are the issues that are important to SAGA really just white male-defined issues but professed to be "inclusive" to racial, ethnic, gender, or class minorities? Before I delve deeper into the mission and organizational strategies of SAGA, I will address the broader issue of diversity in SAGA.

Based on the demographic data I collected from SAGA National, white-male visibility is an issue for SAGA. In my interviews, I asked participants if they perceived the issues that the LGBT movement in general addressed and pursued to be mostly white, middle-class, and gay male dominated. Nearly all respondents, most of whom were white, agreed that this was an issue to contend with, especially for SAGA. In this chapter, I provide answers to this question in the words of the activists who, although recognizing that SAGA may be led by white, middle-class men, believe that the mission is *not* defined by race, class, or gender. Some of the activists I spoke with recognized their privilege in society because of themselves being white, or male, or even straight. But to explain the dearth of people of color and working-class activists, many activists provide hegemonic reasons, suggesting that the organization merely reflects the culture at large.

In the process of answering these questions, an interesting finding was brought to the fore: heterosexual privilege. The straight participants spoke about their willingness to forego heterosexual privilege to some degree upon joining SAGA by downplaying that they were not straight. These gestures were met with resistance by the SAGA activists who believed that being straight was their best asset to the group, and used this privilege as a deployment strategy. However, in this chapter, I explore the foundation of this identity deployment by analyzing how activists conceptualize heterosexual privilege, and how this simultaneous relinquishing/deployment of these privileges actually prevent SAGA from self-destructing because it maintains sexual identity boundaries without replicating heterosexist oppression found in the culture within the organization.

IS SAGA PURSUING A GAY WHITE MALE ISSUE?

Although most of the SAGA chapters that I visited had a dearth of transgender activists, people of color, and members from working-class backgrounds, this was not necessarily true of SAGA National. Reviewing Table 10, it is apparent that, although the majority of the board members and professional staff are gay males, racial/ethnic and gender minorities are present in the organization.

A further analysis of the SAGA National organizational diversity show that gay white men dominate the SAGA National Board of Directors, as well as the professional staff of SAGA National in number. Figures 4 and 5 provide percentages of board members and professional staff according to their race/ethnicity, self-identified gender, and sexuality.

Despite gay white males dominating the staff and board of SAGA National in numbers, from my observations of staff meetings and informal interviews, the leadership by and large respects diverse perspectives. Edit Aloo is a thirty-five year old transgender staff member of SAGA National who works closely with local chapters to ensure that they are following the mission of SAGA in their activist endeavors. She explains that SAGA struggles with diversity, regardless of the organizational level.

Table 10. Organizational Diversity of SAGA National

Categories	Minority				Non-Minority				Totals
	Female	%	Male	%	Female	%	Male	%	
Board of Directors	3	9.09%	3	9.09%	8	24.24%	19	57.58%	33
Professional Staff	4	18.18%	4	18.18%	4	18.18%	10	45.45%	22
Totals	7	12.73%	7	12.73%	12	21.82%	29	52.73%	55

Data Source: SAGA National, 2003

Organizational Diversity in SAGA 59

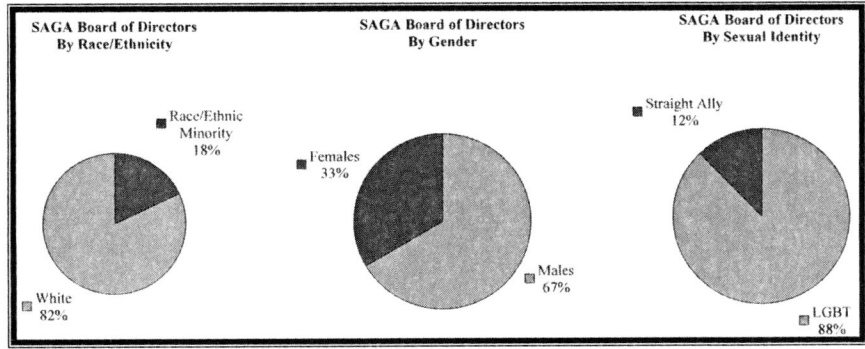

Figure 4. SAGA National Board of Directors; By Race, Gender, and Sexuality

> [SAGA] still, as an entire entity (from the smallest chapter to the national organization board), has its own struggles with diversity and inclusiveness. . . . Although I don't think safe schools work could ever be defined [as male, white, and middle class], by anybody who's in the know. I don't think it's so much our mission that's the problem, because our mission is wonderful. . . . I don't see it as only being a problem of the executive staff of SAGA or the board at SAGA. It's also a problem in our trenches as well.

Edit continues her comments, suggesting that the lack of organizational diversity reflects the hegemonic racism, classism, and genderism in the United States today.

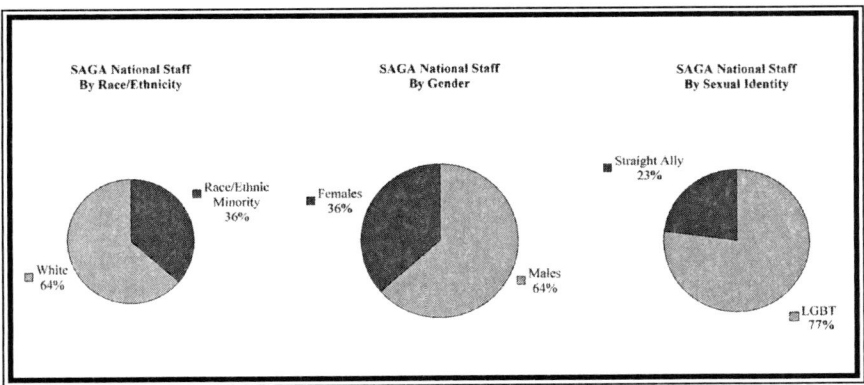

Figure 5. SAGA National Staff Members; By Race, Gender, and Sexuality

> It's a problem that's very much reflective of the problems of the United States to begin with, so. People organize separately. People do everything separately. And you know, it just continues, bottom to top.

Again, Edit reiterates that she does not believe that SAGA's mission lacks attention to diversity, primarily because on the national level, the diverse staff shape the mission to be inclusive:

> But so, I don't think the things we address, like you know, getting teacher training, or trying to get a [youth safety] policy, are white-male driven. . . . So, it is a problem, we're behind some organizations, but I think we're ahead of the country as a whole, so. And I think the staff reflects that, the fact that we're almost fifty percent people of color.

When I followed up with a question asking Edit if the fact that almost half of the SAGA staff members are people of color affects the organization in any way, she said:

> Not with our staff. . . . I would actually say that we have some people from a poor white background who are more liberal than some of the people of color that we have on staff, who are not necessarily that liberal, ironically. So you know one of the diversity considerations I think when we're looking at things is also economics, not strictly color.

As we read in the quotes above, for Edit, diversity in SAGA encompasses more than just racial categories, but economic categories as well. This is an interesting finding, but is not indicative of what I noticed from the demographic data of the SAGA chapters I studied. Cameron Fine, a twenty-three year old transgender and also a staff member of SAGA National, discusses how SAGA's conceptualizations of diversity are implemented at the grassroots level. Cameron works directly with local chapters as a part of his job responsibilities. As the only staff person willing to openly discuss particular chapters during the interview, Cameron is quite frank with me when he states, in his opinion, how he and his colleagues react to local chapters that are more resistant to inclusivity in a general sense:

> [Some chapters] aren't a priority for us, because they're either not really doing the work that we'd hoped that they'd be doing, and they're not in a key location, and they're all white and they're male, and so, sometimes, even when they outreach to us, it's not always the same in return.

And yet, as Edit and Cameron suggest (and from what I learned in my analysis of the chapter accreditation applications, as well as interviews with chapter activists), SAGA's *message* is inclusive, but its *membership* tends not to reflect this idealized goal. One case in point is that the only people to identify as "transgender" in this study were SAGA staff members. Most local chapters knew of *no* transgender people who had joined, or are currently present in SAGA. Why this dissonance between the work toward diversity and inclusivity directives from the national organization, and the reality of the chapters?

Activists tried to make sense of this dissonance in a number of ways. When I questioned broadly whether or not they viewed the issues that the LGBT movement addressed and pursued were mostly male, white, and middle-class issues, almost all activists defended SAGA without me even posing the direct question. Some of the responses from activists were specific, citing the local reasons, such as the location of the chapter or their geographical region they cover (i.e., suburban areas) for the absence of non-white, working-class, or non-gay male members. But beyond attributing the dearth to local circumstances, most of the responses from activists of why their particular chapters are comprised mostly of white males typically followed a similar pattern: The mission of SAGA, to protect LGBT youth from oppression, is not shaped around middle-class white male issues. But, if it is true middle-class white males dominate the chapter, it is only because it is reflecting the culture as a whole. In this section, I explore these findings, and in conclusion, I address how the organizational diversity in SAGA chapters has an effect on implementing the mission of SAGA on the local levels.

An Issue For Everybody

As I began my research project, I wondered if whether or not leadership hierarchies would form in local levels and, if so, whether or not they were stratified according to sexuality, gender, race, and class. By and large, the SAGA activists I spoke with saw the LGBT movement in general addressed and pursued issues that were male-dominated, white, and middle-class concerns. But, in our interviews, nearly every SAGA activist stated that the LGBT movement was simply reflecting the racist, sexist, and classist power structure of the dominant culture. Some activists went so far as to express disappointment with this reality, but believed that changing the system was beyond the control of any organization. Dixon, a SAGA activist (and a gay white male from a working class background) from the Northeastern United States, articulated well the sentiments of many local SAGA activists:

> Gay rights issues suffer from every single thing that every other issue in the country does. . . . You can't have a movement that doesn't have some sort of impact on it from those greater society issues. . . . I don't necessarily think that the white male is saying [to people of color and lesbians], "You can't get on board." . . . You just can't extract our Americanism and our culture and our history, from this particular movement, just like you can't extract it from any other. So, is it defined by the white, male, middle-class guy, yes, but so is everything else.

Dixon suggests that the message of SAGA may be inclusive, and that the board members are not practicing exclusionary tactics. But, his final statement in the quote above seems to suggest that the reason LGBT people of color are not joining SAGA is because of its reflection on the discriminatory social structure at large.

Interestingly, most of the activists who agreed that the LGBT movement is defined by white male, middle-class issues eventually concluded that SAGA was different. The organizational mission of SAGA is built around inclusivity; The fact that the goal of SAGA is to promote safe schools for LGBT students, teachers, and staff means that the mission in itself is *not* seeking an issue that pertains only to the middle-class, white, or male issue. Vincent Pasquarelli, the former co-chair of SAGA El Reto County, makes a comment that reflects the thoughts of other SAGA activists who find SAGA's mission not racist, sexist, or classist:

> I don't think that's true for SAGA. I mean, there is a clear mission and vision for SAGA National. And mainly similar or adapted missions at the local chapter level. And, those visions and missions are ideals, which are not classified as white male issues. Those goals and aspirations are for everybody. It's not a white male issue to say that all students regardless of their sexual orientation should be schooled in a safe environment. That is not a white male issue. That's an issue for everybody.

Similarly, Gloria Wentworth from SAGA Victoria agrees that the mission of SAGA is not defined as a white male issue, but is also an issue that affects everybody regardless of gender, race, or class:

> I'm not big on supporting the male, white middle-class, so that must not be it. Why would I working so hard [in SAGA]? . . . I got involved in advocacy for GLBT youth because of the intense pain that the youth were sharing with me. . . . But I don't think of it as a race or a class

thing at all to see a kid in pain because they're being rejected by their family. It seems like that pain goes across all class and racial/ethnic—I mean, it may be expressed differently, but it seems to me the hurt's got to be the same across all of that.

Three of the youngest members that I spoke with, Chase O'Donnell from SAGA El Reto County, Trey McIntyre from SAGA Victoria, and Justin Petrov from SAGA Piedmont also found the mission of SAGA to be inclusive. Chase, a white gay male who just graduated high school two months before our interview, was audibly baffled by the question since he had never heard this criticism of the LGBT movement before, but attempted to pattern his answer around his experiences in SAGA:

> [. . . *People in the gay and lesbian community have said that the issues that gay and lesbian organizations address are mostly male-defined, white and middle-class issues. What do you think about that?*] I'd never even heard that before. I mean, I think it depends on the organization. Like, for example, SAGA, it helps out everyone: the students, the teachers, I mean I don't think there's any certain specific group. I mean, like I said, I think it just depends on the organization or the group. [*Do you think SAGA has that?*] I don't think so, personally. . . . I mean, I don't think—because I think it helps out everyone. I don't think there's any certain specific category, you know, it doesn't just help out guys or just help out girls, it helps out everyone together.

Trey, recognizing his own identity as a white gay male, attempts to reconcile the gay white male dominance in SAGA Victoria by connecting it to the American culture as what he sees as dominated by "middle-class white males":

> [*Some activists say that the main issues in LGBT organizations are mostly male-defined, white, and middle-class issues. What do you think about that?*] I don't know. I'm male and white, so I guess I kind of fulfill that in some way. But I know that the direct goals of SAGA are not to support middle-class, white males. That's not the sense I got out of the organization. We're coming together to work on something that includes so many more people than obviously white males.

Trey also cites culture as the roots of the lack of diversity in the LGBT movement, but reiterates that SAGA is different because of its organizational mission of inclusivity:

> So I think that, sure, we live in a culture where it's been very centered around middle-class white males, you know, and that's just the way it's been. I also think that's changing. But I think that this specific organization is not. And, whether its constituents typically are middle-class white males, that's not the implied goal of the group, is to work for middle-class white males.

In my follow-up question, asking Trey whether or not he sees SAGA Victoria members as mostly middle-class, white gay males, he hints that the location may have an effect, rather than the mission being defined as a gay white male issue:

> I mean, there's a good number of middle-class white males, but there's a good number of middle-class white males in the country, so, I mean— I see women, like—I don't know. I've definitely—I feel like there's a good mix of females and males involved with this movement. I've definitely noticed that most of the people [in SAGA Victoria] are white, but maybe you can attribute that to the area.

Justin Petrov, a sophomore in college, explains the white male dominance in the LGBT movement on the power structure of the United States society in general, but suggests to me that the geographical location of SAGA in suburbia is a reason for the local dominance of wealthier, gay white people on their chapter's board:

> I think just based on the constructs of history everything is male defined, white, and middle class, or at least it always starts that way. . . . I guess the statement is true but it's certainly not done intentionally. . . . SAGA does a really good job of making sure to outreach to as many schools as it can . . . And the truth is that a lot of the lower class schools don't have the kind of leadership from the faculty and from the students that would allow for a group like SAGA to come in.

Like Trey and Dixon, Justin argues that the mission of SAGA is to assist all students, regardless of race, class, gender, or sexuality differences. If there is any dominance of middle-class white males in the organization, it is because the organization unintentionally reflects the culture at large.

SAGA activists rarely made claims to me that the white male "message" framed the mission, despite the obvious dominance of males in numbers. From what I learned from these interviews is that *where* organizations choose to focus their efforts (such as suburban locations rather than urban

Organizational Diversity in SAGA 65

areas) and which communities they choose to outreach for membership will influence the image to appear gay, white male dominated. In the next section, I explore this idea and choose two case studies of chapters—SAGA El Reto County and SAGA Victoria—and explore how they diverge in their perceptions of the influence of geography in the apparent dominance of white males in their chapters.

Location, Location, Location!

> [Some chapters] aren't a priority for us, because they're either not really doing the work that we'd hoped that they'd be doing, and they're not in a key location, and they're all white and they're male, and so, sometimes, even when they outreach to us, it's not always the same in return. (Interview with Cameron Fine, SAGA National)

In the quote above from Cameron that I explained earlier in this chapter, where a chapter is located can have a profound effect on whether or not there is minority representation in the membership. This, in turn, can affect how much attention a chapter receives from SAGA National. Every chapter that I visited, with the exception of SAGA Piedmont (located in a suburban location), was headquartered within the city limits of a major metropolitan area. Even though five out of the six locations were in city limits, their primary focus was in the school systems outside of the city limits. My analysis of chapter records indicates that this may be because the teachers on the board work and have established networks in these suburban school districts. SAGA Sunntach was the major exception to this "suburban focus" and has made an active effort to increase minority participation in the organization by focusing on the city only. Cameron praises them in his quote below:

> This may sound sad, but it's also really wonderful that a chapter that's in a city, like SAGA Sunntach, is actually doing the work in the city, and not in the suburbs. Because we have had and do have a lot of experience with chapters being SAGA Blank, you know, [representing] this large metropolitan area, and then they work on the outskirts. They work in the white, majority white, suburban communities there. So it's definitely great that SAGA Sunntach really does the SAGA Sunntach work.

And yet, even though the focus is in the "minority-majority" city itself, their location within the city still hinders the active inclusion of minorities on the board. The three activists from Sunntach that I spoke with, all chapter co-chairs at some point, were the only participants to specifically mention meeting location to explain the dearth of non-white members.

For activists in SAGA Sunntach like Sebastian, Marc, and C.J., the reasons why African-Americans and Latinos—who, as racial and ethnic groups, comprise the majority of the population in the city of Sunntach—did not join SAGA in large numbers was because of the inaccessibility of people to get to the meetings. Marc, a past co-chair, cited structural causes, such as the city structure and meeting location in the gentrified gay enclave of northern Sunntach, as a possible reason for the notable absence of people of color:

> Part of it is the way Sunntach is set up. Sunntach is very regionally segregated. . . . Its neighborhoods are segregated. . . . And so, in SAGA (and we talk about changing this but we never do) [Marc chuckles], SAGA is a north-side organization, which is white. . . . Our monthly programs are up here, our meetings are up here—we end up having white people on the board. Do we ever meet on the south side? No. That's where all the black neighborhoods [are]. Not that we don't [meet there] consciously. Do we meet downtown where it's neutral? No. We meet up here. It's also the gay neighborhood. . . . You know, it's like a chicken and egg kind of thing. [Marc chuckles] Where does it start and where does it end? I don't know! [Marc chuckles]

Sebastian was the co-chair of SAGA several years ago, and also finds diversity in SAGA to be a "chicken and the egg" problem. He finds that the meeting location in the gay neighborhood limits the access to include people of color in the organization. Without people of color in attendance, there can be no programming that attracts them. Sebastian explains:

> . . . We have had a couple of people who are always very conscious of how do we support or how do we include programs for people of color. . . . But what's hard is that it's the chicken and the egg problem. How do you do programming for a group when you don't have a member of that group to help you with the programming? And, how do you recruit people when you don't have any programming to get them involved at an attendance level?

For Sebastian, the way to end this problem was two-fold: first, move the meetings to a more accessible location for people of color. And, second, SAGA should take a proactive stand on creating meaningful coalitions and partnerships with people of color.

Organizational Diversity in SAGA

And there's also how do you involve minorities without—like what kind of partnerships can we form? What kind of coalitions can we form? It's something that we struggle with a lot.

And yet, as Sebastian notes, moving the meetings downtown may not be enough to change the racial dominance in SAGA Sunntach because people of color may still see how white the chapter currently is:

In the monthly programs that we've put on [when I was co-chair], we did have a lot of people of color and speakers and presenters. [*How well did that work?*] I think we had some really great programming actually. I thought it worked pretty well. It didn't generate a lot of volunteers for people of color. I'm not sure that it drew people of color to the event. [*Why do you think that might be so?*] Maybe because it was still on the north side. It may have been inconvenient. It may be because they're working—I don't know why they're choosing what issues they're working on. They might perceive it as a white thing.

During our interview, C.J. noted a few reasons how, as co-chair, he has made attempts to change this reality by moving meetings to a neutral location downtown in the hopes of sending that message to people of color that SAGA wants to be inclusive to their needs as well:

We changed the location of our programs this year so we could attract more adults of color and hopefully build a more racially-diverse board. And with our efforts that we'll be focusing on with parents, hopefully we'll be building a board that is more diverse in age as well . . . We are moving it . . . right into the heart of the downtown, which makes it easier for people coming from the south and the west [of Sunntach, which are the minority neighborhoods].

C.J. also looks to cultural reasons for the lack of success in bringing in people of color despite having programming that was presumed to be of interest to the communities of color:

[. . . *What are some of your thoughts about trying to gain more minorities [in SAGA Sunntach?]* . . . I'll give you a few reasons. Location was one thing. . . . [Also], I think it's tougher in the Latino community and in the African American community to be out and be gay or lesbian. For different reasons, I think that they struggle even more than white communities do to accept that. So, I think that people aren't as out and that limits the population you can attract. They're not going to want to come to an event that is pegged as gay or lesbian. I think our programming hasn't always appealed to other populations other than what people want to hear about. We assume that the issues are the same, but we don't really know that.

In addition to citing the structure of the city, Marc is a bit more forthright in his response to why SAGA Sunntach has very few people of color in the organization:

. . . There are several reasons. One is there are unique minority groups, and that's their work. Many of them feel that way. It's like we try to recruit members *out* of these other groups, like [a group] for black lesbians. Well, you know, they're going to want to hang out with other black lesbians! I think. You know? So, we're trying to take them away into our group. But, that's not their culture! They have their group! That's why they're there! I think that's part of it.

As I stated earlier, SAGA Sunntach was the only chapter to specifically note their active attempts to increase minority membership in the organization. I find that this is partially in response to its location in a minority-majority city. But, what if the city in which the chapter is located is overwhelmingly white, such as is the case in SAGA Victoria, a city in the Pacific Northwest? Is it fair to criticize a board that it is comprised almost all of white people if the city is mostly white, too? A few of the activists I spoke with agree that it is a fair criticism of a chapter when the leadership of the chapter fails to be inclusive in its message to the community. Before I delve into the criticisms made by some of the members of SAGA, it is important to explain how the chapter co-chair, Taylor Lynde, perceives organizational diversity.

Although the activists I spoke with believe that Taylor Lynde has good intentions for SAGA Victoria, they feel that both his leadership qualities and conceptualization of what is meant by organizational diversity has had an effect on membership and, in turn, its efficacy in the communities it services. Three activists described meetings as "Taylor's show" because of its top-down dialogue method. Taylor spoke for nearly the whole time with only brief opportunities for discussion amongst members (one of which was a heated discussion of which I described in Chapter Two).

Don Sotheby, a gay male elementary school teacher, spoke with me immediately following the heated scholarship discussion. Still visibly distraught by the night's discussion topic, Don makes his ambivalence toward

Organizational Diversity in SAGA

Taylor very clear to me when he bluntly states that Taylor does not fit his criteria of a successful chapter leader:

> Taylor's great, but he's very—he's got his agenda . . . Eventually things are done and things are supported. But, it takes a long time. . . . I think a successful chair needs to be somebody who can facilitate a discussion and let the members talk and let the members bring up issues. A lot of times, the meetings we have can be over a lot quicker, but he wants to talk. I think, a leader of an organization needs to lead and also to listen and let the group do some stuff and take control . . . and not have to listen to top-down all the time. Let a discussion happen!

Some activists were rather forthright with me that Taylor, as a leader of SAGA, is unclear what SAGA National means by "diversity." Casey Lina, a bisexual activist in SAGA Victoria, suggests during our interview that Taylor is unclear about what is meant by the word "diversity" in activist circles.

> There was a classic thing where . . . somebody sent something to Taylor asking for panel. And, Taylor misunderstood it was a diversity panel and he assumed that some board member should go. . . . So, he put the call out for us to go. And, a couple of us kind of thought, "You know, this really doesn't seem right!" And sure enough, it was actually a racial diversity focus. And he was *really* surprised. And he kept saying, "Are you sure? Are you sure?" And there were two of us that looked at each other and, "Read this description! There's not a single person in this room right now who is going to be able to reflect an African American experience in Victoria. There's just not, really."

Casey immediately stresses the point that if SAGA Victoria activists—all white suburbanites working on LGBT issues—were to present at this panel, it would have been embarrassing to the group and the organization at large:

> And it was telling to me, you know, that he's so gung-ho and trying so hard to make a wonderful impact on people's lives that he saw the word diversity and assumed that included GLBT and was all ready to send one of us and we had to say no. Not only is this not the diversity we're to talk about here, but also look at this board. We can't do this. We can't. It would be embarrassing to offer.

From what I gathered in our interview, Taylor does not define diversity in terms of race, class, or gender. Taylor's understanding of diversity seems to mean "sexual" diversity, and not race, class, or gender. We can see this in the quote below when Taylor describes to me the process by which he sought to increase chapter diversity, which was to draw from a pool of people from which he was personally familiar. As Taylor had a tendency to continue speaking uninterrupted for long periods of time, his quote may be confusing, particularly when edited for content.

> . . . I felt, to keep SAGA alive, that I had to instigate some change. So, what I actually did was go out and I tried to find people that I thought. . . . were more of my thinking . . . Trey McIntyre was the first person that came. . . . But he was a younger person, which I felt—at that point he was the youngest . . . I really felt that we needed more diversity on the board. Most of us were teachers. . . . We were all in that probably maybe mid-thirties to forties range. And I really felt we needed more of an age-diversity on the board.

Taylor continues on with his response, stressing his idea of board diversity. Notice how his conceptualization does not mean race, class, or gender, but age and employment position (i.e., teacher vs. non-teacher).

> . . . So, our board has changed a lot—although I think the diversity of our board is a lot greater now. We have some young folks who are in college that are participating and involved with us. We have teachers who are just beginning teachers all the way up to some pretty veteran teachers.

As Taylor speaks further, he begins to address diversity in more specific terms, focusing on race, gender, and sexuality as a part of organizational diversity. However, in the context of the discussion, this appears to be more of an afterthought in what he truly sees as "diverse" for a lesbian and gay organization. And, the lack of diversity in SAGA Victoria seems to be attributed to the limitations of Taylor's social networks as well.

> We have a school psychiatrist who is actually straight who has a gay son. We have only one female on our board, and she's heterosexual[1]. And she's kind of a new addition to the board. But it's a really nice, to me, a nice balance. I would like to try to move into, and I would like us to have people of color. I would love for us to have some more gay women. That would be interesting to be involved in those kinds of

Organizational Diversity in SAGA

things, too. But, at this point, it's one of those things that will take a lot of work and right now, most of the people that have come have been people who have just fallen into the spot. And I have to admit, most of them are people I know.

In our three-and-a-half hour interview, Taylor spoke in a relatively uninterrupted "stream of consciousness" fashion. At one of these times, he divulges his interpretation of diversity in an LGBT organization, as well as his unawareness of racial histories and issues. In one of the more shocking moments of my interviews, Taylor tried to answer my question "What is an activist" by speaking at length positively about the direction of the gay movement, while also using racial stereotypes to describe what he sees as SAGA's strategy. Since Taylor spoke in a stream of consciousness, the quotes below immediately follow the ones above without interruption.

> . . . [A]s a gay activist, one of the things that you always want the community to see you as is as a respected individual who has *thoughtfully* put together ideas and a plan for the betterment of the community and for it not to be a rioting kind of—disturbing meetings and throwing things. But, you know, damn it, I guess there is a piece of that too!

He immediately connects emotionally-charged rioting with the African American Civil Rights Movement:

> I guess in being an activist, sometimes—I mean, I guess I look at the black movement and I don't think people started listening to black people until they started rioting and breaking and burning and looting and killing. And when they started doing all that kind of stuff, all of a sudden the community started looking at them and saying, "Oh my God, they really mean business!"

Again, Taylor erroneously states that the African American community as a whole, as well as other civil rights movements, is not "educated" about their collective history.

> Now, the part that I don't think the black community has got yet or a lot of communities have gotten, which I think the gay community has finally figured out, which is what SAGA to me is all about, I think you have to educate—and I think you have to take that one step further. You have to educate the gay population into their history and being

proud of their history and who they are, and where they're going, and what they're doing. When you do that, you have that force and you have those allies.

Taylor continues with his uninterrupted monologue, implying that both he and I are both "educated" and have strong self-esteems in that I am willing to "move into research" on LGBT issues, and he is unafraid to be an out gay teacher in a public school:

> And I think also then, when you have moved them to that point of self-esteem where they feel good about themselves, they are willing to move into research. They're willing to move into political offices. They're willing to be out teachers. They're willing to do all of those kinds of things that the community as a whole look upon and look upon with a positive outlook and not a negative saying "Look at those damn faggots! They're tearing things up!"

When Taylor continues on, he evaluates the LGBT movement in comparison to the "black movement," suggesting that the LGBT movement is more evolved because LGBT activists do not, in his mind, incite violence. Likewise, Taylor argues that unlike the "black movement," which he feels is "negative about the gay movement," is not centered around winning political allies or educating people about their issues.

> Which is what I think a lot of people see with the black movement. You know, if they don't get their way, they will go out and burn cars and set people on fire. And so, I think part of the black movement—I think one of the reasons the black movement tends to be so negative about the gay movement is that I think we've seen the education part. I think we've seen the political part.

Continuing his monologue (which, as my field notes attest, had already made me uncomfortable), Taylor goes even further in disparaging the African American Civil Rights Movement by stating that white gay males are more intelligent than African Americans:

> I think that we're also white males that move into that system much easier, much faster, much quicker. But part of it is the—part of it is the intelligent thing. Part of it is most gay people are well-educated. Their parents expect them to go on. They are very well-educated. They are well-spoken. They have goals. They know how to set those goals. They

Organizational Diversity in SAGA

know how to reach those goals. And consequently, the movement, I think, is moving along rapidly because of that.

Taylor's comments can easily be interpreted as race-ignorant, if not flat-out racist. This may help explain the dearth of people of color participating in SAGA Victoria. But what is also interesting in his long statement is his exclusion of straight people in SAGA. For Taylor, straight people are not mentioned as instrumental in the movement cause. In fact, his comments throughout the interview are reminiscent of the "gay liberationist" message of the early LGBT movement (Seidman 1993), which tended to view straight people as the source of oppression, rather than as a possible identity strategy for SAGA.

This ignorance on diversity issues has caught the eye of other SAGA Victoria members, as well as SAGA National. Cameron Fine from SAGA National remarks specifically about his experience at a SAGA Victoria meeting in late 2002:

> Okay, I'll be real. It was like all white people, all men except for one person, who they were trying to get involved, and the co-chair spoke the entire time. Nobody else had anything, barely anything to add. . . . It just seemed like a kind of a dull atmosphere. . . . So we talked a little bit about diversity within the board, and trying to get more . . . people of color involved. There seemed to be just a real lack of understanding about how to go about doing that, or not really knowing why that was important . . .

Brooks Sheppard, a gay white male teacher in his early thirties, mentioned that the voices of racial minorities and women were "sorely missed," and could not understand why they were not present in the organization. But, perhaps no activists were as forthright with me regarding this issue in Victoria than Chrissy Williams and Casey Lina.

I spoke with Chrissy Williams, who works with queer youth in Victoria, at great length about diversity. Diversity is very important for Chrissy in her activist work, as well as her job as a youth organizer. She stopped attending SAGA meetings because of what she saw as a lack of diversity in the organization. When I ask her what she sees might be limiting her from becoming involved in SAGA again, she responds:

> A more diverse group of people involved. [*How is the diversity of SAGA Victoria*—] (Chrissy interrupts)—Or lack thereof! . . . In terms of ethnicity, there is a whole analysis of racism that is probably

missing (Chrissy chuckles nervously) that is really important to me and the other groups that I am involved with. Like gender, they're not diverse in terms of gender at all right now.

As Chrissy continues, she states that the reason SAGA Victoria is not diverse is because of "personalities" in general that seem to inhibit an increase in organizational diversity.

Chrissy is very cautious throughout the interview not to say anything bad about SAGA Victoria. At one point, she said that she "doesn't want to just trash Taylor" or his leadership abilities. However, from what I learned in the interviews with most of the SAGA Victoria members, Taylor's ignorance of diversity issues, as well as his leadership style, may have an effect on the willingness of people of color and women to join SAGA Victoria. Chrissy's comments are interesting because they stress the point that variations going on in organizational successes or failures, even with regards to diversity, are not always attributed to the environment[2]. However, when I asked Chrissy if she believed SAGA as a whole addressed and pursued male-defined, white middle-class issues, she thought that this was true for SAGA Victoria because of the particular issue that Taylor seeks to resolve.

> It seems like SAGA's focus is mainly on school safety . . . And, definitely for students, that seems more inclusive, and also from the adult perspective. One thing that I get from SAGA local is that it's more focused—the people who are there, their personal passion is their own job and feeling safe for themselves in their work. . . . And, I support that, too. . . . So, and insofar as they're white men, safety for them is a white male issue.

In response to her criticism that SAGA Victoria is comprised mostly of white men and headed by an activist who does not appear to focus on race, class, or gender issues, I asked her how could SAGA Victoria become more inclusive. Chrissy answers that it would require substantive organizational changes, as well as individual changes that require relinquishing the privileges attached to being white and male in our society, and to be "multi-issue":

> [*How does SAGA Victoria become inclusive? What makes something inclusive in your mind?*] That's created by a diverse group of people, not just a bunch of white people for example saying, "Oh, we want to make this inclusive so we'll do X and X and X." . . . That it's meaningful,

that it affects the lives of lots of different group of people. It feels like we have to be multi-issue.

As Chrissy continues on, she reflects on a similar strategy suggested by Sebastian in Sunntach: forging alliances with groups inclusive of people of color.

> . . . I think, groups should build alliances with diverse other people, you know. If I want to have a group that is inclusive with all people of color, then I need to be aligning myself with people of color groups that are working on people of color issues, not just queer or other queer people.

Similar to Brooks and Chrissy, Casey Lina from SAGA Victoria believes that the overrepresentation of gay white males in SAGA Victoria is limiting to the organization. During our interview, Casey remarks how "appalled" she is at the race, class, and gender demographics of the board, stating that it reflects the state of the LGBT movement in its earliest stages of organizing in the second half of the 20th century:

> I'm appalled at the demographics of the board in terms of race, and class, and gender, and gender identity and sexual preference. . . . This is a very white state in a very white area, so anyone could start nit-picking about it's a 93% white area and 93% of the board is white, that's technically speaking representative, which is true. But I certainly don't think that we, as a board, represent at all the GLBT community. And I'm ashamed of that.

Casey then discusses her experiences in the organization as a woman:

> I also had felt as a woman stunned at some of the things that the assumptions that are made and things that go on. Nothing horrible or disrespectful, but still very much—and a lot of it may have to do with age differences on the board—represent how I view our community and our activism how it was fifteen or twenty years ago.

In the comment above, Casey states that the way the Victoria board looks demographically reflects the activism during the height of the "gay liberation" movement. Casey believes that it is the age differences on the board that leads to the lack of diversity. Note that earlier on, Taylor specifically cited *more* age diversity was needed in the organization. Like other activists from SAGA Victoria, Casey insinuates that the reason for the lack of membership diversity in SAGA Victoria is attributed to the movement ideology, held by the current leadership, that misconstrues what is presently meant by "diversity."

Even though Casey, like Chrissy, says that Victoria is in a very "white" state, she does not buy that this would be a valid reason for the under-representation of diverse voices in SAGA Victoria. Wondering if Casey is suggesting that SAGA Victoria implement a kind of "affirmative action" policy, in response to her quote above, I asked her whether or not the board of SAGA Victoria should reflect its local constituency in terms of race. She responds:

> . . . What I am about to say is my whole take on life as opposed to being specific to SAGA and its strategy here. I think it should be the local representative. I think it would be bizarre—well, not bizarre—it would seem almost false to me to have a board that was 85% people of color purposefully. If that were in the charter that said that this must be 85% people of color, that would be forced and bizarre. . . . It's disadvantageous to us to say "Be that 90% white board." Even though everybody intellectually knows that it would be the percentile. . . . I would want us to look at children and teachers and think "Wow, who are we not serving?" And "how can we best serve everybody?" And, race and ethnicity to me are two important things, but they are not the only measures.

In my follow-up question, I asked Casey how does she think the board came to be so white, middle-class, male dominated. Casey echoes her earlier comment of being uncomfortable about the ways in which the board deals with gender diversity and issues:

> I don't know. And I was uncomfortable with it the first meeting. I was really surprised. I was surprised to be the only woman in the room . . . and I didn't have the courage to ask. And I've been wanting to. Now I have the courage and I'm thinking about it and I want to ask Taylor, "Gosh, what's going on?"

Like a number of the other activists before, she then attributes the reason for SAGA Victoria's lack of diversity to be rooted in the male-dominant culture at large.

> . . . I also know from my own experience that so many organizations tend to be dominated by gay men and bisexual men and so in a way part of me just thought, "Oh well. This is normal. This is normal here

in Victoria for an organization to be predominately white men and white gay men." So to me that's sort of the discouraging part of this is, "Oh yes, this is falling where I see and where I believe to be a trend of a disproportionate number of men and disproportionate number of white people."

A question that naturally follows these harsh criticisms of the lack of organizational diversity is to ask the activists how they suggest they go about making it different. Similar to Chrissy's response, Casey hints that recognition of the privileges of race, class, and gender by the leadership may be required:

> What should we do now to get things different? Well, again, I'm a big one for planning. . . . I would have us start thinking specifically of who we're going to be serving and what are the demographics going to be in five or ten years. . . . For us to be effective, we have to change the demographics of the board or we need to partner with organizations, or figure out what it is.

Again we find that alliances with other organizations specific to people of color may help change SAGA chapters from comprising of mostly gay white males. Casey continues on, suggesting that the organization must also be self-reflexive:

> . . . You know, maybe it will take my saying, "Hey, does anybody realize I am the only woman who's here and what does it mean within the politics of our community that I'm a bisexual woman and that I'm not a lesbian, and what is that saying about us and how is that good? How does that make a lesbian teacher feel? We need to talk about this as a board."

Casey's last sentence sums up very well the feelings of many activists about how to increase diversity at the local level:

> . . . To me, the process is fairly easy. That's not to say the work is easy. I know it's really hard, really hard.

To summarize this section, I presented case studies of how two chapters addressed the diversity of board and membership demographics at the local levels. Activists from both SAGA Sunntach and SAGA Victoria considered the geography of their region in explaining the dearth of non-white, working class, or female activists involved in SAGA on the local levels despite the inclusivity in SAGA's mission. SAGA Sunntach made proactive changes to move their meetings out of the mostly white gay male enclave into a more "neutral" downtown location. Although it remains to be seen if this will have an effect on membership, it can be viewed as a positive step toward making the organization more inclusive to other voices and interests. Comparatively, SAGA Victoria continues to struggle with diversity, which is attributed by fellow activists as a failure of the chapter leadership.

Although the locations of both the SAGA meetings and organizational objectives may not provide an impetus for people of color or working classes to join in the cause en masse, what I do find is that straight people, most of whom are white, are present in *every* chapter that I visited. This means that, on some level, there is some type of inclusivity within the local chapters. But, for the SAGA activists, this does not mean that any straight person will suffice. From what I learned, the straight people who join SAGA tend to recognize their heterosexual privileges in society, but downplay it upon joining SAGA, and then strategically deploy it when necessary to achieve political goals. In other words, the straight members "shed" their heterosexual privilege on a personal level before becoming members of SAGA, but are expected to recognize it and deploy it on some level when politically advantageous.

MEMBERSHIP HAS (SHED) ITS PRIVILEGES . . .

The idea of privilege and the diversity of sexual identities in SAGA, which are covered in this section, are important recurring themes that I continue to expand upon in Chapters Four, Five, and Six. In this section, I address how the straight members of SAGA have addressed issues of privilege in the organization, and how they have tried to shed it in order to successfully participate in an LGBT movement.

One of the most remarkable quotes that addressed issues of heterosexual privilege came from Greg Adler, a straight married white male schoolteacher in his early thirties. I asked Greg whether or not he saw the movement as pursuing gay, white, middle-class issues. Drawing on his only experience with an LGBT organization—SAGA—Greg focuses on the classist aspects of movement organizing, stating that activists in the LGBT movement should recognize that they can "afford to be an activist."

> . . . I think for the most part . . . a person who's an activist can afford to be an activist. It's somebody who is able to be involved and care enough for those activities—social issues, cultural issues—they have the

time to do it. They have the wherewithal and the educational background to do it. It's not just an issue of interest and having time, but it is also of being—I hate to say this, and I wish it wasn't so—but I think it is also in some way a privilege.

Greg continues to speak about privilege in general, addressing why he finds that the class structure in our society will skew movement participants to be mostly middle-class and not poor:

> You're able to become politically involved and active if you're in a certain socio-economic bracket. . . . I don't think poor people or people who have to hold down three jobs and are just struggling to put food on the table have the time to get involved in political activities or activism. I think that they probably have the interest if they're aware of those things and they may not be aware of them as much because they're so totally involved with staying alive. So, I would say that activism and some of the things that SAGA does is a middle-class issue. . . . I just think that to some extent, privilege affords you time and information.

Privilege, particularly for the straight people involved in SAGA, tended to be at the forefront of their minds during our interviews. But, what do activists think about the privileges of being straight, and then joining an LGBT movement? Is relying on straight people as supporters in the safe schools movement tacitly approving of the heterosexist power structure in American culture? What do the queer SAGA activists think of straight people speaking out for their concerns? Throughout the interviews, I learned that it is not any kind of straight people that are helpful to the movement, but a particular one who speaks *with*, rather than *for*, LGBT people. In other words, activists tended to challenge the concept of the "prime time" activism of celebrities (Meyer and Gamson 1995) where celebrities speak *for* movements and causes, perhaps as honorary members, but not relinquishing their celebrity status by "getting their hands dirty" for the particular cause and joining in the organization. However, by humbly recognizing their power and privilege in society, straight activists in SAGA co-exist with LGBT people in the organization for the benefit of the movement objectives in identity deployment strategies. In the rest of this section, I discuss how activists speak about shedding privilege, particularly heterosexual privilege, in order to fulfill the mission of SAGA.

When I asked Grant Daniels, of SAGA El Reto County, if he thought having one-third of the board (two out of six board members) straight people helps achieve organizational successes, he responded:

> No, it definitely helps. Yeah, it definitely helps. And if we were to go and have a meeting with a politician, I would insist that one of the people who goes be one of those straight people. *[Why is that?]* I think it sends that message. I think it sends, "This is who we're representing." If we're here to lobby for such-and-such specific policy, "Look, we have straight people who agree as well as gay people. We're a combined effort."

Grant then responds that this identity deployment strategy would not really work well if the straight person is not willing to lose some of their privilege.

> I think it's a particular kind of straight person . . . *[What kind of straight person?]* Someone who is open minded and willing to take risks in wanting to lose some of their privilege. *[Do you have those?]* Oh yeah! Yeah! I wouldn't say that's the majority of the straight community in El Reto County though.

Remarkably, he speaks of the identity strategy as a "combined effort" where both LGBT and straight activists are to expect to lose some of this privilege while, at the same time, deploying it to "send that message" that this is not just a gay and lesbian issue, but one that affects everyone. Grant also stresses the difference between any straight person and an ally, which is a point I made in Chapter One regarding the reconceptualization of the sociological term "ally."

Gloria, from the liberal city of Victoria that is surrounded by conservative suburbs, echoes this idea, stating that it is the responsibility for straight people involved in SAGA to risk losing some of their privilege for the greater good of LGBT rights. As a straight woman in SAGA, Gloria discusses her personal recognition of her straight privilege:

> Victoria schools asked if I would be the paid co-leader to some support groups for GLBT youth, and I said, "Boy it sure would be better if you got a GLBT person (it was important to me as a straight to have my co-leader [be GLBT]. See if you can't find someone who's GLBT." So diversity's important to me. . . . I have an awful lot of privilege in my life and I try and remember that.

Likewise, Joshua David, a self-identified partnered gay professional in his early forties and one of the founding members of SAGA, mentions privilege as a tool for LGBT social movements as well, comparing it to the "courageous push" of the oppressed and "compassionate pull" of the privileged in the abolitionist movements in the United States.

> I think that there is also a very unique dynamic . . . called "the courageous push and the compassionate pull." And I had a professor who talked about this as the dynamic of all successful social change movements. The "courageous push" comes from the people who have no power. And he would use the example of the Underground Railroad. Think of the slaves who ran away from slavery risking their lives. But the "compassionate pull" came from people who had privilege who chose to use that privilege to dismantle the system of privilege. And he talked about the white Quakers who would use their homes as their stations on the Underground Railroad because they knew the police would first search the homes of freed blacks for escaped slaves. And that the Underground Railroad never could have worked if there had not been people without power who were pushing against injustice and people *with* privilege who were using that privilege to fight injustice.

Joshua David applies this concept to the circumstances of SAGA:

> And that's the fundamental premise to me in all organizing that we do. . . . And therefore that's why I think it's critical to have straight people help us so much because they are bringing in a new perspective and they play a role that I cannot.

When Joshua attests that straight people can "play a role" that he cannot, this also connects to the idea of identity deployment of straight identities. As I explain later in Chapter Five, participants stated that one of the most successful ways to deploy a straight identity was to stress the fact that straight people, although different from LGBT people, share the same differences. This is one of the reasons why I claim the identity deployment strategies of SAGA is a mixed model of deployment. And, in Joshua's answer, we see that the roles of LGBT and straight people in the movement are different, even if their end movement goals are the same.

Xavier and Adam discuss the importance of straight people speaking out for LGBT issues, especially when LGBT members are not present, either because of their lack of presence or they do not see the salience of the issues SAGA resolves. Looking at the dearth of "out" gay legislators in the city and state governments, Xavier Lucas (a self-identified single gay white field organizer for a local LGBT organization in his mid-twenties) finds "at some levels, [having a straight ally speak out] is all that's possible." Adam

Lieberman discusses how straight people make the work in SAGA so much easier because they "keep it real" by validating the message—a point which I elaborate upon later in this chapter—and provides SAGA chapters additional strength to achieve the organizational goals:

> I don't see a problem with [straight people] speaking out. I think it's important. I think it would be foolish for them not to. I don't see any pitfalls to that at all. . . . The National board has always had incredibly strong representation from the heterosexual community. The local chapters that have been really strong have always had really strong heterosexual folks. I think it's [a SAGA chapter in Alaska] that's entirely straight. There isn't a gay person on it. . . . But there is one chapter that is *completely* straight! (laughs) I mean, it just makes the work so much easier.

Marc, from what I gathered in our three-hour long interview, is one of the more moderate activists with whom I spoke. Marc is an upper-middle-class and upwardly mobile young white male who sometimes sees the strategic use of privilege to be beneficial in order to secure organizational funding. Marc reiterates the belief that the strength of straight people is that they are not gay or lesbian, and therefore make a better spokesperson for SAGA. In the quote below, Marc alludes to the benefit of using straight privilege to the benefit of SAGA.

> I love allies. They're the best. [*Why?*] Because for many people I'm still threatening as a gay man. I'm still not one of them. If I could have a straight person speak on my behalf, that's great. Allies are wonderful.

Interestingly, Marc is the only activist who challenges the idea that straight people should not speak on behalf of LGBT people. His comment is reminiscent of the "prime time" celebrity activist model as discussed by Meyer and Gamson (1995), where celebrity allies use their status to speak out for oppressed people.

Marc continues to speak about a straight woman on SAGA Sunntach's board who, as a straight Republican woman, she is a spokesperson for SAGA within the social networks available to her, but not necessarily to the LGBT people in the organization. In fact, we see how this particular board member can frame the mission of SAGA, as well as deploy a straight identity strategically in such a way as to garner support for SAGA from influential groups.

Organizational Diversity in SAGA

> One of our board members is a 50-year-old Republican straight woman whose daughter is lesbian . . . And she's a [local councilperson] in . . . this fancy suburb. And she wears a SAGA t-shirt to the gym every day. She's *great! Love it!* Ab-so-lute-ly love it! . . . Yeah. I think she's a great spokesperson. And it's even better if she says, "You know what? I am a Republican but that doesn't matter because safe schools are a universal fight."

Anson Ross, a self-identified gay man in his mid-fifties, is also from the Midwest outside of the city of Sunntach. Although he welcomes allies in SAGA, he wants them to be informed about LGBT issues as well.

> We need all the allies we can get. And I don't want them to speak out uninformed. But I'd rather have them talking to the folks than me [a gay man], because I know I'm not going to get anywhere, and I'm just going to get mad. Whereas, again, by being straight, they've got that connection. They're more likely to have some sort of religious position to come from, that I don't have. So there are all kinds of things they could do as allies. And it's important for queer kids to see that there are straight people who are allies, who do care about them, and who will try to help them, no matter what the issue is. And it's good for straight kids to see that there are straight people in the school that won't put up with intolerance and will seek to promote tolerance and acceptance. So I think it's really important.

Immediately following the above comment, Anson says that he does not mind "Cybil Shepherd speaking for me," which suggests that he also find helpful the celebrity activist model as explicated by Meyer and Gamson (1995).

CHAPTER CONCLUSION

In this chapter, I explored the ways in which SAGA activists explain diversity in their chapters and in SAGA generally. Many of the participants admitted that their local chapters are not very diverse in terms of race, ethnicity, gender, or even class. But, how they explained this lack of diversity in their chapters, and made attempts to change this reality, varied widely. I used two chapters as examples of this variance.

SAGA Sunntach, recognizing that its board comprised mostly of gay, white, professional males, made meaningful attempts to change the demographic composition of the board by instituting organizational changes, such as moving the meeting location away from the center of the gay enclave to a more neutral location. However, these changes did not result in any significant gains in diversity. Comparatively, SAGA Victoria has not instituted any organizational changes to change its board diversity. I found that it is the chair's misunderstanding of the contemporary meaning of "diversity," as well as his method for garnering volunteers though his social networks, which inhibits meaningful changes in the organization. As I learned from the examples of both boards, the only way to really demonstrate that SAGA's message of inclusivity is by more than just lip-service but to engage in meaningful dialogue with organizations of color, and forge strong alliances with them in future endeavors.

Another concept explored in this section focused on heterosexual privilege in SAGA. As I argued earlier in Chapter One, the empirical findings elucidated in this chapter suggest that most activists expect that straight allies who join SAGA will relinquish part of their heterosexual privilege upon becoming members. These straight allies speak *with* and not *for* LGBT people and, on some level, personally identifying with the experiences of heteronormativity that LGBT people must endure in a heterosexist society. And yet, as we saw in this chapter (and I point I elaborate further on in Chapter Five), SAGA activists expect that straight allies will hold onto part of this privilege in order for the identity deployment strategies of a straight identity to work successfully. Furthermore, this simultaneous relinquishing/deployment of heterosexual privilege is what keeps SAGA from self-destruction with the addition of straight people into an organization held together by tenuous coalition of identities. Likewise, these findings on diversity provide a solid foundation for understanding the strategies of identity deployment and how they may vary according to the local sociopolitical environment.

This chapter also briefly discussed the ways in which activists construct the ideal straight activist around a heteronormative ideal, as well as notions of a particular race, gender, and class that would maximize political success. Throughout our discussions, I learned the ways in which activists would conceptualize straight activists. Although there were some concerns about gender stereotypes, most activists seemingly presumed straight activists would be like themselves and, therefore, reflect and replicate the gender, racial, and class composition of the chapters. Further research is needed to explicate this phenomenon with data derived from robust feminist analyses of identity.

In the next chapter, I build upon these findings to explore another important concept that assists us in understanding the strategic identity deployment process activists use in SAGA. As I noted in the introduction to the book, I found that activists weave together moral and injustice frames in how they present the goals of SAGA to the public. This, in turn, shapes the ways in which SAGA strategically deploys a straight identity in its particular environments (concepts which I elucidate in Chapters Five and Six). To this end, I will now explain the "mission" of SAGA in Chapter Four.

Chapter Four
"God Is on Our Side": The Mission of SAGA

One of the most surprising findings to develop from this research project did not come out of a specific question in my interview schedule. Throughout the interviews, some participants began to speak about their personal spirituality (mostly derived from Judeo-Christian religions) as influencing their desire to become involved in SAGA. A primary leader of the organization, Joshua David, said that he *personally* believed that SAGA would be victorious in the challenge to secure LGBT rights in schools because "God is on our side." Had I not known I was sitting in the presence of an LGBT leader, I would have imagined that I was sitting with their opposition from the religious right.

Although it is a small aspect of my findings, it is also very interesting and lends support to the idea of identity deployment. Four of the five straight allies with whom I met spoke of their spirituality openly (although one, Ruth Huerta from Davis City, did not do so while tape-recorded for this particular project). The organizational culture is shaped under Joshua David's leadership to be accommodating to those politically liberal and Judeo-Christian religious straight allies. And, my data on the way the mission is framed under these conditions adds empirical support to studies (e.g., Young 2001, 2002) that demonstrates the "moral" and "injustice" frames are not always diametrically opposed as is posited in the "culture war" debates (Hunter 1994).

In this chapter, I delve deeper into the origins and structure of SAGA, as first introduced in Chapter One. I also describe the organizational mission of SAGA (its ultimate goal), and explain how it uniquely utilizes both the moral frame (typically used by religious movements) and the injustice frame (the dominant paradigm for identity and LGBT movements today) in order to fulfill SAGA's goal of achieving school safety and establishing protections of LGBT youth. I engage this literature by providing empirical support that reconceptualizes the "culture war" debates.

WHAT IS SAGA?[1]

SAGA is organized as a national level "parent" organization (heretofore referred as SAGA National) that shapes the mission and goals of SAGA, with local-level chapter affiliations that implement the general mission statement on a local level. Unlike other organizations in the LGBT social movement industry, such as Human Rights Campaign or National Gay and Lesbian Task Force, SAGA is a federated structure. It is organized similar to the NAACP (Morris 1984) or National Organization for Women (Rohlinger 2002) in that it is a national organization that creates and manages local level grassroots organizations that share the name and the mission of the parent level. In SAGA, these local organizations are called "chapters." As I discussed in the Introduction, chapter names in SAGA use a specific nomenclature based on its association with SAGA, and then on its geographic region. Each chapter is responsible only for a particular geographical region that is specified either by National or the interested organizers. Judy Eberhardt, one of the activists I spoke with from the Northeast, described to me in our interview how the process of beginning a chapter works. After attending a meeting where she heard one of the leaders of SAGA National give a presentation at a workshop, she contacted SAGA and asked if she could start a chapter in her town. They told her that SAGA typically starts a chapter when at least three people within a particular geographical area express an interest in founding a chapter. This way, there are enough people to occupy the critical executive chapter positions of chair, treasurer, and secretary (much like the Federal requirements of establishing a corporation, where it is required to have president, treasurer, and secretary positions on the board). When this basic requirement is fulfilled, SAGA begins the accreditation process that establishes a new chapter in the established territory.

Accreditation occurs when this new group of people are considered an "official chartered chapter of SAGA," which means that an organization can "reap all of [the benefits of] not-for-profit corporations" under SAGA National's group federal tax exemption status, also known as 501(c)(3) status (SAGA El Reto County Chapter Affiliation Status memorandum 1997). However, receiving these benefits for chapters under SAGA National's 501(c)(3) non-profit status for taxes is not a simple task. New chapters must complete an eight-step process of accreditation that includes a definition of their territory; a proposed budget for the current and following fiscal year; board demographics to ensure diversity by race, sexual identity, gender identity, and age; and other financial and demographic information about the proposed chapter, including a description of its territorial composition (the communities they are "serving"). In a memorandum to SAGA chapters that congratulates chapters for meeting all requirements for accreditation, National reminds the chapter board leaders why they went through this initiation process: "Falling under SAGA's Group Exemption—even though it may have been frustrating and time-consuming—is much easier than applying to the federal government on your own. You saved a lot of time and money doing it this way" (SAGA Memorandum 1997).

If the accreditation process for new chapters is not onerous enough, every chapter must be re-accredited at the close of the fiscal year or else it is prohibited from using the name of SAGA in its activist work, including fundraising, in the following year. Once an organization is not accredited, the chapter is considered inactive and the accreditation process for the same territory must begin anew. At the close of the fiscal year of 2002–2003, SAGA Davis City—one of the organizations in this study—failed to become reaccredited and now is considered an inactive chapter by SAGA National.

The re-accreditation process also has some positive aspects to it since it requires activists to reflect every year on the successes of the organization and measure its accomplishments. The re-accreditation process changed in 2003 and is less time-consuming because it includes an itemized plan for the next three fiscal years (which mimic the school year of beginning in late summer), rather than the previous method that required re-accreditation every fall. The current three-year plans include two additional steps. First, the group conducts a "needs assessment" of the community to help focus the chapter's goals for the following year on what needs to be accomplished in its territory. This is done through surveys that are sent to every school district in the area to learn of the policies and programs that protect and serve LGBT people and allies within the school system[2]. Second, the group conducts a "chapter self-assessment" that covers six areas: Board Governance and Planning, Mission and Programs, Public Information, Fundraising, Financial Management, and Personnel Management. In completing the additional step of chapter self-assessment, chapter leaders have the opportunity to openly discuss ways they can improve the dynamics in the chapter as a way to avert organizational problems in the future.

When the re-accreditation process is completed as a group effort, members who were frustrated by the lack of tangible successes may find solace in knowing that the organization really does make a difference in school systems, thereby renewing their passions that may be waning from a lack of monumental political success. I interviewed C.J., the co-chair of the SAGA Chapter in Sunntach, who used to be a paid staff member of

SAGA National and was a member of SAGA Sunntach since its inception in 1995. In our interview, C.J. described the positive experience of accreditation through seeing the history of the organization and its successes:

> When I'm talking with current board members about something, I'll often bring up something from the past. You know, something we've learned or some comments that someone made that can kind of help guide us. And, I don't know if anyone would say, "Oh, yeah! C.J. is really valuable because he brings this historical perspective" but it makes a difference in our conversations, even if it's one bit of, "Well, we tried this and that didn't work" or "This was really successful" or "The reason we started this project was . . ." This year I chose to start our [re-accreditation process] off in May with a visual timeline of all the major events and when they first occurred. And, we really got to go back and see . . .

C.J. sums up how the re-accreditation process can also be uplifting to the activists, by demonstrating how far they have come in their journey:

> . . . And, just to see that [look of]: "Wow! They started that [fundraising program] in '96 and seven years later, look at how it's grown!' And so, I just think that really helps give people perspectives of how the organization has got to where it is and how meaningful it really is.

This process, at the end of the year, can really refuel the fire in the members. But the downside is that in the more conservative areas, where few tangible goals can be accomplished year after year (see Chapter Six), it can also be a double-edged sword and show to the activists exactly how much hard work is still necessary for ultimate success. However, re-engaging yearly with the mission benefits the chapter, as we see in the next section.

SAGA'S MISSION

Up to this point, I mentioned the term "mission" as used by activists to describe exactly what members of SAGA want to accomplish. The mission is the whole reason why the organization ideally exists in the first place. Modeling itself after many non-profit and for-profit organizations today, SAGA developed a mission statement that delineates what it seeks to accomplish as a social change organization. In both my conversations with the leaders of SAGA, and analyzing the historical documents from SAGA chapters, the mission statement was alluded to vaguely, but rarely delineated. The organizational mission is on SAGA websites and is very broadly defined, which assists local chapters in implementing this mission into the cultural and political milieus at the local levels.

> [SAGA] strives to assure that each member of every school community is valued and respected regardless of sexual orientation or gender identity/expression. . . . SAGA seeks to develop school climates where difference is valued for the positive contribution it makes in creating a more vibrant and diverse community.

How this mission is implemented on the local levels is up to each chapter "board" (or a "steering committee" as some chapters call it), but SAGA National has a specific guideline: the mission must have a youth-focus because its goal is to protect LGBT people in school systems by educating teachers, administrators, parents, and youth on these issues. According to the National staff members I spoke with, they find that chapters typically fail when they are used as a support group for LGBT teachers rather than as an organization that empowers youth to be the primary source of change within the school systems. Interestingly, nearly all of the chapters in this study arose out of being a type of support group for gay and lesbian educators. Yet, the mission of SAGA has not changed since its inception in the mid 1990s, and the "support group" model of organizing was frowned upon since SAGA's inception (Interview with Joshua David). Although no one I spoke with was certain how or why their SAGA chapter began as a support group, they did agree that by the late 1990s, all active chapters moved away from this model of organizing.

Most of the organizations that participated in this study suggested that this transition occurred with some difficulty. The two chapters that experienced the most difficulty in this transition were those from the cities of Victoria (Pacific Northwest) and Sunntach (Midwest). Teachers, who wanted school safety for students but only in addition to their own job protection, founded these chapters. Taylor Lynde, a retired school teacher from Victoria, stated clearly his understanding of how youth can be protected in schools by first protecting the jobs of the teachers who can foster an environment of safety:

> . . . If [schools] are protective with the sexual orientation clause [for teachers], they're able to be out. They're able to talk about their life and their family. And all of a sudden, the kids see them as very human beings. They put a face to this "gay" thing, whatever it might be. . . . And I think that kind of snowballs down in the sense that

> when teachers feel comfortable and they're able to feel comfortable in keeping [LGBT] kids safe in their classrooms, then [LGBT] kids feel like coming to school. . . . The teacher is helping them to understand that that is who they are and that that's okay.

However, Joshua David, one of the leaders of SAGA National disapproved of this trickle-down method of achieving the mission of SAGA, emphasizing in our interview that "we feel very strongly that's a very bad model." And by the end of the 1990s, those chapters that did not overtly integrate youth into the leadership were strongly urged by SAGA National to make this transition. In our interview, Joshua David says:

> We strongly urge all chapters to have youth. I personally [believe] youth are where it's at. They have a lot more energy, they're a lot less scared, they're a lot more willing to stick their necks out. That's a realistic sign of growth.

Joshua continued speaking, arguing that both the teacher-centered and support-group models are "a fundamentally flawed thing," emphatically arguing:

> . . . If you asked me, let's say, "Joshua, what's the number one indicator that a chapter is not going to make it?" When it's all gay teachers. It will be dead within two years.

One chapter that struggles with this transition is SAGA Victoria because, as I explained earlier in this section, the fervent chair Taylor Lynde still adheres to this model. Although very passionate about creating meaningful change in the minds of parents and students that he reaches as a gay teacher, he fundamentally believes that institutional support of teachers is the necessary first step in ensuring school safety of LGBT students. This is also noted in our interview where Taylor discusses his proposal to implement seminar training of college students in and around Victoria studying for a career in primary and secondary education. SAGA National, Taylor states, continuously rejects this proposal, as it does not fit closely to the mission of youth empowerment for school safety in grades kindergarten through high school. And, as I discuss later in this chapter, SAGA is very strict in its adherence to the organizational mission, and is quite specific with the programming curriculum deemed necessary in youth empowerment on LGBT issues.

In a very long and winding anecdote that is edited below, Taylor describes the transition from a teacher-focused support group to the current goal of being more youth-based (although Victoria falls short from this goal):

> I think a lot of the dissention was kind of an old school/new school kind of train of thought. . . . So, I felt—to keep SAGA alive—that I had to instigate some change. So, what I actually did was go out and I tried to find people . . . that were more of my thinking versus kind of that old thought. . . . And I really felt we needed more of an age diversity on the board. . . . I think that the young people are a real energy base for your group. . . . They have that energy that is very contagious. And so, all of a sudden, the other board members were starting to feel a little bit more energetic about wanting to do things or getting a little bit more involved. . . . And then I talked to another teacher friend of mine who is a teacher, but also a pretty liberal active thinker kind of mover, kind of groover. And so he was on the board.

Taylor continued on, stating that this transition was not as smooth as one would hope, as the previous board members who wanted a teacher-focused group began to leave SAGA:

> And then at that point, we had enough votes and we had enough kind of clout. I guess the other folks [from the old school] kind of saw the writing on the wall because they were actually going to resign from the board.

But, in my interview with Chrissy Williams, a staff member at a local LGBT youth organization, she said that she left SAGA Victoria at that particular time because of the "personalities" of the current board members. Chrissy also sees that the board, under Taylor's leadership, still lacks a youth focus because of Taylor focuses the attentions of SAGA on the jobs of the teachers, rather than the students. Instead of instituting change from within the organization in a similar way as Taylor states he had, Chrissy told me that "there are lots of other places where I can put my energy into doing things that I feel passionately about that don't involve fighting other queer people who are doing their own thing." Chrissy continued on, stating that " . . . there can be room for [SAGA] to do [its] thing and room for me to do my thing. And, we can collaborate superficially when necessary and do our separate things." Chrissy's experience with SAGA Victoria's membership reflected my findings from the self-reported chapter accreditation papers, where only one active board member might qualify as "youth" at age 20.

SAGA Sunntach also experienced a difficult transition into a more youth-focus mission rather than as a teacher-support group. The challengers to this transformation were mostly teachers who were afraid that a meeting with gay and lesbian students might be considered "recruitment" of children to become gay, or even worse, an "out" lesbian or gay student may "out" the teacher who remained secretive about their sexuality. For example, Sebastian, a former co-chair of SAGA Sunntach in its early formative years, explains how this transition led to resignations on the board:

> I think a lot of teachers saw it as a support group. And now, I don't know if there are any teachers on the board. [*Why do you think that's changed?*] It's changed in part because people came to us in thinking it was a support group, and it's not. It's really community activism. It's really trying to change the way that kids and staff are treated in schools.

Sebastian spoke to me briefly about the history of this transformation from a support group focus to a youth empowerment focus. Early on in the transition, a concern of many teachers were that "they didn't want to be outed at work" by the students that were also attending SAGA meetings. But, most of all, says Sebastian, is that the leaders of SAGA were afraid:

> . . . that the organization was going to be attacked because there is always this perceived threat that—there's a lot of fear in activism that other conservative organizations will try to discredit it. Or by saying that we were preying on young children.

And yet, these fears seem to have been unfounded. Even when there was a scandal in Sunntach when one of the board members (who almost immediately resigned) was charged and convicted of having sexual relations with a minor of the same sex, the incident hardly created waves outside the immediate Sunntach communities, except for a few mentions in the Christian right newspapers. However, it did result in a fractured leadership in SAGA Sunntach in the years following, which only was able to overcome in the past several years because the board members at that time disagreed over how to resolve their personal feelings with their professional ones in dealing with the scandal.

Once activists find what SAGA members *can* do to fulfill the mission statement of SAGA, staff leaders in SAGA National believe it may be

"God Is on Our Side" 95

equally important to know what an organization *doesn't* do. Joshua David, one of the leaders of SAGA National, states why SAGA is unique to all other LGBT organizations:

> We've defined ourselves as an education organization that works on LGBT issues. We don't define ourselves as an LGBT rights group. We're an education group. We have a very specific piece of education that we're working on, but we're an education organization. . . . And so I don't really think I can speak to the broader gay movement strategy because I don't sit at those tables. I sit at a very specific table of . . . education, which is the only issue we speak to.

What makes Joshua's comments so interesting is that he claims that SAGA sets itself outside of the typical LGBT activist organizations in the United States, such as Human Rights Campaign (HRC) or National Gay and Lesbian Task Force (NGLTF), which do not have local chapter affiliations and seek broader LGBT civil rights victories.

Activist after activist that I had spoken with had repeated this message: SAGA is an "education organization" and not a "gay rights organization." And, yet, as I spoke of earlier in the book, the evidence I gathered highly suggests that SAGA *is* an LGBT organization, even though they may state publicly that they are an "education organization working on LGBT issues." For example, in my interview with Joshua David, he states how he attends monthly meetings with other LGBT organizational leaders in the city where SAGA National is located. In addition, every chapter has records of marching in the local gay pride parades. And, furthermore, the inter-organizational alliances formed by SAGA National and the local chapters are typically forged with other local LGBT organizations.

Most activists did not *specifically* address this strategy of situating its mission outside of LGBT civil rights causes, but everyone agreed that "straight" allies who volunteered for SAGA were integral to the success and image of SAGA as an "education organization." However, activists such as Adam Lieberman and Melissa Eggert from SAGA El Reto County, and Amanda Candor from SAGA Davis City explicitly agreed that it is a successful public relations strategy for dealing with policymakers on local levels. By situating the organization outside of the gay and lesbian movement, SAGA hopes to increase the likelihood of gaining entry into school systems where they can affect social change. By being an "education" organization instead of a "gay" organization, SAGA is less threatening to teachers and school administrators who may believe that SAGA is trying to "teach homosexuality" to young children. When SAGA states that they operate outside of the gay and lesbian movement, and have straight people who support the mission of SAGA, they can deflect some of the intolerance expressed by school administrators.

Melissa Eggert is a self-identified single lesbian in her mid-twenties. Melissa calls herself "a walking contradiction" because of her paradoxical identities (She states, "I'm a practicing Catholic [and lesbian], for God's sake!"), and like Adam, she finds "radicals" as hurting their cause for safe schools, and seeks social change incrementally and with moderation. Being in a conservative region of the Southwest, Melissa sees SAGA's self-labeling as outside of the "gay rights movement" an asset to their cause because "we're kind of hard to get mad at because we are not a political organization." Melissa speaks on, suggesting that as a non-partisan educational organization, " . . . people can't really say, "Oh you know what, I don't want my kids to be safe at school." Or, "I don't think that someone should get beat up for whatever reason, let alone being gay." Instead, by changing their "tag line [to], We're an educational network dealing with LGBT issues" rather than the obverse, Melissa thinks that it:

> . . . seriously helps [gain allies], even for people that aren't exactly liberal, [such as] more conservative-leaning [people] who might not think homosexuality in and of itself is correct or, we're burning in hell or what have you. I've found that even if they do hold that view, they still don't think a kid should be beat up for it or a teacher should be fired for it.

Adam's response to my question about what it is like to be a board member of SAGA El Reto County echoed this similar idea of being on the outside of the LGBT movement is an asset because it makes the issue less offensive to those who may find homosexuality to be morally wrong, but believe all students should be safe in schools:

> By *explicit* design we are not a gay organization working on education issues. Our focus is on education with LGBT issues as our cause within it, but we try to be seen as an education organization because that's the way we're going to get into school and districts that are less friendly to us.

By situating its message outside of the LGBT mainstream movements, SAGA allows for a unique strategy that, as I suggest in Chapter Six, is especially beneficial in conservative political environments dominated by the religious right.

This unusual strategy also gives the movement greater flexibility with their strategic message, and permits SAGA greater opportunities to use their opponents' symbolism and shape the movement into their favor, thereby helping to circumvent the idea of a "culture war." The cultural message is the same—the safety of children is the number one priority. It may not neutralize the symbolic weapons, but it certainly weakens the attack, which gives SAGA an advantage over other LGBT organizations in this particular issue.

Part of this separation from the mainstream LGBT organizations is traced to the personal history of one of its leaders, who shaped the organizational culture around Christian morality, and uses this symbolism to effect social change. In the next section, I develop this idea further, and argue that this is not a strategic "toolkit" of symbolic structures in meaning construction, but that this unique moral environment in SAGA permits the strategic deployment of straight people in an LGBT social movement.

CHRISTIAN MORAL SYMBOLISM IN SAGA

It was not my original intent to study the role of religion in LGBT social movements when I first began my research. And yet, in my research on the identity deployment strategies of activists in the LGBT organization SAGA, it was not a surprise that many of the participants supported their arguments around an injustice frame that is articulated within the organizational mission. This is because, as Rohlinger (2002) demonstrates in her research on the abortion debate, it is the prevalent frame for the sides of the "culture war." Interestingly, activists sometimes conveyed a moral necessity and urgency to explain their participation in SAGA. Although nearly every activist I spoke with referenced "SAGA's mission" in a broad organizational sense, in some instances such as the ones highlighted in the above quotes, they communicated a moral mission as well. Joshua David, one of the founders of SAGA, considers the safe schools movement for LGBT students a moral crusade, stating that the movement is a "David going up against an enormous Goliath." Had I not known I was interviewing activists working toward LGBT causes, I would have imagined that I was talking with the leaders of the religious right countermovements, especially when the leader Joshua David tells me his most valuable skill as a leader of SAGA:

> . . . My most valuable skill is that I'm a very effective evangelist. I am definitely my father's son [who was a Protestant minister]. And in fact I was invited to give the guest sermon at the Unitarian Church, . . .

which was a mile from the church where my father preached. And my mom and her friends came. One of them said, "You know, He's just like his daddy! He's just got a little bit of a different sermon!" (Joshua laughs) So, it was kind of a funny moment! And that ability to inspire and motivate people whether it be in a local community or a donor who has his checkbook in his back pocket is the thing I bring to the table that is most valuable.

The leader of an organization working *toward* LGBT social issues sees his most valuable skill is that he is an effective *evangelist?* What is going on here? Is this LGBT organization modeling itself after moralistic movements, such as those of abolition, temperance, and suffrage, rather than focusing on the social justice frames that have dominated the LGBT movement organizations since its earliest beginnings? If so, could a movement associated with LGBT concerns use moral and/or religious frames in such a way as to shape the organizational culture, while enticing both straight people *and* LGBT activists at the same time?

In this section, I address these questions by arguing that this "little bit of a different sermon" is exemplified in the organizational mission of SAGA, and there is evidence that this moral frame is imbued within the typical injustice frame of modern identity-based movements. What makes this all the more interesting is that this frame is constructed *unstrategically* by a small group of LGBT activists and straight people who believe in SAGA's mission that seeks safety for LGBT youth in schools. Even though SAGA activists disparage religious right activists, some of them profess their own religious beliefs, and seemingly meld it into their activist work. Lastly, I provide evidence that it may benefit particular grassroots organization during critical moments of interactions with highly contentious religious countermovements.

A Little Bit of a Different Sermon

Almost like a musical movement, the words of the activists when they described the mission of SAGA sounded like a moral melody, with the passages of the Bible as the harmonic movements. But, why would a modern mainstream gay and lesbian movement use a moral framework in such a way to their benefit; typically, they are fighting the moral frames of the Religious Right. After meeting with Joshua David, one of the founders and leaders of SAGA National, I believed that this was not by chance, and nor was it strategy. The moral beliefs of the organizational leaders helped transform the culture of the organization, and by operating outside of the LGBT mainstream, it created an environment conducive to inclusion beyond identity, making successes (whether political, mobilizing, or cultural) in even the most hostile environments possible. To stress the earlier quote from Joshua David, we can see how an individual's religious identity can benefit an LGBT organization when he says " . . . my most valuable skill is that I'm a very effective evangelist."

Joshua David attributes his evangelical ability to inspire people to helping build SAGA exponentially over the past several years. Early on in our discussion, Judy Eberhardt described how she was one of those converts to SAGA through Joshua's passionate evangelical speeches:

> I first joined [SAGA] because our son came out to us in '96. And, when he came out to us, I said "I have to do *something*. First, I have to understand what's going on with him and what [being gay] means." And after I figured that out, I said, "Well, here I am in a school as a social worker—and Joshua David was speaking at a conference in April of . . . '97 . . . and it was all about gay issues. So I said, "Wow, I have to go to that." And as he does for many people, he changes your life. I listened to him and said, "Wow! This is exactly what I need to be doing! I'm going home and starting my own chapter."

Judy describers her relationship with her gay son as "very close;" she says that she and her son Kyle are "kindred spirits." Judy has used that relationship as the foundation of her passion for social change. Toward the close of the interview, when I asked Judy if she considers herself an activist, we hear Judy repeat how SAGA has become her passion and infuses her words with moral symbolism:

> I always said that when the boys were getting older, I need to find a passion, Joe [my husband] has a passion, Kyle [my son] has a passion, Matt [my son] has a passion. I need a passion! And I didn't really have it . . . Once I heard Joshua, I was like "Oh yeah! There it is! I just needed to sit here and listen to it and hear it." . . . And, if you have faith and the belief that you're going to succeed I think that's another thing [to succeeding] . . .

But, at the same time, Judy was sure to mention that this was not a religious experience per se, especially for activists in general. Rather, activism in SAGA becomes a "sense of purposefulness" that is altruistic and unselfish, which suggests that there is a moral immediacy infused within secular activist injustice frame within the safe schools movement.

> . . . It's been my experience that people that are really solid right there all the time do feel—not a religious calling—but there definitely is a sense of purposefulness that they know this is something they need to be doing. It's broader than for themselves. It's beyond themselves.

On the other hand, Joshua does find a quasi-religious element to activism in SAGA that may be palpable because of its origination outside of the LGBT movement:

> . . . There is a crusading element to this, and we are the youngest of the large national gay rights groups. We did not arise out of the gay community. We arose out of students and teachers, many of whom were straight. And there is this crusading mentality around us. I think people are drawn to us with a deep sense of injustice, a deep sense of rage, a deep sense of hurt.

Joshua connects his experiences with speaking on the crusading element of SAGA's mission to "coming out of the closet," so to speak:

> . . . It's been that only recently that I've been more comfortable talking about it in public. . . . I've had to come out of the closet as somebody who has religious faith because it's kind of unacceptable in some ways within LGBT circles to be a religious person.

Again, the moral frame is ever-so-gently infused within the injustice frame that resonates most with modern identity-based civil rights movements. The personal attributes of Joshua David influences how he envisions the safe schools movement in Christian terms.

When I asked Joshua about what were the most memorable failures of SAGA in its political goals, he refers to them as "setbacks" rather than defeats because he believes the organization will win no matter what, so long as a dialogue on the issues continue. But, his response to the question is surprising because he believes that God is on their side in this fight, almost dismissing the moral claims of the religious right in their perception of a culture war:

> There are plenty of failures. . . . In our case, where we very much a "David" going up against an enormous Goliath, we're not going to win most of the time. We're not going to win most of the time. But, to me, raising the dialogue is a win. So, I don't take those setbacks—I see them as setbacks and not defeats—which gives us an opportunity to

"God Is on Our Side"

educate. . . . It might take a little longer but we're going to win in the end. I know that.

When I asked Joshua about why he thought that the LGBT movement would win in the end, he stated that it is "because we're right." But why does SAGA consider their perspective of LGBT social justice to be correct? Joshua continues:

> Because every human being has worth and deserves to be treated with respect. Period. End of story. Exceptions to that rule are not allowed, in my book. I really do feel that—although I would never really say this in public, as my opponents say the same thing, but I really do feel that God is on our side—on a very personal level. That's not what the organization thinks. That's not what the executive director of SAGA thinks. It's what Joshua David thinks. And that faith sustains me.

As we see in the quote above by Joshua, a moral frame is not a strategy the organization uses, but rather, a personal belief of one of the original founders and current leaders of SAGA. But, I argue that this *does* have an effect on the message and the organizational culture. SAGA exists outside of the mainstream LGBT movement organizations and also the safe schools movements that advocate against gun violence (see Figure 1). This means that it straddles outside of the LGBT movement organizations, and must ally themselves with parents, who by mere statistics, are going to be straight for the most part. By being inclusive to straight people (who are primarily parents and teachers), the organization opens itself up to additional social networks that are not typically open to most lesbian and gays. The organization culture is flexible, which permits straight and LGBT, religious and non-religious to join the safe schools movement. This flexibility in defining us-versus-them identity politics based on sexuality is one of the reasons why the board president of SAGA is a straight man, because with that position, he brings to SAGA connections that many LGBT people may not be privy.

Four out of the five straight activists I interviewed had either overtly mentioned their personal affiliation with a religious organization or suggested that religious activists leaders inspired their activism. Gloria Wentworth is a straight retired school social worker in her mid-fifties in the city of Victoria in the Pacific Northwest. Where she lives it is somewhat more conservative than what we might find in the more liberal cities of Portland, Oregon or Seattle, Washington. As Thomas Linneman (2003) and Arlene Stein (2001) have found in their research in the Pacific Northwest, there are vocal activists in this region on both sides of the "culture war." From our discussions, Gloria appeared to be a woman with strong religious faith, which comes out in our discussion about her altruistic involvement in SAGA. A parent of two straight sons, she tells the story of how she began her involvement in LGBT youth organizing after witnessing "the intense pain" of the students who came to visit with her over the years.

> I got involved in advocacy for GLBT youth, because of the intense pain that the youth were sharing with me. And I think in the school environment, in the faith-community environment, whether I'm working with the youth themselves, or their parents, I just kind of have this equal mix [of compassion] . . .

One case in particular demonstrates how comfortable she was in her abilities to challenge a religious argument from a parent with her own religious position. In a long anecdote, she discusses how her faith was used to educate religious parents on how to accept their LGBT children:

> I had a youth, lesbian woman . . . come to the support group at the high school initially all excited, she was going to come out to her family, and then she came out to her mom, and her mom was fine, and then she showed up the next week and things weren't so good after all. You know, it sunk in, and mom had gone berserk and was devastated. I offered (in a weak moment) to saying, "You know, I'm involved in my faith community (and obviously faith was a big issue with your mom struggling with all of this) and if she ever wants to come talk with me, you tell her she's welcome to come do that."

Gloria then describes the meeting she had with the mother, who was personally struggling with pinpointing an answer to explain the cause of her daughter's sexuality:

> . . . She was very polite and friendly, but she also said, "Don't you think that one of the reasons that my daughter's coming so easily to deciding that she's a lesbian is because the school is so friendly and supportive of it?" I said, "No, I think that it's good that she feels safe to do it, but that doesn't make her lesbian. She's who she is." . . . And I also said "I'm never in the business of pushing kids to be anything. I hope I give them a safe space to take their time to be at peace with themselves and their questions and find their way."

"God Is on Our Side"

Gloria concludes the anecdote with an interesting resolution. The mother had come full-circle by bringing her church friends to a Gay Pride parade. The family shares this moment with Gloria:

> A couple of years later I'm at Gay Pride, and this, I hear this voice saying, "Gloria! Gloria!" And, this young woman comes running up to me and says, "I just wanted to say hi and update you on what I'm doing. I didn't go to that religious college, and I'm here in town and I'm working at this bike shop and I'm happy, and mom's here and she's brought a bunch of people from the church to be at the Gay Pride parade." That was just awesome.

Similar to Judy, Gloria points to her activism in SAGA as fulfilling her passions, especially when it comes to caring for youth. In the quote below, Gloria uses moral symbolism to describe her passion to fight religious right organizations such as Focus on the Family. She states that she feels compelled to do more for the oppressed, but her fervor can sometimes make her feel as if she is "holding up the world" as well:

> . . . My faith is something that's important to me, but I don't put it out there for other people. I mean, I don't hide it, but it's just not in my daily language at all. But my bumper sticker on my car says, "To believe is to care, and to care is to do." So, it's just, you can't *not* be doing those things. . . . I still have to work on not taking on too much, because the Focus on the Family, the people in Colorado, are coming to do a reparative therapy conference, and so [we are] going to do a counter conference. So my instinct is, "Oh, I've got to get involved and go work on that . . ." . . . A friend in the faith community says, "Okay Gloria, it's time to stop holding up the world. It's okay, you don't have to do that. Someone else will do that."

The bumper sticker on her car is quite a testament to her religious faith: "To believe is to care, and to care is to do." Like Joshua David, Gloria's religious convictions are the foundation of her activism in LGBT causes. But unlike Joshua, Gloria never had a *personal* stake in the movement—neither she, nor her children identify as LGBT (She says, "to my knowledge"). But, as Gloria told me in our interview, "My family supports what I do. My husband marches with me in the Gay Pride parade with our faith community." Gloria's support group—straight religious people—are now interconnected with the LGBT movement through her connections, opening up additional opportunities for alliances and positive change in a conservative area.

Judy Eberhardt was less vocal about her religious connections, but in the liberal area of Piedmont in the Northeast, fighting religious fire with religious fire is not as much of an imperative. But Judy finds religious groups as an important ally in the safe schools movement as well:

> I think that we have to go to these [other] organizations . . . We need to find people that have connections in these other organizations, and then ask to be invited to them to talk to them. . . . It could be church groups. I'd love to do church groups.

Judy is familiar with and comfortable in church communities. In fact, rather than merely saying that she spoke at a local church, in our interview she clearly states that she was invited to a local Presbyterian church and "preached" about SAGA's mission. The results were positive because in this wealthy Northeastern suburban location, Judy perceives the minister and congregation both as fairly open-minded and liberal:

> . . . I think one couple left the congregation because of it. So that was good. . . . They have a really gay-friendly, straight gay-friendly assistant minister, a woman. She's wonderful. So that might be a great venue for connecting with other groups . . . I just think that that's what we need to do, to get out there and make some change.

This is not out of the realm of experience for Judy, as she has experience leading her church groups. She continued on saying, "I like that . . . That's just what I always do." And, as Judy stated above, she finds that churches are an important venue for making change for SAGA. As a straight woman who is both active in her church, in her SAGA chapter, and now on the SAGA National board, this can open up new avenues for the organization as a whole that were previously out of reach.

Another straight activist who spoke in religious terms was Paul Freeman. Similar to Gloria Wentworth in Victoria, Paul is a retired educator and has no LGBT children. Paul is from SAGA El Reto County where there is an organized religious right in power that have a 6-to-1 "supermajority" on the local school board. As a self-identified follower of peaceful leaders like "Martin Luther King and Gandhi," Paul is described by one of the activists as the "soul" of the organization because of his penchant for protesting against social injustices and has an established history in the African American Civil Rights Movement. Paul makes a number of connections between his experiences in the African American Civil Rights Movement and the current antigay situation in one of the school districts in El Reto County:

> Tierra Blanca is kind of what we're fixated on because they've drawn so much attention to themselves and been so evil about it. . . . It's like Mississippi for the black people in the 40s in the Tierra Blanca school district for gay students. . . . They're really Christian right. . . . One [school board member] is a minister at one of those churches that are sworn to uphold Leviticus (Paul chuckles). And, they're proud of it!

By and large, Paul discusses his activism in the LGBT movement in injustice frames, connecting his participation in relationship to his experiences as a young African-American man in the Southwest. When I ask him how he feels about being a straight man speaking on behalf of LGBT people, he responds, "I have no problems with it at all. I feel that it's—to me, it's being a member of a group who have been discriminated against. I feel that it's pretty much an obligation." And, similar to what Judy mentioned in our interview, Paul's continued response is imbued with religious symbolism as well, describing it as a "calling":

> It's like a calling, if you will. I feel like I have to. . . . As a child bumping into racism, it was just very baffling to me . . . how my mother and my grandfather and my dad (when he was around) and my neighbors just thought I was a gift from God, and I'd go and try to spend a quarter in some café and somebody would tell me to get my little black ass out of there.

Paul's comments are infused with moral symbolism amidst his references to the injustice frame in his comparisons to the racism he experienced as a youth. At another point in the interview, when I asked Paul to comment on why others call him a "radical" when he considers himself "a strong liberal," Paul speaks of "a spirit of love and caring:"

> It seems like to me that really something is wrong when you're trying to do as much as you can to create a better world and you are trying to do so in a spirit of love and caring and somebody calls you a radical.

Although the sample of organizations is too limited to make broad generalizations to all of SAGA, I noticed that in SAGA El Reto County, the one geographical region where there is a vocal and active religious right in political power in the school districts, the LGBT activists infuse moral symbolism in the face of their lack of successful political impacts. By using moral symbols, activists are able to construct these symbolic meanings to fit different circumstances. In her analysis of the Irish Land War of 1879–1882, Anne Kane finds that "the locus of meaning and therefore the condition for meaning construction is symbolic structures," and that the metaphoric nature and patterned interactions of these symbols "is a fundamental key to how meaning is constructed and why it can change" (Kane 1997: 250). There is some evidence in SAGA El Reto County that the activists transform the religious symbolic structures of the religious right in the face of extreme opposition.

Adam Lieberman is one of the youngest SAGA chapter co-chairs in the country. Adam expressed the severity of the situation in one of the local high schools that SAGA has struggled to transform with the board being so right-wing:

> When I've gone out to Las Palmas High [in the Tierra Blanca school district], . . . I got out of there so fast because I was sitting there in this meeting and these people, if they knew that I was Jewish, much less gay, would have lynched me! They were talking about Jesus openly in their board meeting. What do you do? So I got up and I made my plea and I was out of that auditorium. Whew! I didn't even go back to my seat. And I walked through the campus with my keys in my hand so that if somebody tried to attack me, I had some kind of weapon. And I have not felt that way since I was in high school.

Adam continues on, interpreting the beliefs of the Christian board members as a sign of a flawed mental state, rather than a difference of opinion:

> These people are crazy. They believe that they have two-way communication with Jesus. They believe that they are the judgers and they honestly believe that we are trying to convert their children and that they are protecting their children.

But, Adam expresses more compassion toward the children who may feel victimized or helpless in the conservative environment of Tierra Blanca.

> . . . Quite honestly, I couldn't give a shit if their kid is gay. I want to make sure their kid isn't going to get killed. I want to make sure that we don't have another kid that goes off the deep end. And I want to

make sure that gay kid who is sitting in the corner scared doesn't just say, "This isn't worth it."

Adam extends this point further when he reflects on why he continues to work in Tierra Blanca despite the many setbacks that the organization must endure:

> That's what keeps me going with SAGA is—(Adam pauses) If I can turn around and say that there was one kid who I helped somehow, whether I knew that he's okay or not, then I am doing the right thing. And I know that I'm reaching kids.

When Adam continues speaking, notice how he echoes the statements by Paul when he tells me: "[The safe schools movement] is much bigger than me. I do know that. I'm well aware of that."

Adam is Jewish, and although he expressed this identity as an ethnicity at the start of our interview, and in the earlier quotes, he later mentions praying as a way to deal with the horrible situation for LGBT youth in the Tierra Blanca school district:

> [*If you could do anything differently regarding Tierra Blanca, what would you do?*] (Adam sighs) I've spent a lot of time thinking about this. And I've done workshops on it. It's not that I would do things differently, I would just do more. . . . And, you have to pray. You have to pray the kids are going to be okay.

Although some readers may interpret Adam's comment about praying as an idiomatic expression synonymous with saying "I hope," both the timbre of his voice and context of the discussion leave me little doubt that his intended message was rooted in his Jewish faith. At this point in our interview, Adam beings to sigh more heavily, his voice trailing off to almost a whisper and, with a quiet, mournful voice, repeats twice to me that praying for the safety of the children is sometimes all one can do in the hopeless political environment of Tierra Blanca.

Another reason why I remain convinced that Adam used the word "pray" in the literal sense is tangentially connected to our post-interview discussion. Adam and I met on the Friday evening before Palm Sunday. As a guest in the city, I asked Adam if he could refer me to a "welcoming" (codeword for gay-accepting) Roman Catholic Church for me to attend Palm Sunday mass. He immediately called Grant Daniels, who off the top of his head referred me to three different churches in the area.

This further suggests to me that the open profession of ones' religious faith is not uncommon in the organization, and that Adam's comment about praying is not meant figuratively.

While interviewing activists in El Reto County, I did not ask questions directly about religiosity since it did not directly address my research questions[3]. But still, four out of the six SAGA activists in El Reto County made a direct reference to religious affiliation in a conservative city within a conservative county, including Adam Lieberman as quoted earlier. So, it came as no surprise to me that when I interviewed Melissa Eggert via telephone in the summer of 2003, that some people on the board were unabashedly affiliated with organized religions.

Melissa is a white lesbian "liberal Republican" in her mid-twenties and a practicing Catholic. When I asked her about the issues of the organization being mostly white, gay male-defined, and middle class, she responded that this was not the case for El Reto County, citing the religious affiliation of her and another lesbian activist:

> . . . SAGA El Reto County definitely differs from that. But if you actually went through and looked at our board you wouldn't think that at all, I'm sure. I mean, for Christ's sake, the two lesbians on the board are white, Catholic. Yeah, I mean, seriously!

Greg Adler is a straight schoolteacher in his early thirties who, as an atheist, considers his being Jewish only in ethnic terms. Yet, in his quote below from a follow-up interview we had about board diversity, we see that despite his own religious beliefs, he respects the views of others on the board:

> . . . Right now we have people on the board who speaks strongly of some of their religious backgrounds. I, myself, have virtually no interest in religion, so I am much more like an atheist than anything. But, there are people on the board who come from Catholic backgrounds, Jewish backgrounds. . . . But, at the same time, having spoken with these people, I would never question their motive because their eyes are on the prize in the same way that mine are. It's just that they come from a different view and it's fascinating to get that view.

Greg continues on, stating that he believes the religious views of the other members can benefit the organization because it brings some insights into the minds of the opposition:

So, it affords us an opportunity to look at where Tierra Blanca is going with this [Christian Right] voucher kind of thing, and people coming from that background have some insights that I would *never* have.

My visit to SAGA El Reto County was one of my first trips on this research endeavor, and it was an anomaly to learn about the overt embracement of religious symbolism in the chapter. But is it a strategy? From the data I have found, I conclude that it is not an overt strategy. But what an interesting strategy it could be on one level by connecting together two diametrically opposed hot-button issues that were never-before successfully linked: sexuality and children. Despite some obvious limitations, in some ways, it could be a recipe for success: By helping to build an organization outside of the LGBT movement, and building it upon a foundation of morality, and including straight people such as parents and teachers as allies, while appealing to the American value of equality that is the centerpiece of LGBT movements, and blending it together with the drive for children's safety, some form of success is possible.

Another city I visited, Victoria, is considered liberal, but the surrounding suburbs where SAGA Victoria operates are conservative, especially in the rural areas. In all of the five interviews I gathered from Victoria, only Gloria Wentworth and Taylor Lynde made a direct mention of their religious affiliation. Although we learned that Gloria infuses her liberal political beliefs with her religious faith, Taylor Lynde provides us with a more expected response form many lesbians and gays who, for many activists, the symbolism of Christianity today is the epitome of homophobia and intolerance (see Adam 1987: Ch. 5).

As a lifelong resident of Victoria, Taylor confesses that he, a self-identified gay retired schoolteacher in his early-fifties, was once religious. So, he now believes he can see the danger of the current drive from religious right Christians of whom he once was a part:

> I was a Campus Crusader for Christ—Oh my God, I was a Bible Thumper from the word "Go!" But, you see, . . . I kind of understand. I understand that drive, I understand that fervor in the religious population because I was exposed to a lot of that. And I also see the danger. I also see how that whole piece can be so kind of devastating to our movement.

When Taylor continues, he suggests that SAGA has the answer to the drive and fervor of the religious right to challenge the LGBT rights movement:

> See, I truly believe that SAGA has the answer. I mean, SAGA is right. I truly believe that we've got to start in the schools and start turning out kids that are caring, thoughtful, respectful individuals. . . . And before you know it, you've got generations of kids that are looking and being respectful and voting for people to have equal rights and those kinds of things.

Implicitly mentioned in his comment above is his fear that the religious right, if left unchecked in the school systems, will create children who hate. As we see in Taylor's quote below, which continues immediately from the one above, his fears of the fervor of religious activists comes out forcefully in his voice and hands, followed shortly after with an apathetic resolution that there is nothing people can do to convince church communities that LGBT people are not an "awful element:"

> (Thumping the table with his fist) *I-don't-think* (thumping ends) I am going to change one church-going Bible-thumper's idea about what is going to go on. And the hard part is that I want to. My original thing was, "What can we do to convince the church community that we're not the awful element that they're up against?," so to speak. And there is nothing we can do. There is really nothing that we're going to be able to do.

Also present in Taylor's quote is the dominant theme today of movement-countermovement dynamics—the "culture war"—where one side fights for morality while the other challenges the injustice making claims to individualistic freedom:

> But what we do have to send to that group is the message to them is that we're not going to be run over by them. We're not going to allow them to demoralize or to degrade us because of their religious beliefs. And they can believe however they want, but they will not infringe on my right to be who I am and what I want to be either.

Xavier Lucas from SAGA Davis City in the South appears to challenge the culture war dichotomy. Xavier is a self-identified gay man in his early-twenties and, as one of my last interviews for this research project, I asked him what he thought of religion in the LGBT community. Xavier, like Greg Adler, is not religious himself, saying, "Religion has never been a part of my life. I never even went to church as a kid." Yet, Xavier finds that there are a lot more options for LGBT people to find positive churches, even though he never explicitly states that this may benefit the LGBT social movement cause:

> For the people for whom it's important, then it's important that they find a positive alternative to the Southern Baptist Church, within the gay community, and there are a lot more options for them now. I mean there are gay churches like the Metropolitan Community Church, and there are so many gay-friendly churches, maybe not as an institution. . . . So there are a lot of more actively, pro-actively gay friendly churches than there used to be, and that's very important to a lot of people. They don't just have to join a gay church, if they want to find spiritual acceptance.

But, not all LGBT activists consider religiosity as nonchalantly as Greg Adler or Xavier Lucas. In the experience of Joshua David, one of the leaders of SAGA National, members of many local and national LGBT organizations scoff at his religious beliefs. As we see in the quote below, Joshua explains in an anecdote how the local LGBT organizations have regular meetings amongst the leaders. One of those meetings coincided with a religious holiday that led Joshua to make a difficult decision of whether or not to profess his religious affiliation.

> There is a biweekly meeting of executive directors of gay rights groups and AIDS groups . . . This year the retreat was scheduled on a meeting I was not at—it was scheduled on Good Friday. And there was all this peer pressure like, "You gonna come? You gonna come? You gonna come? You gonna come?" Finally at one of the meetings, I said, (speaking to me in a measured tone) "I-can't-come! It's-Good-Friday!" And, there is a little bit of a snort in the room from some people. And I had a long talk with my partner about all of it—"Should I make up some story that I'll be away giving a speech?" Whereas, if it was on Yom Kippur, clearly there would be riots about how insensitive we were. I decided to say, "No, it's Good Friday. It's one of the holiest days of the year and I will be going to church for part of the day and I'm not going to be going to work. So, I can't come."

Joshua further explains how he perceived the other meeting invitees thought of him personally, as well as the organization:

> I think in a lot of ways, frankly, it seems a little bit odd by a lot of the executive directors anyway because I didn't come out of the gay

movement. I came out of schools. . . . So, it's just one more thing about, "Joshua David is kind of strange. He [leads] this group that has this straight guy as the board president. What's up with them?"

Earlier in the chapter, I noted that Joshua related his admission to gay colleagues about his deep religious faith to coming out. He surprised me in his response as he cites an academic source, giving him further evidence of the "crusading element" to SAGA's mission:

> Well, first of all there is a great a book out there titled *Hell Fire Nation* by Professor [James] Morone, which is all about how every controversy in [American] history is turned into a moral crusade. All. It's a part of our national character. But, I also do think there is a crusading element to this, and we are the youngest of the large national gay rights groups. We did not arise out of the gay community. We arose out of students and teachers, many of whom were straight. And there is this crusading mentality around us. I think people are drawn to us with a deep sense of injustice, a deep sense of rage, a deep sense of hurt.

James Morone in his book *Hell Fire Nation* (2003) considers most of the American movements—conservative or liberal—to be steeped in images of sin, redemption, and morality. Other sociologists have found a religious component to other liberal (rights expansion) movements, such as the early Suffragist movement (Buechler 1990), the Abolitionist movement (Young 2001), and the Civil Rights Movement (Morris 1984). But in the LGBT movement, coming out as religious would be akin to sympathizing with the enemy, or perhaps even an act of treason. And yet, in some instances, SAGA chapters like El Reto County may eventually find it a necessity to fight fire with fire by using a similar moral frame in what Xavier Lucas (and, in the 1992 Republican National Convention, Pat Robertson) calls "a battle for the spirit of America."

CHAPTER CONCLUSION

To paraphrase Joshua David's earlier quote, what is up with SAGA? The data that I collected suggests that activists utilize moral symbolism *unstrategically*, mainly because they see it as their *personal* belief, and not an extension of the dominant ideology of the organization. But, there is evidence that the personal beliefs of one of the original founders of SAGA might actually influences the organizational culture by building on a Christian moral framework. This may, in turn, create a welcoming environment to straight allies who sense a moral reason to fight the social injustice, while not going so far as to isolate or offend the non-religious members of the organization. The research on the effects of the "culture war" debates within modern identity-based movements such as the LGBT movement (e.g., Linneman 2003; Stein 2001; see also Rohlinger 2002) has not fully theorized the incorporation of a Christian moral framework *within* the LGBT organizational culture. These unusual findings suggest that in some instances, the LGBT movement and Christianity can be intricately connected in the organizational culture, which may have an effect on the success of the organization in particularly hostile religiously conservative political environments. Further research is needed to buttress these findings with additional empirical support.

The method by which SAGA utilizes both the moral and injustice frames simultaneously is under-theorized in the research on modern identity-based movement organizations, particularly within the culture war debates. However, I must stress the point that as my data suggests, this utilization is *not a strategic decision* by SAGA members. Rather, it is the outcome of some of the personal beliefs of some activists, which may "spill over" into the organization to affect its culture. This result may have an effect on the strategic deployment of a straight identity. However, with the limited amount of data gathered in this project, more research on SAGA is warranted to understand the connection between the use of these two frames and the strategic identity deployment methods of SAGA activists.

In light of my findings from the SAGA chapter in the conservative area El Reto County, it would be interesting to learn if the imbuement of the moral and injustice frames could be applied differently within particular political environments in order to garner success. This possibility remains under-theorized in the areas of political sociology, framing analysis, and social movement studies on movement/countermovement dynamics. Additional research in these areas on the issue of varied strategic moral framing in political environments should consider my findings to ascertain whether or not this possibility exists. Likewise, activists in organizations on the so-called "secular" side of the war, particularly the abortion or safe-sex education movements, might consider these findings and see if it could feasibly *become* a viable strategy for their organizations and, if so, what the negative implications of such a strategy might be.

In the next chapter, I build upon the idea of using organizational strategies and social networks in achieving the mission of SAGA. Building upon the concepts of diversity and frames from the previous chapters, I discuss identity deployment strategies first theorized in Chapters One and Two. Using empirical data derived from my interviews with thirty activists,

I explore the reasons why activists deploy a straight identity in order to achieve the goals of SAGA. And, as I introduced in Chapter Three, I provide additional evidence to address how the potential pitfall of this identity deployment is mitigated by the benefits of this strategy.

Chapter Five
No Joking About the "S" in SAGA: "Straight" Strategy

In this chapter I explore what SAGA activists see are the strengths of deploying straight identities as a strategic social movement tool. These strengths are difficult to isolate into individual strategies because, as the activists and I are aware, they are interconnected social movement tools. However, as I focus on these strengths individually, I also recognize that many times these strengths are viewed holistically by the activists and therefore deployed as such. Also in this chapter, I discuss what activists see are the weaknesses of deploying straight identities in a movement designed to secure LGBT rights, as well as how activists feel about straight people speaking for them in their activist work. The last sections of this chapter address the more subtle nuances of strategic deployment of straight identities. I address how some of the activists alluded to these processes being gendered in their deployment, and this strategy may be an effect of the sociopolitical environment.

As I discussed at the beginning of Chapter One, I thought, why would a lesbian and gay organization treasure the visibility of straight people? In the quotes below, the visibility of straight people in an organization can be a treasure, especially in a conservative political environment like El Reto County in the Southwest where gay people are assumed to have a "gay agenda" when speaking about LGBT issues. Adam Lieberman, the chair of SAGA El Reto County, states:

> When I go to meet with the superintendent of schools here, I take Greg with me! You know, it's a very strategic thing, and I've told him that! You know, "You are a straight married man with a child. There is *no way* anybody can claim you're gay. And you saying, 'This is wrong, and I'm not going to allow it' makes it that much more real. And legitimate. . . . There is no joking about the "S" in SAGA. It's not a token.

115

Greg Adler, one of the straight board members of SAGA El Reto County, told me:

> I had initially made a resolution to myself that I wouldn't even divulge that I was straight . . . because I felt that people would somehow see it as me trying to distance myself from the [LGBT] people I was working with. . . . I spoke at length with numerous people about it—mostly LGBT people. And they said, "You need to say you're straight." Overwhelmingly, people said "You need to say you're straight." [*Why was that?*] Their reasoning was because this needs to be a human issue and not a straight-versus-LGBT issue.

In the quotes above, the deployment strategies of straightness is quite clear. Adam, the co-chair of SAGA El Reto County, speaks specifically about using Greg's sexuality to make the mission more "legitimate." Greg, a married straight man with a young child, is also aware of his sexuality in the context of the movement, and makes a conscious effort to keep his heterosexuality hidden as to not distance himself from the LGBT community with whom he is working. But, the LGBT people he speaks with encourage him to make his straightness publicly known to politicians and school boards. The message that SAGA wants to send to the straight and LGBT communities alike is that straight people bring strength to the movement through their social networks and influential numbers.

THE STRENGTHS STRAIGHT PEOPLE BRING TO SAGA

Most of the interview responses from activists could be grouped into the following categories: 1) Weight in Numbers, 2) Appearing Objective, 3) Straight Parents Bring Political Influence, 4) Universalize SAGA's Message, and 5) Bring Access to Unavailable Social Networks. I elaborate on each of these categories in the following pages. However, it is important to note that in our interviews, activists did not parse these categories themselves, as most of them cited a combination of categories when explaining the strengths of including straight activists in SAGA. It is my data analysis that hones these categories in this way so that the reader can better understand the ways in which the identity deployment of straightness might maximize organizational success.

Weight in Numbers

Many activists noted that the presence of straight people gives the organization some "weight" since they are the majority of the population. Cameron

Fine from SAGA National stated "that they're the vast majority of the U.S., of the world, and the majority of people in power . . ." Xavier Lucas from SAGA Davis City considers the strength of straight people that "there are more of them. So you can have a lot more people who can do work, *if you can get them in.*" Xavier makes an important caveat—getting straight activists into the organization is easier said than done. As I mentioned in Chapter One, every chapter in this study had at least one active board member who identified as heterosexual.

Some of the activists quantified the number of straight people by referring to the often misinterpreted 10 percent statistic of the United States population who self-identified sexual experiences with the same sex at least once since puberty (Kinsey, Pomeroy, and Martin 1948). Marc Andersen, an activist from Sunntach, suggests, "the more people [we] can identify as constituents and as our base and as our allies, the better. . . . If we [LGBT activists] remain at 10 percent of the vote, we're never going to get the majority." As we see in Marc's quote, he assumes that ten percent of voters are LGBT people. Scholars who study the political behaviors of LGBT people estimate that the actual number is nearly half that amount (Sherrill 1996). C.J. (from Sunntach) also cites the "ten percent" statistic as evidence of the political influence straight people will have in the school systems.

> Straight people are in a lot of powerful positions of influence. They're often the decision makers in the school. Take the large percentage and say it's ten percent of America that's gay or lesbian, and so ninety percent of the people out there aren't. And so it's pretty safe to assume that a majority of decision makers are going to be straight.

Reid, from Piedmont, was reluctant to answer the question about the strengths of straight people, and would not explain why. However, when I gently probed for an answer, he sighed and spurted out his thoughts, citing their majority statistic:

> I mean, let's face it. Gays and lesbians are wonderful. So are transgenders and bisexuals and everybody else in between. But—I don't know what the statistics are—somewhere around 90% of the population is straight. So if you think that the majority of the people on the school board or in a school community or in a civic organization—wherever you're talking—is straight, I think it's less threatening to the people that you're talking to.

Dixon Harrington is a partnered self-identified gay social worker in his early thirties and also from Piedmont. Dixon thought I should ask participants whether the straight component is too large or too small of a component in SAGA. I asked him what he thought about the number of straight people in SAGA and he, too, referred to the fact that straight people are the majority and therefore a political asset in the LGBT movement:

> I think it's probably too small. [*Why do you think it needs to be larger?*] Two reasons: A bigger representation of the straight factor in SAGA informs the organization in a different way. It also again, feeds back to that population in a different way. And, you know, in the nitty-gritty demographic world, there are more straight people than there are gay [people], and so it's not a bad thing to have that be a part of your makeup. . . . A local chapter of all gays and lesbians and one straight person sends a very different message to youth about who's interested in their well-being and who, currently in going forward, they can expect to have an ally. If they don't see straight people involved in SAGA on a large scale, then how can we ever expect to explain that that's a possibility, or display it as a possibility?

In his response to my question about the strengths of straight people to SAGA, Justin Petrov from Piedmont looked to his college coursework on social movement history to find the role of allies in movements by using their power in positive ways for the movement. In this quote, he alludes to the majority status of straight people as being political weight:

> . . . Someone like Clinton (who was certainly working in gay people's favor), while he may have not gone out on the front lines and put his own reputation at risk, he was definitely trying to help things out. And now (when things are changing) it's more likely that you could have someone's vote in Congress to come from a gay person and be influential. But there's still 2 or 3 that are openly out. There may be way more that are not [out], but that's not your weight. Your weight's [sic] the straight people. . . . So I think that straight people have the ability to do something very special for gay people, which is why it's so important to have straight people on our board, which is to have people listen.

It is also interesting to note the connection Justin makes between celebrity status, politics, and speaking out for LGBT issues. Like Meyer and Gamson's article (1995) that discusses the role of celebrities in shaping social movements, Justin cites Bill Clinton—a political leader in his own right as the former President of the United States but also a larger-than-life celebrity figure—as using his status as a benefit to a particular movement through publicity and name recognition.

Does ones' own straightness have an effect on policymakers? Interestingly, Paul Freeman, a retired straight principal from El Reto, does not think so. However, as we see in the quote below, he believes that he does have some influence because of his former position in the school system as a principal. When I asked Paul the question that heads this paragraph, he shook his head no, and chuckled:

> No. They put us [SAGA activists] all in this kind of [box]. That's not to say that I don't have some [influence]. I'm not talking so much on this issue that I don't have some influence. I get called a lot to take part in a problem-solving kind of thing. But, no.

Greg thinks that his straightness has an effect on policymakers, but in a different way than he would have hoped. He feels sometimes that he's also put into "this kind of box" and lumped together with the LGBT activists with accusation that he has "been brainwashed by the gay agenda or something like that."

From his earlier quote at the beginning of this section, we note that Greg wants to *not* offend by announcing his straight sexuality. In our interview, Greg expresses annoyance with the assumptions that are made by policymakers when a person from SAGA speaks.

> . . . Some of that stuff kind of makes you go, "Well, is my presence here in some way going to be a comment about my own sexual identity?" And I've thought about that as I go along, and I've wondered about what other people think about my identifying with this group, but I really don't give a shit! (laughs) In the end, I (measured) *really don't care!* . . . I'm really just there to kind of do my work and to get my job done. . . . I think when I'm doing my job and trying hard, and they see that I'm going to continue doing what I'm doing, they'll know that the mission is much more important than the person itself.

Although his words below suggest that he does not care about how others perceive his sexuality, the measured tone of his voice suggested he was a bit offended by the assumptions of others (including activists in SAGA) because of what his participation in the organization might suggest about his sexuality.

Zero Self-Interest: Appearing Objective to the Public

Another reason why straight people are seen by SAGA as having political influence is that they are *not* gay or lesbian, and therefore cannot be seen as seeking a personal agenda. Joshua David from SAGA National connects together two common themes in the responses of activists, one being their position as a majority, but also by the fact of *not* being LGBT:

> First of all, straight people are the majority. We're not going to win unless we get them on our side. Number two, so many people who are gay are drawn to this work as a way of working through their personal issues. And, I find that straight people often tend to be just more interested in seeing the work get done. They're not working on their identity issues through activism. Some of the parents are, frankly. . . . But I find that's rare. Most of the straight people are in it because they believe in the cause. And, you know, they aren't kind of working through their identity issues in the same way a lot of gay people are.

Joshua sees the "working through their identity issues" as a liability to the movement as it can hamper progress. The presence of straight people can "lower the temperature" in the room by curbing the "passion [from] people who have been directly affected" by homophobia. Joshua goes on further stating that in order for the movement to progress, sometimes "it's important for someone to be able to say, 'Whoa, let's take a step back'" from the salience or urgency of homophobia in our culture.

Brooks Sheppard from Victoria sees straight activists as having a "super-positive role in SAGA for the most part" because they do not come across as having a personal agenda and therefore are not immediately interrupted when speaking with policymakers at school board meetings. C.J. Fleisher from Sunntach echoes this idea when he says, "their main strength is that when they speak about our mission, they have zero self-interest." Xavier Lucas from Davis City also states a similar pattern when he says that the motivation of straight people is "more altruistic, generally, for a sense of social responsibility . . . whereas for gay people, it's usually more personal: 'This affects me and that's why I'm involved.'"

Raul Gomez is a self-identified single gay therapist in his early thirties. Raul finds that the same message coming from gay people is heard differently when a straight person says it: "Hearing it from another straight person is going to sometimes make more sense than hearing it from just [gay people]." Anson Meyers from a rural SAGA chapter outside of Sunntach, considers straight people as being more objective than gay people because of their outsider status in an LGBT organization:

> A straight person can explain better what the issues are because they're able to do it perhaps a bit more objectively. You know, it's not coming from their personal experience, and the things that shaped me as a gay person aren't shaping them. They can look at it perhaps more dispassionately then, and then serve in the role of ally, as well as SAGA member and stakeholder.

Don Sotheby, a gay elementary school teacher from Victoria in his mid-twenties and an LGBT activist for nearly a decade, finds his sexuality a liability in the school system when he tries to correct homophobic behavior expressed by young children. He sometimes meets with resistance from the school administration, who often see him as seeking a personal agenda.

> When I came out to my kids, and when I was the one disciplining kids for calling each other gay and using derogatory terms, it was seen as "Well, you're just doing that because you're gay." But when a straight person does it, it has a stronger effect, you know? This is a person that *isn't* gay, but they know this is an important issue and other students who know they're not gay can say, "Wait a minute! So-and-so is standing up for this so maybe it's something that I should, too."

But, Don states that allies are always present in movements, suggesting that when allies with privilege speak out for the oppressed, it has a stronger effect:

> I think any movement that you just have—you know, the civil rights movement wasn't just African-Americans. It was other people that were helping, too. And I think seeing white people in the movement helped show others, "Well, wait a minute. Maybe I need to question what I'm thinking."

In the quote below, Don finds that straight people in the LGBT movement are what white people were to the civil rights movement.

> And the same thing with gay issues. I think if you see a straight person standing up and supporting this, it's going to cause people to question because of this visibility out there. It's not just that this is only an issue for gay people. It's an issue for everybody because I think everybody is

affected in one way or another by a gay person, whether they want to admit it or not. I think it's straight people who help people see that.

But, unlike the civil rights movement, straight activists in SAGA are not speaking *for* gay people but *with* them, and therefore not reifying the heterosexual dominance found in the mainstream culture (see Chapter 3 for further discussion).

Grant Daniels from El Reto welcomes straight people speaking up for LGBT rights in the community because a straight person is "an objective outsider." This reassures him that the equal rights he wants is not too much to ask:

> I think personally I feel a little bit (what's the word?)—reassured—because growing up in the society that I've grown up in, and fighting for the rights that I fight for, there is questioning and there is doubt. It's like, "Am I pushing too hard? Am I being unreasonable? Am I asking for special circumstances or special rights?" And you begin to start with some of the rhetoric. . . . And when I hear a straight person get up and talk, it's reassuring that, you know, I'm not off my rocker! There is some validity here. And what I'm asking for isn't that far-fetched. And, look, this is someone who for all intents and purposes is a third party, an objective outsider. And they even agree with me!

Grant continues further, saying that it is a "relief" to know that he is not engaging in an "internalized oppression" (Moraga 1983) when he witnesses straight allies speaking out:

> There's some relief. I don't always have to be the one on guard. I don't have to walk into a room and constantly be watching for the homophobia or heterosexism and be prepared to confront it and deal with it. I don't have to always have that responsibility. There are other people who are going to share it with me.

Appearing "objective" can provide credibility to the movement, especially in the conservative area of El Reto County in the Southwestern United States. Chase, Melissa, Grant, Adam, and Greg are all from El Reto and find straight people to be crucial in validating SAGA's message. Chase struggled to find the right words to explain how others in power might perceive the presence of gay people in SAGA. Chase says that "to mingle the two communities together . . . [creates] a lot more support" and brings a sense of impartiality to the message of SAGA. Melissa has a problem as seeing

No Joking About the "S" in SAGA

"people as gay or straight" because of her perception of a false categorical dichotomy of sexuality. However, when she looks at the "real world" benefits of straight people, Melissa finds that the inclusion of straight people:

> . . . validates your mission in a broader sense so you're not just targeting a certain segment of the community. . . . If we all thought that was the only segment of the community we could target, I think we would be selling ourselves very short. I think [straight people] help validate our mission in that particular community.

Adam finds the active presence of straight people one of the reasons for its successes:

> The word that comes to mind immediately is credibility because in terms of the work that we do, the heterosexual allies are the ones that make it sellable to a greater audience. It no longer becomes 'the gay agenda.' It becomes a human agenda.

Grant suggests that the credibility of straight people is their biggest strength:

> I think probably the biggest strength that a straight person can bring to SAGA is a detached sense of personal investment. . . . I think that when we're talking about trying to shift the power dynamic and trying to fight for gay and lesbian rights, a straight person can lend some creditability to the movement so that it doesn't just look like a gay person's personal agenda.

As a straight man in SAGA, Greg is ambivalent about his credibility because of his sexuality. First, Greg is also concerned about what this powerful message says to those people who are unfamiliar with LGBT concerns because he thinks that it may weaken the message of LGBT activists in SAGA:

> It's kind of a dichotomy because in some ways, by identifying as straight, I would imagine that in some people's minds that I further myself from retaliation or from people's negative impressions. I'm not trying to do that. But some people could then look at the issue and go, "Oh, well, you know he's not gay so I can approach him." Or, "I can relate to this person somehow." And I feel that in some ways that could be detrimental to the LGBT folks that are on SAGA or who are invested in this issue.

Not only does his straight identity make him more approachable, but Greg feels his speaking out as a straight ally also lends him "more credence" than a gay person fighting for LGBT rights:

> . . . When a person sees a person who is straight in SAGA, I can almost imagine the other side—and I'm not saying everybody does this—But I can just imagine people who may be sort of inclined to less-tolerant views of the world, I can almost imagine how they would lend me more credence than somebody who was directly affected by it, if that makes sense.

Straight Parents Bring Political Influence

Not having a perceived personal agenda was an important strategy for SAGA activists because it validates SAGA's message to the public, especially to parents who, as a social group, have tremendous pull in the school system. But some straight parents, like Judy Eberhardt from Piedmont, have gay children and therefore *may* have a personal stake in the success of the LGBT movement. But, the hope is that by being straight, parents can influence policymakers more effectively, and perhaps even bring in more straight people who do not have a personal venture in the LGBT movement.

It is important to note that the implicit message here is that *straight* parents, and not necessarily same-sex parent couples, bring political influence. The symbolic meaning of "parents" in the activists' minds were constructed around a heterosexist notion of family, particularly because their statements were made almost exclusively following my query of what the greatest strengths straight people bring to SAGA. I believe it is important to note that this is a clear example of the pervasiveness of heterosexism in the definition of the modern American family unit. However, given the framework limitations in gathering this information, it is not possible to provide a more in-depth analysis of the reasons why straight and gay activists adhered to a heterosexual family model.

The activists I spoke with consider the school system to be conservative places. Both Taylor Lynde from Victoria and Paul Freeman from El Reto compared schools to the military because of their conservativism, intolerance, and methods of social control to both teachers and students. But in school systems, parents typically have the final say in what information about sexuality is given to students. Cameron Fine from SAGA National suggests that when straight parents become LGBT allies and speak "in alliance with them," then the influence is much greater than having only LGBT activists lobby school policymakers for social change:

> I mean it's also just really crucial to have parents involved, and the majority of parents of LGBT youth are straight, so I think students' voices and parents' voices are often the most critical for getting like policy passage, not some random gay activist, who's not even part of the school system. So it's always important to have people who are active in school systems, but for these issues you also need to have other avenues.

Sebastian St. James from Sunntach echoed this idea when he spoke about his decision to confront his former high school ten years after graduating valedictorian about how poorly they dealt with LGBT issues and students like him. Sebastian recognized that his status as valedictorian and being gay had an emotional effect on the principal and superintendent during his return back to his alma mater, but it was his mother who was the most successful in reaching out to the current administration in creating social change:

> I think that she's the one that people listen to because she's speaking on behalf of her child. And that's something the audience can relate to really strongly. And so I think that—well, anytime you can make a really personal connection with your listeners, then you have a chance to open their minds and change their way of thinking.

C.J. finds there to be too few allies in the LGBT movement. Although students sometimes may organize a gay-straight alliance club at their school, C.J. considers parents as a group to have the most effective power in school systems. When I ask him for his thought about straight people in SAGA, he responded:

> I think it's great! I think we need more of them. . . . We absolutely need to. Parents are the most persuasive people in a school community. . . . If we get parents on the side of the teachers and the students, they're going to go to back and they're going to be the people that administrators are listening to. You know, it's easier for a student to be dismissed with their ideas or their wishes. But, parents are often the ones that are most listened to, so I think it will be incredibly valuable to bring more parents into our work.

During our interview, Justin Petrov refers to Judy, the co-chair of SAGA Piedmont, as having influence because parents can identify with her being a concerned parent:

[Judy] has this inspiration though she herself is not gay, . . . everyone listens to her. So parents will listen to her, friends will listen to her, random strangers will listen to her because they can identify with her because she's a parent, she's straight, [and] she has a family . . .

Brooks Sheppard, Chrissy Williams, and Don Sotheby work with middle and high school students in Victoria and consider straight people to be beneficial in the school systems they work in. Brooks, a teacher in a private school, finds that vocal straight people "play a big role" in bringing ideas about LGBT equality into schools. Reiterating the idea of straight privilege, Chrissy, a youth organizer at a local health service center, believes that straight people provide "a lot of credibility," especially in the school system. Chrissy recalls a straight man who leads a GSA (gay-straight alliance) in the local high school:

I think that straight people have a lot of credibility. That's a privilege. They have to have credibility with other straight people that they can have a lot of power and influence that way. There's one of the people involved [in SAGA] who is a straight school psych [and] who is involved with [the school's] GSA. His son came out in his same high school. And he's great. The students really feel supported by him. And, he's very vocal in his school. And, I don't care who is saying we need to make schools safer! It's a great, it's an important message, and he's doing it really effectively.

Reid and Judy from Piedmont, as well as Anson from outside of Sunntach, work in education and consider allies important to gain entry into schools. Reid is a retired schoolteacher from Piedmont, and he also finds schools to be conservative places. I first asked Reid about the strengths he thought straight allies brought to the LGBT safe-schools movement. He listed a number of reasons, one of which was the strength that parents bring to the movement:

And the fact that in this case Judy [the co-chair of SAGA Piedmont] is a parent of a gay child, I think they also associate with the idea of parent. Almost everybody knows "parent" whether it's their parent they are thinking of or they are a parent. So, I think that there's an empathy there. I think that's the strength they bring.

When I asked Reid what he thought about straight people in general speaking actively for the LGBT community, his answer was ambivalent. He loved

No Joking About the "S" in SAGA 127

allies speaking up because of their credibility, but he also expressed guilt from his reluctance to go into schools and talk about LGBT issues when straight people are willing to put their careers on the line for the mission. Reid responds to my question about straight people in SAGA:

> *I love it.* I think it's critically important. I think that straight people are our best allies. [*Why is that?*] Like it or not, I think they are listened to more. I think they come into the straight community with (pauses) not necessarily credentials, but almost without an axe to grind or something like that? Maybe that's not the right phrase. [*An agenda?*] Yeah! She [Judy Eberhardt] *does* have an agenda.

Here Reid begins to express his ambivalence, as he states that he's "just as good" as Judy in speaking, but that straight people have that objectivity necessary for success in the school system:

> And, maybe it's just me personally, the way I feel a little hesitant going into the school and acknowledging that I'm a gay man and I'm looking for support for the gay-straight alliance, or something like that. To me it's better if there's a straight person doing it. And I'm not 100% proud of that feeling. I think it's something I have to work on as an individual. I mean, I'm just as good as she is. But there is just something about a straight person doing that.

Reid, who is a single gay man in his mid-fifties, finds that straight parents help activists "get the foot in the door" in the school system:

> . . . The mission of SAGA is to create safer schools and if we accept the fact that the population in schools is mostly straight and that the parents are mostly straight, then I think it helps to have a straight at least to get the foot in the door. Because the straight can introduce the gay person, bisexual, transgendered person, and say "See, they don't have horns" and "See, they're not out to recruit your child" and "See, they do have moral values" and "See, they do have a family" and "They espoused values like you do in your straight family."

Universalize SAGA's Message

As we saw in many of the quotes above, activists see the right kind of straight people—those who are altruistic and willing to relinquish some of their privilege for the greater good—have political influence, which moderated and validated the message of LGBT activists who are often accused of seeking a "personal agenda" when appealing to politicians. Connecting together the theme of the outsider as beneficial to a movement identity, Joshua looks at the LGBT community as isolated from the dominant culture. And, in order for change to occur on a broad scale, LGBT people must reach out to the mainstream culture through education and inclusion. Joshua explains why it is important to include straight people in SAGA:

> [Having straight people in SAGA] really universalizes the message. There is a tendency within the LGBT community to talk to ourselves a lot and get caught up in our own language and lingo and issues. And then you have some straight people who might not even know what the "T" is [transgender], it forces you to ground yourself back into talking in a way that most people can understand, which frankly is something as a community we're not great at. We tend to talk in a way that we understand.

Dixon Harrington from Piedmont also thinks that the presence of straight people in SAGA universalize the message:

> [Straight people are] also are really good for saying, "This isn't going to play for a straight crowd." Or, "That's too much for them. Let's not be so controversial." . . . And I say that probably because I travel in a more straight world than most gay men do, so that's probably why I value the straight members as much as I do. . . . Many, many of my close dear friends are straight, so I understand that perspective, and I'm probably more excited to hear the straight people on the board's voices.

However, Greg also finds that by having no personal stake in LGBT issues, and through the social networks he has in the straight community, he lends some power behind the movement's message:

> We [straight people] also have some sway over people that may not necessarily be swayed by someone from the GLBT community. And interestingly, because we have no personal stake in this (I mean, personal in so much as we're not directly affected by it ourselves). In some ways there's a little bit of power behind our message because what that it's sort of like, "Here we are, we're involved in this. Why aren't you guys?" You know, "Is there a reason that you have to be GLBT in order

No Joking About the "S" in SAGA   129

to be concerned about this issue?" And our answer is "No." And I think that's a powerful message . . .

Bring Access to Unavailable Social Networks

Interestingly, a continuation from the Greg's quote above captures another important theme that other activists have mentioned was politically advantageous:

> You know, every community has its own networks, and I know now that working with SAGA, I've made some inroads into the LGBT community as an outsider. . . . And in some ways, we [straight people] try to make some connections with the people we know.

Straight people have the added strength of providing access to social networks and institutions, which are most often unavailable to many people in the LGBT community. This broadens the base of possible allies by educating people who may be removed from the gay and lesbian enclaves and issues. Sebastian St. James from Sunntach also sees straight people as giving LGBT people access to other social networks.

> . . . [Another] thing that straight people bring [SAGA] is that they're connected to so many different social networks that we're not connected to . . . because they belong to churches and PTAs. So they get [SAGA] access to whole different groups of people that gay people don't necessarily have within their circle. . . . There's a lot of potential allies. I don't think we've done our job to really tap them as well. I guess it's because of what is easiest for is our social networks. And our social networks don't always, at least my group of gay friends seems to be fairly self-contained in the gay community. That's probably not such a good thing.

Sometimes straight people bring the added benefit of making the "straight world" much more familiar to LGBT people who are often outside of the "straight" culture in their urban enclaves. Several of the activists expressed a "disconnection" with the gay communities where they live, and find that to be a benefit to the organization. C.J. and Dixon, find it easier to bridge gay and straight worlds because they live in a "straight world." As a gay man, C.J. finds his strength to be that his "life is really integrated in both the gay and the straight communities. And, so I see that influencing the people that were working to get involved in the organization doing more outreach to the straight community than to a lot of other gay organizations do." Similar to Joshua, Dixon finds the strengths of straight people in SAGA to be a "thermometer of the level of heterosexism in our culture" because of their connections with other straight social networks that many LGBT people do not typically live within.

But, Dixon—a partnered gay man in suburbia—*does* live in the "straight world" as we saw in his earlier quote, and explains how their presence in SAGA is a "thermometer" of heterosexism because of their being in a "straight world."

> I think they bring an excellent sort of thermometer of the level of heterosexism in our culture. Not so much of theirs, because I think we all have heterosexism in us. But many of the straight members, obviously, travel in a more "straight world" than some of the gay and lesbian members do, so they can reflect and state sort of what the straight perspective is out there now, and whether it has evolved, or gone backwards, or what the snapshot is now.

Paul Freeman and Judy Eberhardt are both straight SAGA activists, and find their strengths to be their outsider identity of "straight" because of the social worlds in which they operate their day-to-day lives. Paul, an African-American in his mid-sixties, speaks for himself when he says that his role in the straight world is "keeping it honest."

> . . . We are the kind of contacts or the people who might be able to promote understanding in the non-gay part of our community because I find myself having to speak out sometimes even with friends. For instance, not too long ago I was at a luncheon with some of my colleagues from the school system—black principals. And I forget what it was, but something was [said] about homosexuality and somebody made a snide remark. And, I had to say, "Come on now! We've had to go through that!" And the guy said, "Yeah, I know." You know, that type of thing—Keeping it honest.

Judy uses almost any opportunity to talk about SAGA. Her gay son, Kyle, and his partner, Sal, tease her sometimes for using her accessibility to straight communities as often as she does.

> . . . Kyle is thrilled and very proud that I'm involved. . . . If he were sitting here, talking to him, he would be saying, "I think it's great what she's doing." But I am a little over the top. He was going off on me last

night because we were at a benefit. I think it was the first fundraising event since I've got involved with SAGA that I haven't said anything to anybody about SAGA. Last night it just didn't come out. I didn't have an opportunity. Kyle's partner Sal was teasing me like "Okay, who did she talk to this night?!" And I said, "Nobody! Nobody!" They were like, "Whoa!"

Despite the occasional teasing from her son and his partner, Judy finds her greatest strength to be this accessibility:

> The benefit I think is for me to be a co-chair, the benefit is that I'm accessible to other straight people, to talk about this mission and why it's important for all of us. I'm sometimes, for some people, it's easier [for] straight people to get to talk to me about it and understand it, like they might not ask the same questions if someone were gay. . . . It's a different advantage. It's not like it's better, I don't think about it that way.

As Judy continues, she makes it a point to mention that the movement cannot be "just a gay thing" because of the interconnections between straight and gay people:

> . . . There are so many straight people that have gay friends, gay family members, you know that kind of thing, have gay parents—that they're going to be a part of this [movement], too. It's not just a gay thing. In terms of it shouldn't just be a gay community that's doing this. It should be all of us doing it. And, it is.

During the interviews, SAGA activists had no trouble listing the strengths that they see straight people bring into LGBT movements. From my observations, using straight people strategically is a beneficial social movement tool for SAGA in achieving its mission. But are there weaknesses to having straight people in SAGA? If so, do SAGA activists see a problem with increasing the visibility of straight people in an LGBT social movement organization? I address these questions in the next section.

THEIR GREATEST STRENGTH IS THEIR GREATEST WEAKNESS

When I asked activists in SAGA the question, "What are the strengths/weaknesses that straight people bring to SAGA," I noticed a different response from my other questions that asked about the strengths and weaknesses of gays and lesbians. As I mentioned earlier in Chapter Three, most activists in the interviews assumed that when I was asking about straight people in SAGA that they already *were* the "particular kind of straight person" willing to shed their social privilege. Cameron Fine was aware of privilege during our interview. It irritates Cameron when straight people continuously mentioning their sexuality, while saying that their sexuality doesn't really matter.

> I think in general, it irritates me when straight people are allies and proclaim their straighthood. Like, publicly, if a famous person is like talking about, "Yes, everybody should be treated equal. It doesn't matter if you're gay. I'm straight, but it doesn't matter." That usually bothers me. Like the "straight, but not narrow" pins. They bother me. Like, why are you proclaiming your straightness?

However, he also states, "if you want to get something across to somebody in power, often if you have someone who is like them or appears to be like them, you can influence them better." Ambivalence like this is a recurring theme throughout my interviews, as they recognize that the strengths of deploying straight identities in an identity movement are also weaknesses.

Why Does it Have to Be That Way?: Depending on Allies

Reid Roberts, who is a single gay man in his mid-fifties and still reluctant to publicly identify his sexuality to family and colleagues, continues to expresses a sense of regret that gay people like him need straight people:

> I haven't really thought about this too much, but there's a certain—not a resentment, but "Gee, it's too bad that gay people have to have or that gay people are depending on straight people to represent them."

Casey Lina, a single bisexual woman in her mid-thirties, expresses a different view from most of the other activists in how she perceives straight people in effecting change within school systems. Her ambivalence might stem from her "left" political activity as a younger woman in the bisexual rights movement. Casey, who identifies as a "bi-dyke," still feels the "tug" toward separatism, even though she believes that this would be a poor strategy for political success.

> I go back and forth on that a lot. Part of me is, within the SAGA board, I'm really happy that there is someone that is straight who . . . takes time to show up to SAGA board meeting and participate because, I view schools as pretty conservative places and scared places. So, I

think for SAGA to have-obviously the "Sss" in SAGA, to have those straight people is going to make all the difference. Part of me still has the, "Damn it, why does it have to be that way?" My good separatist self still rails against that and says, "NO! Ugh! God damn it, no! I just want the G, L, B and the T and that's it!" . . . I think within most organizations, straight people are great but not necessary.

Out of all my interviews, Taylor is the only activist to explicitly embrace the "gay liberationist" model of political action, which advocates separatism from straight communities. In our three-hour interview, Taylor tended to follow his own path filled with tangents and side stories. In an excerpt from one of these stories, which is about confronting the conservative school board in suburban Victoria where he works as a teacher, Taylor explains how he sometimes is militant in his desire to end heterosexist oppression of LGBT people:

I think gay people have always been 'Oh, can you help us?' *Pttth!* We don't need your fucking help! We have the right to be here! We have the right to have a life. We have the right to be the people we are. We don't have to ask them for our rights for what we have! That belongs to us! And I think part of it is us finding those avenues—and I guess that's the little militant that comes out of me, I guess—I think you have to play a real fine line between being out of control and being so over that people don't take you seriously. And that militant where you look at them and say, "I'm not going away! This isn't over with! We're just starting! So you better decide just how far you want this to go! And you decide now! I want an answer from you *now!*

As we have seen in this chapter thus far, "the little militant" part that comes out of Taylor is unique from all the other activists who advocated inclusiveness and unity in the fight for safe schools. For the most part, activists expressed ambivalence when describing the weaknesses of straight people, saying that their outsider status is both a strength, but also a weakness.

Outsiders Within

Nearly all of the activists found it difficult to find weaknesses that outweigh the strengths. When I asked Paul if he saw any weaknesses of straight people in SAGA, he (as a straight man) stated that "No, I don't. I just think that any help is a strength. Any understanding or acceptance or tolerance is a strength." In fact, most activists saw no substantial weaknesses with the inclusion of straight people in the LGBT organization.

However, what many saw as the greatest strength of allies was also their perceived weakness: Their straight identity is, at times, problematic because they are outsiders of LGBT communities. Anson Meyers, a SAGA activist from outside Sunntach, expressed ambivalence when he said:

> Well, one of the things that's sort of the flip side of that [is] the same thing that could be a strength [of straight people] could also be a weakness. They probably wouldn't have experienced the harassment and discrimination that most gay adults have had at some point in their lives. And therefore, their experience is essentially an intellectual experience, rather than an emotional experience. It's not both. Whereas for a gay person, it almost has to be both.

The most difficult part of the interview for Judy Eberhardt was when I asked her how she felt as a straight person speaking out for the LGBT community as a SAGA board member. She finds her perspective as a straight mother raising a gay child as an advantage, but also a concern because she only knows the experiences of LGBT people "once removed." As we see in the quote below, the presence of LGBT people in leadership positions validates her message as well because it ensures that what she is saying is not offensive to LGBT communities:

> How do I feel about that? Like am I unsure? Do I feel proud of it? There's all those. I have a lot to learn. I'm not a gay person. I have to be very respectful . . . of that because especially leading this group, as a straight person that should make you double-think everything. You know, "Am I really on target here?" . . . So that's the disadvantage of being straight. I have to be careful because I'm not gay. I can't really speak that voice. I can speak it once removed. I raised a gay son. I'm very close to him so I know that piece as a mother. . . . At least my experience adds some credibility to that too, so that's an advantage.

Edit Aloo is a staff member from SAGA National, and a single "gender fluid" person around 35 years old. She has patience with allies who are struggling to figure out LGBT subcultures. Edit finds that the weakness of straight people is "sometimes a little education curve . . . sometimes they don't get why there are habits that queer people have sometimes, self-preservation habits, defense mechanisms. And, so that's the learning curve."

Adam Lieberman from El Reto also sees straight people having a tendency to view LGBT concepts "a little too basically" because of their heterosexual privilege, but that the benefits of straight people joining SAGA outweigh the weaknesses:

> I think the one weakness is that they do have a tendency to view things a little too (how do I say this correctly?) (Adam pauses) a little too basically. . . . I think that that's their weakness in terms of not having a full understanding of how minority groups function and having to fight for empowerment, as opposed to empowerment being an entitlement. . . . That said, I think that's relatively minor in terms of the strengths that they bring to the table.

Grant Daniels from El Reto considers straight people as "crucial" to SAGA's mission. But, he also discusses how heterosexual privilege can be a potential hindrance to the LGBT movement, but that any "gap" between queer and straight identities is "just one of the challenges" in the fight for equality:

> A straight person has never and will never experience heterosexism in the way that a gay or lesbian person would. And while we can do as many exercises and we can explain as many stories and be as anecdotal as possible, I think that there's just a visceral understanding that they will never get. And so, I think that the way that it plays out kind of in a day-to-day process is there are reactions to events and circumstances and situations that gay and lesbian people have that might not be totally understood by the straight person.

But he also feels that gay people may not understand straight people, too:

> And vice versa. Straight people might react in particular ways. And, gay people might be like, "What the hell?! Why don't you get this?" So, yeah, I think there is a bit of a gap there. Not impossible—just one of the challenges.

When I ask Grant if he sees it as a positive having straight people in SAGA, despite the challenges, he quickly retorts that the challenges are outweighed by the "crucial" benefits that straight people bring to SAGA:

> Oh yeah! Definitely! I don't think we could do the work without straight people, honestly. Even though there is that gap, and they're never going to be able to fully understand it. They can get close, but they are never going to be able to fully understand it. Even with that caveat,

I don't think we'd be where we are today if it wasn't for straight people. Yeah, I think they're crucial.

When I asked Sebastian what he considered was the main weakness of straight people in SAGA, he responded, "they're just really hard to find . . . because they have other causes, I guess." But, he continued that their weakness is a lack of a personal story of why they are involved in the movement. And yet, Sebastian is ambivalent about this weakness as we saw in his earlier quote about the strengths in his mother's personal story about being a heterosexual *parent*. But, he still sees the weakness is that they can never truly know the personal pain that LGBT people must endure from oppression:

> And I guess the other weakness must be that—Well, I think the strength that a gay or lesbian person has is they have their personal story and their personal experiences to draw from. So, I can tell you what it was like for me as a gay student in high school. And a straight person can only tell you what it was like for their friends—Unless there was someone who was harassed because they were perceived to be gay.

Cameron echoes this idea of knowing personally the harassment and discrimination of being perceived as LGBT, or in his example, "queer" gender identity:

> . . . Unless they are perceived to be LGBT, they are, or were when they were young (then that's a different case), they don't necessarily know what it's like to be discriminated against or harassed because of actual or perceived gender identity. . . . Obviously, nobody can know anyone else's experience as well as they know, but they don't have that knowledge, because they haven't experienced it.

Trey McIntyre is a college student in his early twenties at a local community college in Victoria and identifies himself as an "all-American gay white boy" on his demographic questionnaire. Trey is an athlete who is open about his sexuality, and uses this opportunity to educate his peers about homophobia and intolerance. When I asked Trey how helpful he sees straight people in the gay and lesbian movement, he responded that it was a "tricky question. . . . It's really hard to decide because they don't have any real concept of what it's like to be homosexual, and when you don't have some sort of . . . that personal aspect of the whole issue, I think it makes it harder to fight for it."

Some of the other younger activists I spoke with, such as Chase O'Donnell and Justin Petrov, were also ambivalent about the weakness straight people bring to SAGA. Although they see that the outsider status of not being LGBT can be a problem, it is not insurmountable because the benefits far outweighed the weaknesses. Chase and Justin are two young activists and based on their experiences in high school gay-straight alliances, they are ambivalent about whether or not being an outsider truly is a problem in SAGA. Chase O'Donnell is a self-identified gay man in his late teens that became involved in SAGA after horrible experiences he received from school administrators in El Reto County when he came out while still a high school student. Chase originally sees no weaknesses for including allies in SAGA, but when probed further, he seems to make broad generalizations by reflecting back to his limited experiences with straight people:

> . . . There aren't any weaknesses that I can see that they bring. I think it helps more than anything else. [*What about straight people in general?*] . . . I mean, I think with everything, there's strengths and weaknesses. I think they can bring some very good things, and I think they can bring some really weak things. . . . I think straight people can be kind of closed minded, and not being as open to stuff, and just kind of having, with that, comes, you know, this like, kind of a negativity. I mean, not all the time, but with not being as open, you know, and to being able to see a different side, or to even think about it. Something like that.

Like Chase, Justin also came out in high school, but lived in the relatively liberal suburban county of Essex in the Northeast. Justin, also a high school athlete, began the first gay-straight alliance in Essex County along with two straight friends—one female friend and one male friend. They created the gay-straight alliance to be more "political" and "go out there and [do] the most talking" rather than as a "feely-touchy" support group for LGBT youth. The result was that only one-sixth of the membership was gay, lesbian, or questioning youth. When I ask him what he thinks are the weaknesses that straight people bring to SAGA, he sees his *own* weaknesses paralleling those of straight people because he, as a gay youth, is not very well connected to the gay community at large:

> Probably a lot of similar weaknesses that I bring in the sense of not having a very good connection with the gay community. Not *really* being able to understand what it's like to have a *really* hard time with something that's so not you're choice. It seems like anyone that's willing to

be involved in an organization that's so controversial and active really doesn't have too many weaknesses.

But, like Chase, Justin is ambivalent about whether or not they are weaknesses at all:

> It really comes down to like what they as a person have to offer. . . . [Allies] don't know what it's like not to have any single person that you can even consider having a crush on because you have no idea who's gay or not and you're too afraid to think about that. . . . So that's limiting but certainly something that people can learn.

C.J. is an activist in his mid-thirties, and is far removed from his high school experiences unlike Chase and Justin. However, one can also recognize the ambivalence in his response about the weaknesses of straight people:

> I think that they don't have quite as much understanding of what it's like to be gay or lesbian in a school. And, they can do a really good job of trying to understand. And I think the ones who get involved have done that. And it actually impresses me much more so than to see their commitment just because they don't have as much at stake for their own life. It might be for someone that they love, which I guess is a big motivator too, but you know, I really don't see weaknesses. I think they can only help our cause.

CHAPTER CONCLUSION

When I asked Joshua David during our interview to tell me what his greatest strength is as one of the leaders of SAGA, he said, "I believe in the old Chinese proverb: 'Your greatest strength is your greatest weakness.'" By and large, I learned that the LGBT activists I interviewed believed that straight people are a benefit to SAGA, but that their greatest strength is their greatest weakness. Activists sometimes expressed ambivalence with the presence of vocal straight allies in SAGA, but felt that the benefits far outweigh the potential costs.

As I explained in Chapter Three, and explored further in this chapter, I found that the deployment of a straight identity—one that speaks *with* LGBT activists and not necessarily *for* them—is a successful strategy that activists use in their interactions with the public and policymakers.

However, this strategy of identity deployment differs from the model of organizations as theorized by Mary Bernstein (1997) because the identity being deployed is *different* than the identity-based movement itself. Bernstein (1997) finds that activists, over time, may deploy a collective identity for education, an identity for critique, or a mixed model that deploys both types depending on the organization and political circumstances of the time. The activists all share a common group identity, such as a coalition of non-normative sexual identities (lesbian and gay) in the lesbian and gay rights movement or of women in the feminist movement. Unlike Bernstein's findings, the primary identity strategy of SAGA activists is based on the deployment of a *straight* identity held by their straight ally members, rather than their own collective LGBT identity.

Activists found that straight people bring with them political influence and social networks because they are often perceived by the public and policymakers as objective outsiders. However, their greatest strength of being an objective outsider was also considered to be their greatest weakness. As my findings in this chapter suggest, the activists in SAGA continue to define identity boundaries of straight and gay, particularly in finding that the greatest weakness of straight people were that they were not one of them. Surprisingly, most activists considered this weakness as very minor in comparison to the benefits of having straight people in helping to achieve SAGA's mission. This finding comports with Joshua Gamson's research on queer movements (J. Gamson 1995, 1997a, 1997b) insofar as boundary maintenance is maintained within the organization to separate the identities of "us" and "them." Including straight people into SAGA, while also maintaining the distinct "queer" character of the organization, permits the strategic deployment of straight identity in order to achieve political goals. It also ensures that the organization or movement does not self-destruct because identity boundaries remain clearly defined in the organizational identity and the strategies used by the activists. Likewise, by combining the identities of "straight" and "LGBT" within SAGA, yet maintaining the distinct boundaries of "us-versus-them" necessary for movement success (J. Gamson 1995), I find further evidence that a mixed model of identity deployment is utilized by SAGA because it combines both the identity for education and an identity for critique strategies when deploying a straight identity.

In the following chapter, I build upon the identity deployment findings, and consider the ways in which SAGA activists may use straight people strategically in varied political environments. One of the activists, Casey Lina, from the conservative suburbs of Victoria in the Pacific Northwest, encapsulates this idea beautifully when she says:

> I think within SAGA, even ignoring that S [in SAGA], it's critical. Especially in Victoria, there are some very conservative segments in the population [so] having straight people, having straight people on the board, having people who don't make a big deal out of being straight . . . that's going to make all the difference in getting us into schools and getting us into help kids. It's just the reality.

As I mentioned in the introduction to this chapter, we learn that Adam (the co-chair of SAGA El Reto County), uses the straight member Greg as an impression management strategy when speaking with the conservative school district superintendent. As we see by both comments from Casey and Adam, it is important to theoretically consider the ways in which political environments affect the success of an organization to survive and, in turn, how a liberal or conservative environment may affect the deployment of straight identities. Building on the political ecology research of Debra Minkoff (1993, 1997), I demonstrate in the next chapter how SAGA chapters in conservative political environments recognize that the "S" in SAGA is critical for any type of success. On the other hand, although still important in the more liberal areas, SAGA activists rely more on straight social networks for success in these areas, rather than as a politically legitimizing identity deployment strategy.

Chapter Six
Political Environments Shape Identity Deployment

Amanda Candor, from SAGA Davis City in the Southern United States, eloquently describes the reality of politics in a conservative environment:

> What we really had to do . . . [was] realize that policy in Davis City is incremental and that it's not going to make the huge steps . . . where they're passing this and they're passing that and they've got legislation, non-discrimination, hate crimes law, and in Davis City, we're like, "Could you not beat us? Could we go *that* far?! We know it will take another eight years to get, 'Could you not call us names?' But, could we go violent crime far? Can we do that?"

In Davis City, progress is slow to come by, with activists often having to forego their political agenda to negotiating very small, incremental accomplishments. Amanda continued to express that this political reality in the South is very disheartening to the activists:

> You must have [tangible goals] in order to give an organization momentum. In order to keep people interested and involved, you must have concrete, winnable goals and you must achieve them. And you can have long-term goals. And that's great and something an organization needs, but you have to be able to get somewhere to show people we're making some sort of progress here.

Let us briefly compare the conservative political reality of the South to what activists in the liberal city of Sunntach in the Midwest experience. Approximately three-fourths of the Sunntach state representatives are Democrats. According to the current co-chair C.J. Fleischer, the schools are changing in how they handle gay and lesbian youth, both in

141

reaction to legal challenges and the social environment of more youth coming out:

> The environment in schools is shifting. Schools are starting to become a lot more accepting of gay/straight alliances and having youth being out. Administrators are losing battles in court when they're not protecting youth. And so, there's a lot more visibility to our issues.

C.J. continues to speak about how the social environment in the United States are a buoy to SAGA Sunntach's challenges to activate changes in the school system:

> And then on top of that, the larger social environment is really changing, obviously with the Supreme Court [sodomy] decision . . . And I know that if we're pushing in the right way over the next couple of years, we could just *explode*—explode in a positive way, that is.

C.J. is cautious to note that as long as they remain true to the organizational mission, he envisions a positive "explosion" of social change. We see that particularly in his comment of "pushing the right way" in marketing on the recent social changes regarding LGBT rights.

In the midst of their respective political environments, SAGA Davis City disbanded, while SAGA Sunntach flourishes with an $80,000 budget for the 2003 fiscal year. Why did these chapters have such disparate outcomes? What I learned is that the political environments can either stifle or fuel the growth of chapters. But, also included in these outcomes are how a straight identity is deployed differently in these chapters. For chapters in conservative areas, straight people may be a necessity for giving the chapter political legitimacy in the face of strong adversaries, assisting the chapter to "stay afloat" in rough seas. Yet, what I find is that for chapters in liberal areas, straight activists are used less as a legitimizing component, and more for their social networks to increase member mobilization and the broader cultural goals of educating people on LGBT issues.

In this chapter, I assess the political nature of each location based on the perceptions of the activists. This method of analysis is not unprecedented in the sociological literature (see Linneman 2003). However, typically one would expect additional sources to corroborate that these areas are, indeed, conservative or liberal. In good faith I attempt to utilize quantitative data to substantiate the political environment claims by activists, such as census data on the number of LGBT families within the chapter's territory, as well as the political representation in the state and federal legislative branches of government. The reader will find this information at the beginning of each subsection below.

However, due to the IRB restrictions for the confidentiality of participants in this book, I cannot be more explicit in my analysis. The reasoning behind this is that the more specific one gets with the data, the more likely readers will correctly guess the city's name, and from there deduce other information, such as the name of the organization and/or participants in the study. Another reason is that it is difficult to assess whether or not local governing bodies, such as school boards, are conservative or liberal without attending several public meetings, or acquiring historical documents or these public meetings, such as minutes or transcripts. Both of these options were beyond the scope of the book. That said, I believe that there is enough evidence I provide to corroborate the environmental perceptions of the activists to draw reasonable conclusions regarding the success of organizations to accomplish the movement goals, and to deploy straight people strategically.

This chapter is separated into two sections: conservative and liberal political environments. I begin each section by introducing the specific political environments within which SAGA activists operate, focusing on both the similarities and differences of the geopolitical milieu. Next, within both sections, I discuss the ways in which political environments affect the identity deployment of straight people.

CONSERVATIVE POLITICAL ENVIRONMENTS

There are two chapters that reside squarely within conservative political environments and therefore share a number of similarities in the organizational trajectories: SAGA Davis City in the South and SAGA El Reto County in the Southwestern United States. SAGA Victoria in the Pacific Northwest is more difficult to categorize because technically, it is responsible for the city of Victoria and its surrounding suburban counties. However, it does not focus its energies working in the liberal city of Victoria and, instead, concentrates on the conservative suburban areas. However, it shares commonalities with the other two chapters in the types of struggles it encounters.

SAGA chapters in conservative regions share a number of similar organizational trajectories and experiences due in part to the political environment. First, chapters that operate within conservative political environments struggle with achieving tangible political objectives, which affect the ability to mobilize additional LGBT activists and secure straight people, and in turn, make it difficult to achieve broader cultural goals such as educating people on LGBT issues. Organizations in the conservative political environments had a tendency to experience shrinking memberships from which to obtain money that is necessary to expand the chapter and assist it with reaching their political goals. In other words, chapters in conservative political areas experienced a stunting in their growth, unable to move beyond the infancy stages of organizing, even if they have been an accredited chapter for many years.

In the next section, I describe the political environments of each chapter, and describe the ways in which activists struggle to accomplish the political, mobilizing, and cultural movement impacts. In each of these subsections, I reflect back on the findings from previous chapters, which describe how activists from these conservative environments consider the ways in which the organization could strategically deploy a straight identity as a way to maximize successes of these three movement impacts.

The South: Davis City

The South in 2004 is often referred to on television news talk shows as the "Red States," which are those states that went for George W. Bush in the 2000 and 2004 elections. In our informal conversation, Amanda called Davis City a "liberal oasis in a sea of conservatives." Many of the laws that SAGA works to obtain, such as allowing the establishment of gay-straight student alliances (GSAs) in high schools and employment non-discrimination clauses in teachers' contracts already exist in the relatively liberal city within a conservative state and region of the United States. However, even though Davis City is relatively liberal, it exists in a Southern state where social change is skewed toward conservative ideology. Lacking the tangible successes as momentum for their cause, the activists explained to me that the organization collapsed because they could not mobilize straight or gay activists in the absence of legislative successes. In this section of the chapter, I discuss how the political realities in which Davis City operates stifled the opportunities for successful straight identity deployment before it even had a chance to be used strategically by the organization.

The land area territory of which SAGA Davis City is responsible is nearly 300 square miles. Out of all the geographical areas covered in this research project, Davis City is the only city to have more than one percent of same-sex unmarried partnerships (Census 2000). This was the largest percentage of any location in this research project. It is mostly white, but a growing number of residents are Latino or African-American (Census 2000). The median household income for Davis City is over $40,000 (Census 2000). Very few state and federal representatives from Davis City are liberal. Fifty-eight percent of the state representatives in Davis City are

Republicans; likewise, seventy-five percent of the national representatives are Republican.

SAGA Davis City is the only inactive organization I studied after not applying for re-accreditation in 2003. Only three board members, Amanda Candor, Ruth Huerta, and Xavier Lucas remained on the board after a dispute over leadership among the board members fractured the organization. Part of the problem for the failure of SAGA Davis City, Amanda notes, was that the co-chair "didn't do their research" on the politics of Davis City and the state, and with being new to organizing on the grassroots level, was unfamiliar with the distinctions between short term and long term goals. The inability to achieve concrete, winnable goals in the political arena was a source of frustration for the members of SAGA, leading to its eventual demise.

Amanda, a self-identified single bisexual white woman in her mid-twenties is regularly active in community activism. In her quote below, we see Amanda's organizing strengths in trying to accommodate the unique political environment of SAGA Davis City into the aspirations of the inexperienced, but passionate, SAGA activists. When I asked Amanda to tell me her opinions of SAGA Davis City, she answers with a frustrated tone in her voice:

> [SAGA Davis City] is an organization that came about with good ideas . . . but whose founders really didn't do their research. Davis City School District has a non-discrimination policy, for example. . . . As an organization with 15 members, we're not going to make those kinds of gains and we're not going to be the catalyst for those kinds of things.

Amanda continues by describing the ways in which she and Xavier tried to shape the organization to reach tangible goals for social change in their conservative state environment, regardless of the school district's liberal non-discrimination policy.

> . . . I think a lot of it was Xavier and I going, "Okay. All right, we'll try it for this. Let's give that a month." And people going, "Wow, we can't do that." "Right. So, let's go back to this. Okay. Maybe we can do this? Good! All right! So, we've accomplished . . ."

For Amanda, success "was about teaching people that you have to have concrete winnable goals . . . in order to give an organization momentum." Furthermore, Amanda and Xavier believed that achieving small, winnable goals is necessary to keep people interested and involved in the organization.

Although people in the state where Davis City is located might consider the city to be "liberal," when compared to other areas of the country, it is not. Ruth Huerta, a self-identified straight married Latina in her mid-forties, comments:

> "I certainly knew generally that Davis City was liberal. It's *extremely* conservative when compared to *real* liberal places like Northeast or something, but it's liberal by [this state's] standards."

When I asked Amanda to comment on how she assesses the political environment in Davis City, she comments on its relationship to the state politics. Amanda considers the city "conservative-at-heart," believing that the local politicians put on a façade of liberalness in order to acclimate to the changing political temperature of a conservative Southern state. The liberal stalwarts in the city may want to support LGBT rights, but they are not willing to risk their political careers on being proactive in the light of the anti-gay agenda promoted in the state capital. She states:

> Davis City politics is a lot about . . . balancing the fact that most people in Davis City are . . . politically correct. And so we will have a policy that says "We will not discriminate. We will have these things that look politically correct. We will not support them. If it comes right down to it, we're not going to put the money behind it." . . . And so, it's that give-and-take of "We're politically correct, but we're still essentially conservative."

Amanda feels that the politicians of Davis City may say they support LGBT anti-discrimination policies, but that it is really not an urgent issue in the front of their minds. Amanda describes below that she sees politics in the city versus the state as fundamentally different. Achieving concrete, winnable goals on the state level requires being reactive, rather than proactive:

> . . . It really comes down to Davis City against the rest of [the state] . . . The liberal left-wing, the people who would generally support LGBT rights are not being proactive, and not able to be proactive . . . [It's] more of "What can we stop?" . . . "How can we prevent a catastrophe?" as opposed to "How can we make things better?" . . . So, it's a very reactive instead of proactive situation . . .

Political Environments Shape Identity Deployment   147

In both the city and the state, Amanda sees the hopelessness of forging ahead in a political environment that will not let activists be proactive, but to continuously remain on the defensive from anti-LGBT initiatives. As a volunteer lobbyist with a statewide LGBT lobbyist organization, Amanda now compares the ways in which politics is controlled by special interests in the state to "a broken candy machine [where] people pay us [lobbyists] because we know how to kick the machine and get the candy out." The way gays and lesbians get legislation passed in their favor on the statewide level is through compromises, most of which are not seen positively by the LGBT constituents the organization serves. With an audible sense of frustration over recent legislation negotiations in the state capital, Amanda considers the process by which activists and lobbyists must face the harsh political realities. She laments what she says to legislators:

> We're aware—to put it less than delicately—your constituency requires that you look like a bigot. So, here's what you can do. You can vote for [an anti-gay bill]. Fine! We don't care! . . . Go ahead, cast your vote loud and clear . . . but vote the right way on the [LGBT-positive] bill." And so, the policymaking in Davis City is a lot about, "Let me show you how to keep your job while still doing something right."
> . . . It's sort of the situation in Davis City where it is very much give-and-take and what we can get and working a really long time for a very small victory.

The strategy of dealing with this political environment means that SAGA Davis City must change their strategy when fitting into the mission of SAGA National. However, as in other places in 2001, the political ramifications of decennial district gerrymandering made the possibility of LGBT successes dismal in both Davis City and the state. According to Amanda, SAGA Davis City had to explain to National in the re-accreditation process for 2000–2001 why their successes in the coming fiscal year were nearly impossible to accomplish:

> What we really had to do to change was to take the mission of SAGA National, which is fighting for very, very basic things and realize that policy in [this state] is incremental and that it's not going to make the huge steps that people in [other liberal areas] are making where they're passing this and they're passing that and they've got legislation, non-discrimination, hate crimes law, and [here], we're like, "Could you not beat us? Could we go *that* far?" . . . So I think that was a big change

from the National organization, which is like, "Go! Organize! Win!" And we're sort of like, "Go! Don't lose! Get *something!*"

This can make for challenges between the chapter and the national organization because the structure of SAGA does not say which level has the final say if disagreements arise in the implementation of the mission (Personal interview with Joshua David).

The political environment in the southern state where Davis City is located is frustrating for activists like Ruth. One of the few times Ruth ever tried to lobby her state representative, she experienced an interaction with a legislative aid that she could only describe as "harassment:"

> I was talking to [legislators] about a bill that would prohibit discrimination against students in schools based on a whole range of the normal things—religion, and all that stuff, but including sexual orientation . . . A legislative aid said . . . "Well, of course, you know, I agree. I don't think teachers should be sexually molesting students." [I responded], "That has absolutely nothing to do with what we're talking about. And of course, I don't want teachers sexually molesting students either, but that has *nothing* to do with any of this." And then I don't even know *how* he started to talk about, "Of course, we believe abstinence is what needs to be taught in school." . . . I get very upset when somebody like this man says things that are insulting because . . . I consider it harassment. I consider myself being harassed by this individual who is supposed to be my elected official . . .

SAGA activists describe exchanges like these fairly often. According to those I interviewed in Davis City, Republican politicians typically equate the term "sexual orientation" with pedophilia or believe that LGBT activists only want to distribute sexually graphic materials in the classroom. Staff members in SAGA National agree that this is not uncommon nationally either. This harsh political environment makes it difficult to be proactive in this southern state and often flame the feelings of frustration experienced by the activists.

Davis City is unique in that it failed to garner member support and mobilize LGBT and straight people in successful ways. As far as the political environment is concerned, it similar to the southwestern El Reto County in that it operates in a conservative milieu. But, as we see below, SAGA El Reto County has achieved moderate mobilization and political successes within a Republican-dominated city and county government because of its development of organizational alliances and a vocal straight

Political Environments Shape Identity Deployment 149

constituency within the organization. I explore this political environment in the section below.

The Southwest: El Reto County

El Reto County encompasses over 4,000 square miles, making this the largest chapter in area that I interviewed for this project. According to the staff member Cameron Fine from SAGA National (who works closely with local chapters), and Vincent Pasquarelli, a former co-chair of SAGA El Reto County, there are over 40 school districts in the county, and sprawls over more land area than the state of Delaware. The 2000 Census data show that only nine out of every 1,000 households in El Reto County are same-sex unmarried partner households. Over half of the county residents are white, but Latinos are the largest minority group comprising of over a quarter of the residents. The median household income of El Reto County is about $47,000. Very few state representatives from El Reto County are liberal, but on the federal level, most of the representatives are Democrats. Two-thirds of the state politicians representing El Reto County are Republicans; however, fifty-seven percent of the federal representatives are Democrats. Yet, when we exclude U.S. Senators and focus only on the U.S. House Representatives, only forty percent of the representatives from El Reto County are members of the Democratic Party. It is interesting to note that some of the local representatives who are Republican are also openly gay or lesbian.

The largest city in El Reto County is the city of El Reto, and is also where the headquarters of SAGA El Reto County is located. When I first began my interviews, I was surprised to see that the headquarters of SAGA in a suite within a modern ten-story office park, even if the single rented room was a modest size. I figured that this chapter had a lot of money available through donations. But, as Adam Lieberman, the chair of SAGA El Reto County noted, they "were lucky" to find a sympathetic ally who provided them small office space at a low cost. The city of El Reto has openly lesbian and gay elected officials that represent the district in the state and national governments. One of the straight activists, Paul, struggled to explain to me why he thought this relatively conservative city in the Southwest has a number of openly gay politicians—some of whom are Republicans:

> There are a couple of openly gay politicians. . . . They've been the ones who've stood out in the gay community here and went on about it openly but didn't talk about it a lot in their campaigns . . . They're just kind of matter-of-fact people and talk. And I haven't seen—I'm

trying to think if I'm being accurate. Those [politicians] didn't run it on their being gay. But they certainly—everybody knew from the beginning that they were and that didn't seem to be a hindrance to their aspirations at all.

Vincent Pasquale, a self-identified partnered gay principal in his early thirties and a former co-chair of SAGA, expects that he will be one of those not running for office "on their being gay" when he anticipates ten years from now to be a district administrator for a school system. Reflecting on his political goal, Vincent comments on how the gay politicians in El Reto County broaden their focus outside of lesbian and gay issues in order to appeal to a voter base that is comprised mostly of straight families:

. . . Doing my career but also at the same time, using my position as a principal and/or district administrator, [I will] work for kids and families and all of their issues. Sometimes those issues are gay and lesbian issues. Sometimes they're poverty issues. Sometimes they're, you know, lots of things [such as] special education issues. You take someone like [the state representative] who is a politician in El Reto . . . and [the city councilmember] . . . they all have their constituencies. You don't hear [them] just talking about gay and lesbian issues. They talk about the lights on the street or the dog parks, as well as gay and lesbian issues because that's what they're representing.

Like many SAGA chapters, SAGA El Reto County focuses their efforts in the suburban school districts where most of the SAGA members on the board tend to live, and, if they are teachers, work. However, SAGA El Reto County is different in that their focus is not because of one particular leader's vested interests in the suburban school district but, rather for two reasons: SAGA El Reto County does not have easy access into the school districts of El Reto without the assistance of more well-known organizations, and the particular school board for the district of Tierra Blanca—immediately outside of the city limits of El Reto—is currently controlled by religious right leaders. I take these two issues to point in the following paragraphs.

SAGA El Reto County finds it difficult to gain entry by themselves into the school districts of El Reto, despite the fact that some of the local politicians are openly gay and lesbian. Yet, as Vincent said earlier, they take great care in appealing to a broad constituency that, at times, can sometimes make them appear to the LGBT community as "overly objective" on gay issues. Grant Daniels, a self-identified single gay man in his late-twenties whose career is in an activist organization, echoes this idea as well:

I think . . . there's a little bit of placating going on. Not so much with [the State Representative], but with [the city council member] and especially [the county politician], they're lesbians in office and they have to be real careful that the non-gay people in the world don't see them as having a gay agenda. So, they are usually really objective whenever it comes to dealing—I think maybe even *overly objective* when it comes to a gay and lesbian organization—so as not to be seen as giving them favoritism by the rest of the constituents (emphasis added).

The limits into the school districts within the city of El Reto goes beyond gay and lesbian politicians distancing themselves from LGBT issues in order to have broader appeal to a conservative constituency. In some places within the city of El Reto, just like in Davis City, there are politicians who are vehemently opposed to LGBT issues being mentioned in the school districts. An example that really bothered Greg Adler, a self-identified married straight teacher, was the waffling of the mayor around the use of public land for the Boy Scouts. Despite a local law that prohibits the use or leasing of city property to organizations that discriminate against LGBT people, the city continued to permit leasing city property for use of the Boy Scouts. Angry with the city council's lackadaisical position on an issue so close to his heart (as a straight man, he gave up his Eagle Scout badge out of protest to their discrimination policies), Greg airs his frustration with the mayor whom he sees as failed to make do on their positions when it mattered most:

. . . [Greg sighs] Oh man, our mayor (who is just a big idiot) makes these kinds of grand statements about being very supportive, but then when it comes down to decision making things, like the Boy Scout thing, he did the *wrong* thing.

Greg continues on, mentioning the local city councilmember who makes no apologies about his position on leasing public land to people who discriminate. As a teacher in a school within the councilmember's district, he is quite angry when the councilmember makes an appearance:

And then there was . . . this asshole who is a city councilmember who was just this vehemently ultra-Christian right guy with these horrible, hateful words about the LGBT community. You know, sin and all that bullshit. He spoke when it came down to the Boy Scout headquarters being on city property, he spoke in favor of the city continuing to associate with the Boy Scouts, mostly on his religious grounds. Man, this guy was as hateful a person as you could possibly imagine and it was all in the name of religion. So, when that guy (who happens to be the councilmember for the district in which my school [that I teach in] is located) . . . came to a classroom to do some sort of a presentation, . . . I wrote a letter to my principal and said basically what I just told to you about this guy. . . . And she came back and said, "I didn't know that. I can definitely hear the emotion in your voice, and I will definitely consider this when we have people speak to a group of students in the future." Whether she is going to follow through on that, I don't know.

Although the activists in SAGA El Reto County typically explained their reasons for focusing on the suburban area on the political structure of the city, Paul Freeman hones in on one particular person—the superintendent of El Reto city schools—as the reason why SAGA must focus its work in other areas of the county. Paul is an African-American retired public school principal in his mid-sixties. Having been somewhat nudged into an early retirement by what was described as poor interpersonal skills, Paul has no qualms about taking shots at Superintendent Pete Chadwick in our interview:

El Reto city schools has a superintendent who *says* he's for all people and this type of thing. And he marched in Pride, but he hasn't done one things as a superintendent to make gay students feel any safer. As a matter of fact, he just became the superintendent in the 1998–1999 school year and disbanded a committee we had that took on these issues that was led by Terri Vassiliki [the former SAGA co-chair]. . . . He didn't just pick on us. He stopped *all* existing committees. And, never formed any other committees except his committees. . . . You have to meet this guy! He's all PR. Somebody will see him and say, "That Pete Chadwick, he's all right!" . . . It's just, you hate to see BS.

Forced out of working within the city limits, SAGA El Reto County began to focus their concerns in the suburban areas just outside the city that are vehemently opposed to any LGBT concerns. This means that achieving their political goals for LGBT-positive school district laws are nearly impossible to accomplish. One school district of particular concern is Tierra Blanca, which borders the city of El Reto. Currently, Tierra Blanca has a religious right "supermajority" on the school board whose goals, according to activists Greg and Melissa, are to dismantle the public school system according to the steps dictated by the religious right. Figuring out how to

Political Environments Shape Identity Deployment 153

deal with this volatile situation nearly caused SAGA El Reto County to dissolve in the midst of internal disagreements. Paul describes one school board meeting where he quickly learned how the passions involved in these meetings can quickly heat up:

> A couple of the most frightening experiences in my life have been at a couple of their board meetings in a gym where they had this whole bleacher full of kids who called themselves gay or lesbian or questioning and their friends. And they were trying to get language in their school's—I guess you call it safety policy. And they were trying to get language that specified that it would include them. And the numbers of people—and this was in a cheering/jeering environment. There were people quoting Leviticus and calling these kids sodomites and they're protected automatically, and they are abominations, and stuff. And, even with my experience as an African-American, I had never been in any kind of riotous kind of situation like that . . .

Adam Lieberman, a self-identified single gay man in his early 20s, describes the school board in Tierra Blanca:

> It's a scary place. . . . They have no concept of the severity of emotional distress that they inflict on their students on a regular basis. And they don't really want to hear that anybody disagrees with them.

Greg, before he even became involved in LGBT social movement organizing, moved into the Tierra Blanca school district because housing was more affordable there than in the city itself. Shortly after moving there, he was surprised about the political environment that he and his wife moved into.

> In general, on a wide variety of political issues, we have a long ways to go out here [in Tierra Blanca]. It was particularly disconcerting when I am driving down the street in Tierra Blanca on my way to work, probably in my first three or four months at living here, and I see recruiting signs for the local white supremacist movement—little stickers on the city traffic signs. Somebody had stuck these stickers on it and I was like, "Oh man, what have I moved into?"

At the conclusion of our conversation, he mentions how he talks with his neighbors about SAGA and broader LGBT issues in El Reto County and sometimes realizes that his own safety may be in jeopardy when he said:

> . . . You hope your house isn't firebombed the next day, but at the same time there are people though on the block who I do know . . . love to talk about those issues."

Greg's visibility activity in SAGA has made him concerned about the safety of his wife (also a school teacher in the city of El Reto) and baby daughter:

> I can tell you I am at least mildly concerned about Samantha [my wife] and Charlotte [my daughter]. Being verbally accosted a couple of times down in Tierra Blanca, . . . I'm always thinking about the possibility . . . [that] there are less stable elements out there that are more willing to take matters into more violent territories. . . . I am a father of an almost year old kid, and I've got to think about my safety also as far as how outspoken I've been and how visible I've been in the community. I mean, I could be an easy target. So, it is in the back of my mind.

Greg continues on, repeating continuously about his fear of retaliation by others for his outspokenness for LGBT rights. Unlike the lesbian and gay activists in El Reto that I spoke with, his fear is mostly for his family's safety, rather than his own. But, he begins his statement assuring me that his fears will not waver him from what he sees as the right thing to do:

> Honestly, I think about that, but I don't want to give up on that. I think people need to see a commitment to something. And if people mess with me, I think I deal with most of it myself. It is a concern in the back of my mind, though, about my family and maybe even doing something to my family or doing something to me so that I can't help my family, or that kind of stuff. It is there everyday. But I try not to let it worry me too much. I think about it more on my way home from the Tierra Blanca meetings, those public school board meetings. I probably . . . obsess about it much more on my way home from those, and worry about it for that night and go to sleep, wake up the next day, and feel like it's all going to be okay after all.

Both SAGA El Reto County in the Southwest and SAGA Victoria in the Pacific Northwest focus their efforts in suburban areas. This is where the similarities end. SAGA El Reto County, whose constituents in the major city of El Reto and the suburbs are primarily Republican, relies heavily on alliances with both well-known organizations and straight people to gain access into school systems and provide a sense of political legitimacy in their organizational infancy. Victoria is a liberal city in the Northwest with conservative rural and suburban outskirts. A young chapter as well, SAGA Victoria does not follow a similar model as El Reto County in using well-known organizations and straight people as political legitimacy. Instead, as I explain in the next section, SAGA Victoria lacks the fore-sighted leadership needed to forge organizational alliances and mobilize straight and gay members to the cause to make substantive political gains in the Victoria region.

The Northwest: Victoria

SAGA Victoria is responsible for a geographical area of about 3,000 square miles. Less than nine out of 1,000 households are identified as same-sex unmarried partner households in the Victoria metropolitan area (Census 2000). Over three-quarters of the residents in the Victoria area identify as white on the 2000 Census. Latinos are the largest minority group in the area, with slightly less Asian and Pacific Islanders, and very few African-American residents. The median income of the Victoria metropolitan area is more than $50,000, and the outlying suburban locations have the highest median household income compared to Victoria (Census 2000). In contrast to the other conservative areas, most of the state and federal representatives from the large geographic territory for which SAGA Victoria is responsible are liberal. Only twenty-eight percent of the state politicians representing the multi-county Victoria area are Republicans, and even less (twenty percent) of the federal representatives are Republicans. Yet, on the local levels of the suburban areas, the experiences of the activists suggest that Victoria, although rather liberal in its representation, must still contend with a conservative populace, at least in terms of LGBT issues. Furthermore, the organizational pattern of SAGA Victoria follows more closely to the conservative model. However, it is interesting to note that the stunted growth of SAGA Victoria may not always be due to the environment; organizational leadership may also have an effect.

Earlier in the book I explained how many activists generally liked the co-chair of SAGA Victoria—Taylor Lynde. But they felt that he was a weak leader insofar as his inability to fulfill the mission of SAGA in meaningful ways. Taylor, as I also noted in my observations of one of the meetings, did not provide membership with the opportunities for dialogue or new ideas. Although people do, myself included, like Taylor as a person, he does not transform this likeability into an organizational benefit by drawing in alliances with other organizations. Chrissy Williams, who was once a member of SAGA and now works for another organization dedicated to LGBT youth, commented on the potential of SAGA Victoria to create meaningful alliances with other organizations to achieve their political goals:

> [*What is the organization that you're mostly focused on right now that is closely aligned with SAGA?*] Well, my program serving GLBT youth is somewhat aligned. I mean, it's aligned politically. We don't necessarily work together very much. But, I'm on the steering committee of Victoria Safe Communities and Schools Association (VSCSA). And we don't even necessarily work that closely with the people in SAGA.

When I ask Chrissy why she believes SAGA and VSCSA are not working in tandem, despite being aligned politically, she chooses her words carefully:

> . . . It seems like ideally they would be large and diverse and well-organized and doing lots of things that would overlap with the kinds of things that I'm working on. . . . It's interesting because there are some times, you know, certain events SAGA [Victoria] will pair up with someone but other than that, it seems like they're not doing a lot. . . . They'll co-sponsor and event. Or there will be—like the Night of Noise that was just organized, SAGA helps sponsor it so their name was on it, along with the name of Victoria Safe Communities and Schools Association. I don't know if that makes them linked or allied. I mean, kind of superficially.

Similarly, as I noted earlier in the book, Taylor draws new membership from his friendship network, which are primarily gay men. From what I observed, SAGA Victoria was "stuck in neutral," having all the intentions and visions to go very far but the inability to adequately "kick into gear" by developing these necessary alliances. This makes it harder for SAGA Victoria to traverse both the liberal city political environment (because few people know about SAGA in Victoria), and achieve inroads in the conservative suburbs because they have no alliances to provide them with political legitimacy.

As I stated earlier, SAGA Victoria is in a liberal city but surrounded by conservative suburbs. Relatively new to the area (she comes from Southern California), Casey Lina, a single bisexual woman in her mid-thirties, finds that it is difficult to assess the local politics of Victoria:

> [Victoria] is *extremely* diverse politically . . . [A] national organization or even a regional organization might not be aware of some of the subtleties and the differences even within a ten-mile radius.

Gloria Wentworth is actively involved in social justice causes, including SAGA, as well as her "faith community." Her social movement experience gives her first hand knowledge of the varied political environment in Victoria. In our interview, Gloria is adamant about "keeping it local," meaning that the strategies that SAGA activists are given on how to deal with school systems cannot be "canned" by a national or statewide organization. She discusses the geography of Victoria:

> . . . Suburban counties in Victoria are part suburb and part rural. You know, it's kind of like there's a ring of suburb and then there's a ring of rural as well, in the same county. Sitka County, which includes Ketchikan and Anchorage, has . . . a huge [high] tech deal, so that's made a huge impact in liberalizing Sitka County. So you've got a lot of professionals, a lot of high tech educated, thinking folks. So then you have Olympia County, and you have eastern Klamath County, but it's not the city of Victoria. . . . So, Olympia County is more conservative, and the rural areas are more conservative. . . . So that's why when we present at trainings [for SAGA Victoria], we don't have a canned package for everybody.

Like Arlene Stein's findings in her study of Timbertown, Oregon, Gloria sees the many locations around Victoria quite conservative on LGBT social issues even though the majority of elected officials in the Victoria region are Democrats.

Keeping the focus local is important to Gloria because she recalls a time when a National LGBT organization "from the East Coast somewhere" visited Victoria and gave them a "canned package" much to the chagrin of the local activists in order to challenge an anti-gay law being considered during an election year. Defeating the proposed law required effective public relations in the communities in which activists lived and worked. Despite what Gloria felt was a need to focus on the community one individual at a time, the organization treated the activists as if they were ignorant on the way politics are done in the city. This, she states, lead to animosity from the activists:

> As a volunteer coming in to help, if these outside folks came and they'd been in your shoes, and they integrated the grassroots of what life is [like in the Pacific Northwest], it [would have been] wonderful, but one week—I don't remember the group, and it's just as well I don't—they came in and they knew better how things should be done, and that was very alienating. And to me as a volunteer, it was like, you know,

"I don't need this." I wasn't paid staff for the campaign, and it was unpleasant, and I just thought, "Okay!" And I faded away. . . . The more you're tuned in to what people are going through and the local need, you know, the better it is.

As evidence of these different sociopolitical environments existing within a relatively small geographical area, Brooks Sheppard recalls a horrendous experience of being a new teacher, fresh out of college, working in a small town outside of Victoria and being labeled "different" by the students from a more suburban area. Brooks, a self-identified single gay teacher in his early thirties, recalls his experiences in a conservative school district:

> . . . [T]he last shining movement before I left the [junior-high school I taught at] is that [sixth-grade students] had written on my windows "Child molester. Faggot" across the big windows and in each window pane. And I went to my boss, and I said, "Listen, this is harassment. This is not okay." And he had one of the custodians wash the windows and he said, "Well, we can't do anything about it but we can keep our ear to the ground." And I didn't think that was an okay answer . . . And at the [new] school I moved to, it was expected that I was the faculty adviser for the gay/straight alliance. It was a *very* different climate. I didn't have to deal with any of that.

Brooks left this position for a private school within the city of Victoria where he now has a positive experience of being out to his junior-high students and finds little in the form of homophobic sentiment. Taylor Lynde, a retired public school teacher in his early-fifties, interjects his experiences into his answer and says that this is due to the types of parents that send their children to private school:

> Being a private school, I think the parents are very in-tune to wanting their kids to be acceptant and very involved in diversity kinds of issues and those kinds of things.

Similar to Amanda and Ruth from Davis City, Taylor sees politicians on the state level as influenced by money. However, unlike the activists from Davis City, Taylor uses his personal money as a means of social change in Victoria, rather than using the name of SAGA to obtain social change. In response to my question regarding his view of the organization's

Political Environments Shape Identity Deployment 159

successes, Taylor comments that he influences change in politicians through monetary donations:

> I don't think [politicians] took an *active* partnership in moving the [LGBT] movement ahead until there was a shit load of money that was being poured into their political and their re-election campaigns . . . So this two-hour interview boils down to money. Money tends to be the part the people listen to. School board members that are sympathetic—that talk to me—are people I've written checks to. So, I've taken a lot of money that I have earned and I look at school board members and I say, "What can I do to help you win because we need you and we need your support?"

Taylor sees the political landscape in Victoria to be optimistic because of the influence of money on politicians' decisions, but is cautious about the voting patterns of the electorate, whom he sees as quite ignorant of LGBT issues on a statewide level. In his mind, it is the religious conservatives that are a hindrance to LGBT progress:

> I don't think Victorians care what other people think about them. . . . I think Victorians are truly have a feeling of right and wrong, and I think they tend to vote right and wrong. . . . There are a lot of still that conservative religious—and that's our biggest, that is our *biggest* foe—is that religious right. They are such advocates—and there's not reasoning with them. You could give them ten down-to-earth killer reasons why they should support us and it would not make any difference to them because their minister has told them that these gay people are bad folks.

And yet, almost mirroring the remarks of Amanda from Davis City about having to negotiate deals with politicians to battle the onslaught of anti-gay legislation in her southern state, Taylor continues stating that:

> . . . I really think the vast majority of our political allies have been people that we [queer people] say, "We [queer people] are going to support you." But also it took out gay people to take that step forward and step into the political arena. And they worked really hard. And there was that gay agenda that they were going to move that to the point where we weren't just trying to save face—we're not trying to lose ground—that we're moving ahead. I really think in Victoria, we're

moving ahead. We're moving ahead to secure rights for everyone to change schools to do those kinds of things. We're no longer settling for—"Well, let's vote for this because it's the least damaging of the three things on the ballot measure."

But I wonder if Taylor really believed that, or if it was my own discussions about my research project that prompted him to say this. When we first met, Taylor had many questions for me about the project, and wanted to discuss some of my findings. In a brief synopsis, I explained my research hypotheses, and how some activists have expressed that their fights in conservative areas were more reactive than proactive. Given that the interview occurred after our lengthy discussions, I am left to wonder if this might have influenced his perception of Victoria in relation to what I might have said in general about the experiences of activists in El Reto or Davis City.

Continuing from Taylor's quote above, he continues, regaling about a confrontation with a school board member in the suburban outskirts of Victoria, where her religious convictions seem to echo the experiences of the activists from SAGA El Reto County. The only difference is that the new state laws protecting his job as a gay teacher were a source of his empowerment to confront her inflammatory statements:

> There was a school board member in the [suburban Victoria] schools, and she kind of came after me. . . . You know, we were trying to pass the sexual orientation thing for teachers, and she said, "You know, Taylor Lynde contacted me and if he thinks I will *ever, ever* allow a pedophile to put pictures of his boyfriend or friends and things on his desk like other people do, *he is wrong!*"

In the face of this accusation, Taylor finds the strength in his voice to challenge the discrimination waged by the school board member:

> But again, it was like, one of the first times I ever kind of felt empowered to look back at her and say, "You know, of all the people in the . . . school district, there has never been a gay or lesbian man that has been dismissed from his position because of an impropriety with a student. We've had a lot of straight people that have been dismissed because of improprieties with their students. So, really, Sue, we need to fire all these heterosexuals that are working in the . . . school district and we need to hire all homosexuals because *you* guys are the pedophiles! *We* aren't!" She still looked and thought that there was nothing wrong with that.

Political Environments Shape Identity Deployment 161

Taylor continues in his train of thought uninterrupted, and recalls another time when he was involved with an issue in the suburban Victoria school district in which he works:

> . . . Because of my religious background, I've been told what a bad person I am and how awful I am. And that I'm never going to be anything and I'm never going to amount to anything. And they're all wrong! Because I've amounted to a lot and I've had an *incredible* impact on children. I've had an *incredible* impact on their parents. I think that I've had an *incredible* impact on my community. I think the [suburban Victoria] community is a better place because I live there and because I spoke out about the kinds of things to me that were very important, that needed to be addressed, that people were afraid to talk about. And I think [Victoria] will be a better place because of who I was and what I did.

As Taylor mentions below, he recalls an anecdote in which he finds his strength to challenge school administrators in a fight to keep a poster up in the classroom that provides information to LGBT students about mental health and coming out:

> I'm sure there are a lot of people who wished I never done that and that I've never been there because I cause a lot of controversy. . . . There's a . . . health poster that advertises for a gay support group. And I had a parent that wanted me to take it down because it had the word "gay" or "lesbian" on it. And I said no! I said [to the principal], "Take it down if you want. But if you take it down, I'll file a grievance because I have academic freedom." And I said, "This is a support group for kids. It is a county-based organization that is doing good work with kids. You can take it down if you want to, but I mean, I just want you to know that I won't just let it go." So he decided to go back to the administration, and of course it just blew up in their face! And all the posters are up.

Trey McIntyre, a young gay college student, also mentions the incident with the posters, and comments that it is the ignorance of the parents, and not the school district, that are to blame for the conservative "feel" of suburban Victoria:

> There is a parent that's very upset that the . . . posters were in classrooms, and they kind of voiced their opinion and wanted the posters

taken down. But then again, you always have people who aren't really educated on the LGBT issues, and who have some sort of bias against gay and lesbian people, and in my opinion, I don't know.

Trey tries to balance his rights to freedom of expression as a gay man versus the parents' rights to educate their children on moral issues. He eventually boils the argument down to an issue of bigotry and ignorance, rejecting the belief that a parent has a right to demand that a poster be removed because of non-graphic homosexual content:

> Sure, these people have a right to voice their opinion, and they can be concerned and wonder, but to me it's kind of like, if you're educated enough on these issues, I feel like you would come to some sort of higher consciousness on it, and I just think it's foolish to be like, someone who was against SAGA [or] the GLBT community, [and] say that these posters should be taken down and all this, because whether they like it or not, homosexuality still exists, you know. And so sure, there's people who are definitely against it, but I don't know whether to attribute it to you know, like conventional hand-me-downs from past generations of discrimination in a family, or if it's just like lack of education, [or a] lack of exposure to homosexual people . . .

Casey Lina recalls the incident with the posters as well, but this time considering it one of SAGA Victoria's most successful moments:

> . . . There has been a problem with Taylor and what happened with his school district in terms of the posters he was putting up. I'm sure he's talked with you about that. . . . And the organization has been good at responding whether it is letter writing campaigns or formal statement or getting out there and helping people. So, that's been a positive.

But Chrissy Williams, the coordinator for the program which was advertised on the posters, is skeptical about SAGA's impact on the result, and takes a jab at Taylor in particular, and his role in the controversy:

> It was interesting because recently this big controversy in Beaverton about posters for my program. And he was one of the teachers who had the poster up in his room. . . . So, they told him to take the poster down. He was fighting it. There was a bunch of other teachers—Actually, a *bunch* of other teachers who actually had the poster up. But,

for him, it was very much about him and about him having the poster, [and] his right to have it up.

Chrissy immediately counterbalances her comment by trying to assure me that Taylor, despite what she sees as his personality flaws, truly means well when fighting for the issues of LGBT students:

> And in some ways, it's really important the work that he's doing. He's really visible. He's brave. He's in a really hard position. So, that's useful. And then in some ways, if I feel like his personality makes him a liability to our movement. Things balance out. But, I guess in that situation, it would have been great if . . . SAGA could have been really active in taking this as an issue—as a broader issue—that that could have been a useful role for SAGA to have. And, the role that SAGA had was more about him—that he could use it then as a platform for him talking about himself, rather than the larger issue of school safety . . .

As I gathered from the interviews, the activists see SAGA Victoria as an organization that both benefits and suffers from the leadership. The leadership of SAGA Victoria struggles to see the bigger picture or strategize ways to combat the conservativism of the suburban school districts by building meaningful alliances with other organizations and straight people. Instead, I perceived SAGA Victoria as reactive, rather than proactive, in how it handles issues that arise within its jurisdiction. This differs from the SAGA chapters in a primarily liberal sociopolitical environment. Here, chapters are more professionalized and can more readily move beyond reactionary efforts of influencing politics and work within the political institutions themselves.

LIBERAL POLITICAL ENVIRONMENTS

SAGA Sunntach in the Midwest and SAGA Piedmont in the Northeast operate within liberal political environments. SAGA Sunntach focuses its energies in the liberal city of Sunntach, while SAGA Piedmont focuses on a suburban region just outside of a major metropolitan area of the Northeast.

SAGA chapters in liberal regions share a number of similar organizational trajectories and experiences due in part to the political environment. First, chapters that operate within liberal political environments have a number of organizational allies that comport with the findings of Minkoff (1997; 1999), which suggest that the organizational density (as long as the organizations are not overwhelming in number or have too much overlap in shared goals) is a benefit to the lifespan of emerging social movement organizations. In addition, SAGA chapters in these areas do not have very many active countermovements to contend with and, therefore focus more attention and money on achieving broader goals, such as mobilizing LGBT and straight members, and cultural goals such as educating people on LGBT issues. These chapters tended to have larger budgets and paid staff members to operate the mundane aspects of social movement organizing, such as keeping tabs of memberships, sending out meeting reminders, and the like. The larger yearly budgets are derived primarily from donations from wealthy members and allies, corporations, and grants (rather than from membership dues as in the chapters from conservative areas).

SAGA chapters in the liberal political environments tended to focus on developing workshops with allied organizations. These workshops would educate teachers and high school youth on sexuality issues. In addition, SAGA chapters in these liberal areas would rely more on straight people for their social networks to secure financial and political resources, rather than as a source of political legitimacy. In other words, chapters in liberal political areas experienced steady growth, moving beyond the infancy stages of organizing, and becoming more professionalized over the years of accreditation.

In the next section, I describe the political environments of each chapter, and describe the ways in which activists from the liberal environments accomplish their political, mobilizing, and cultural movement goals. In these subsections, I reflect back on the findings from previous chapters, which describe how activists from these liberal environments consider the ways in which the organization could strategically deploy a straight identity as a way to maximize successes of these three movement impacts. In this next section, I explain how in the liberal environment of Sunntach and Piedmont, SAGA focus its energies more on professional fundraising, spending their large budget pools educating the public on particular LGBT youth issues, rather than investing time and money into combating anti-gay foes as we see in the conservative areas.

The Midwest: Sunntach

SAGA Sunntach's primary area of focus is the city of Sunntach, which is approximately 200 square miles. About one out of every 100 households are same-sex unmarried partner households (Census 2000). Sunntach is a minority-majority city, meaning that the majority of the residents of the city are people of color, and the largest racial group in the city is African-American (Census 2000). The median household income for the city is just over $35,000 (Census 2000). Nearly all of the state and federal representatives

Political Environments Shape Identity Deployment

from Sunntach are liberal. Seventy-two percent of the state politicians representing Sunntach are Democrats, and eighty percent of the federal representatives are Democrats.

Marc Andersen, a self-identified single gay man in his mid-twenties who was the former co-chair of SAGA Sunntach, finds that the only opposition SAGA has to achieving its goals are the political structures they are up against. In an informal part of the interview where it was revealed that there was a "scandal" when one of the former board members was convicted of a sex crime, Marc gives his opinion on the issue's quick demise:

> We don't really have anyone we're working against. We work against bureaucracy. We work against those who are resistant to change in general. But we don't have an adversary. If we did, we could have been crushed by this whole thing . . . People know about it. People read about it. But nobody continues to use it. After the newspapers published, that was the only time I've ever seen it published. And it went away. And we got off easy. In other places, that would *still* be in a pamphlet somewhere.

Sebastian St. James, a self-identified single gay teacher in his early thirties, states that the conviction of this activist was reported, "in some Christian Right newsletter [which] they used . . . as part of their evidence that we're perverts." But, like Marc, Sebastian is amazed and thankful that the issue blew over fairly quickly in the media even though within the organization, the emotions surrounding the issue continued on for years. Indeed, in an internet search I could only find one reference of the sex crime from a Christian "reporter" who used it as the sole evidence that gays and lesbians are hopelessly lascivious.

Out of all the places I visited for this research project, Sunntach had the most personal connections with local politicians. While acting as co-chair of SAGA, Marc was a paid campaign manager for a candidate to city council, which raised little problems for SAGA and their image. Only once was Marc reprimanded for making a shared appearance with the candidate at a SAGA function:

> I invited the candidate and introduced him around for votes. I was like, I knew everyone in the room because of SAGA, but it was just a party! I was like, "Where do you draw that line?" And the woman [who reprimanded me] was like, "This is inappropriate. Tonight you are co-chair of SAGA. So, by you introducing this guy, it makes it look like SAGA endorses him. Which, we don't. We don't endorse candidates,

period." And I said, "But I'm not co-chair. I'm just Marc. This is a holiday party." And she was like, "You don't have that freedom anymore. At least not while you are here."

After that episode, Marc never made an appearance with the candidate at a SAGA function. When the opponent won the seat instead, Marc had no worries about this loss because of his own ambitions: "Fifteen years from now? Hopefully I'll be on a ballot."

If Marc wins an election before his fifteen years are up, he would not be the only politician to have sat on the SAGA Sunntach board. Sunntach is the only place I studied where politicians were also volunteer activists and board members of SAGA. Although the woman mentioned in the quote below declined to be included in an interview for the project, Marc provides his own thoughts on why he believes she is an asset to the organization:

> One of our board members is a 50-year-old Republican straight woman whose daughter is lesbian. . . . And she's a [city politician in] this fancy suburb. And she wears a SAGA t-shirt to the gym every day. She's *great! Love it!* Ab-so-lute-ly love it! . . . I think she's a great spokesperson. And it's even better if she says, "You know what? I am a Republican but that doesn't matter because [our mission is] a universal fight."

Although I elaborated on this point in Chapter Five, we see in Marc's comments that it's great when a spokesperson can universalize the mission by deploying a straight identity to achieve broader cultural goals to educate straight parents and school workers on LGBT issues.

Just because board members have connections with politicians does not mean that SAGA Sunntach has any significant "in-roads" into local politics. According to Sebastian, there continues to be no one who could call up a local politician or a state representative and expect a meeting, despite these political connections. Marc expresses his disappointment because the politicians in the city:

> . . . don't see us as having any power. You know, take us out to lunch, shake our hand, [and say] 'I've met with those constituents. I'm done with them.' We're not anyone that has to be listened to.

For SAGA Sunntach, their ability to fundraise and their nearly nonexistent opposition allowed them to move beyond lobbying for LGBT-inclusive legislation and into more cultural goals. In the next region of the

Political Environments Shape Identity Deployment 167

Piedmont in the northeast, we see how fundraising acumen and fostering intimate relationships with political leaders of a territory can lead to remarkable successes in grassroots organizing.

The Northeast: Piedmont

SAGA Piedmont has one of the largest geographical areas of coverage in this study, covering six counties and over 3,500 square miles (Census 2000). The Piedmont region in the Northeast is vast geographically, and subsequently varies politically. SAGA Piedmont covers several counties, and the farthest reaches of the geographical area extend over 200 miles. Only about six out of every 1,000 of all households are same-sex unmarried partner household (Census 2000), which was the lowest percentage of all the regions in this research project. Nearly three-quarters of the Piedmont is white, and about one-fifth of the residents are African-Americans and Latinos (Census 2000). The median household income for the region is roughly $60,000, which is the highest out of all the regions I visited (Census 2000). Only about two-fifths of the state representatives from Piedmont (forty-two percent) are Democrat, but from what I learned from the interviews and meeting minutes from SAGA, it seems that on LGBT issues, a number of the state-level Republicans are surprisingly liberal. However, seventy-one percent of the federal representatives of Piedmont are Democrats.

According to SAGA National, Piedmont is the only chapter to have separated into subchapters in order to prevent fracturing based on geographical differences. As I learned in my interview with Judy Eberhardt, the SAGA Piedmont co-chair, the division of the chapter into subchapters is not because of a shared geographical identity: "People [in the Piedmont] identify with counties, they don't identify with the whole Piedmont." As one of the architects for this division shortly after she became co-chair in 1997, Judy suggested that the Piedmont chapter split into subchapters for financial and logistical reasons since it was difficult to have all members within six counties to meet at a central location once a month. And, if each county split into its own chapter, some of the resources from other counties would be too little to be effective for the region's hundreds of school districts. So, the Piedmont chapter split into subchapters so that they could pool their resources together but develop appropriate strategies in a more localized fashion.

I asked activists how they perceived the political environment of the Piedmont. Judy responds in a bullet-point fashion, looking at each county as a separate entity and gaging her response on whether or not the areas were tolerant of LGBT issues:

> I used to think that way, I mean now because we have the human rights commission in Essex and we have the liaison—I think we are one of [the few places] in the country that has a full-time liaison to the gay community. . . . I don't know how conservative you could really call that. I think that we're more liberal. I know . . . that's not true of all of Piedmont. I mean certainly Oxford County is pretty good. I think Bristol County is a little more conservative for sure. And Hancock County for sure is more conservative. Norfolk County I'm not quite sure on. Chittenden County I think is a little more liberal, sort of the feeling I get.

When I question Judy further to what evidence she uses to make these opinions, she reminds me that it's just "the feeling she gets" from her experiences talking with people who live in these areas. But the farther away from the major metropolitan areas, the more likely Judy was to gage them as politically conservative. She is not off the mark, however. The more rural the counties, the more likely the state and federal representative was Republican and socially conservative. In relationship to other research, Judy's perceptions are similar to what we see in Linneman's research on the political environments of Washington State. As perceived from gays and religious conservatives, the perception of political environments is often made by "feelings" in relationship to how oppressed or restricted one feels (Linneman 2003).

The political environment of the Piedmont is diverse since some of the state legislature and federal house districts are gerrymandered into the more rural areas of the state while others are gerrymandered into sections of its large metropolitan areas. Here, each house in the bicameral legislature is controlled by the opposite political party, which, in turn, has an effect on the shapes of the representative districts. So, in the Piedmont, the majority of the state house representatives are Democrats but the state senators are almost exclusively Republican. Almost sixty percent of the state representatives of the Piedmont are Republican. On the national levels, the numbers are reversed; over seventy percent of the federal politicians are Democrats. Unlike the rest of the Piedmont, Essex County hires a full-time LGBT liaison who reports on the status of LGBT county residents directly to the County Commissioner. This gives SAGA Piedmont some sway in region politically, but most of the politician connections, such as the relationships created in the Essex County Commissioner's office, end up benefiting the Essex subchapter more than the others because of this relationship with the LGBT liaison.

For this book, I primarily discuss the Essex County subchapter as this ends up to be the strongest politically and also, all the activists I spoke with are board members of the Essex County subchapter. Looking at the basic demographic data of Essex, it is similar to the Piedmont as a whole. The 2000 Census data show that only about seven out of every 1,000 households in Essex County are same-sex unmarried partner households. Approximately two-thirds of residents are white (Census 2000). Latinos are the largest minority category in Essex County at sixteen percent, followed closely by African-Americans. The median household income of Essex County is more than $60,000 (Census 2000).

Reid Roberts is a self-identified single gay man in his mid-fifties and a retired teacher in one of the local school districts in Piedmont. I asked Reid if he thought the Piedmont was conservative or liberal regarding gay and lesbian issues, and he abruptly answered, "Yes," referring really to Essex County and not the region as a whole. I probed further and he explained that geography and income make this region more conservative than the nearest urban neighbors of Piedmont:

> You know, it's so near to [the major metropolitan area] that you would think they might be more liberal. I think they *think* they're liberal. But I believe they are more conservative than they *believe* they are. Essex County is a bedroom community of [the city]. A lot of people commute into [the city] to work. I think it's considered a "family-friendly" county, even though it's got quite a few populations of minorities. And, it's diverse in that sense. The median income is still on the high end. It's just my experience that it just seems more conservative than not . . .

However, we must note how Reid's answer differs starkly in its understanding of liberal as compared to Judy's response earlier. I asked him why he finds Essex conservative when it has a liaison to the LGBT community. Reid considers having the liaison progressive but that the different counties still have a small-town feel to them which makes being out (what he considers to be the bell-weather of liberalness) very difficult. If we compare his assessment to Judy's, we can see that as a straight person, Judy does not experience first-hand the acute discrimination LGBT people may face. As a school employee and a parent of a gay child, Judy admits that she can feel the pain compassionately. Yet, Reid is a retired gay teacher from Essex County who never came out to students in his school district. He came out only to a handful of teachers who were also gay and not out in the school district. He could only attribute his perception of the conservative feel of Essex County to be a manifestation of "internalized homophobia" since the local teacher's union, Essex County, and the state have laws prohibiting discrimination at work based on one's sexual orientation.

Justin Petrov is a self-identified single gay college student in his late teens. As a former board member before leaving for college, Justin helped increase SAGA's visibility in local school districts by involving the organization with his local gay-straight alliance that he founded. When I asked Justin about his perception of the political environment of Piedmont, he focuses primarily on Essex County. As the founder of one of the first GSAs in Essex County, his experience in the political environment of public schools in Essex County differed starkly with Reid's. Justin believed the opposite of Reid in that geography and money make Essex County and the rest of the Piedmont more liberal than it otherwise would be, and he gaged this by the exponential growth of GSAs in local public high schools over the past few years:

> Once you have those two combinations—leadership and money—I think you can do anything . . . I think also Essex County is waiting for [change], like . . . it's liberal, relatively—I mean, it's a conservative area but the kids in the new generation are waiting for change so it was just a matter [of time].

SAGA Piedmont operates on a budget of about forty thousand dollars a year, and their connection with the local politicians means that they achieve more political successes. In order to mobilize more allies and achieve their cultural goals, they host a very popular conference for educators and students about dealing with LGBT concerns in public schools every year. In addition, SAGA sponsors a weekend retreat for LGBT high school students and straight people with workshops on how to build coalitions with peers. And, in nearly every high school there are active and well-funded GSAs throughout the region. What makes this situation different than SAGA Sunntach is that the socially liberal attitudes of this wealthier suburban area and easy access to politicians through an LGBT community liaison, SAGA Piedmont achieves many successes that are recognized by SAGA National. In fact, in recognition of her success as a chapter leader, Judy accepted an invitation to be a board member of SAGA National in the coming year.

CHAPTER CONCLUSION

SAGA chapters in conservative regions share a number of similar organizational trajectories and experiences due in part to the political environment. First, chapters that operate within conservative political environments struggle with achieving tangible political objectives, which affect the ability to mobilize additional LGBT activists and secure straight allies, and in turn, make it difficult to achieve broader cultural goals such as educating people on LGBT issues. Organizations in the conservative political environments had a tendency to experience shrinking memberships from which to obtain money that is necessary to expand the chapter and assist it with reaching their political goals. In other words, chapters in conservative political areas experienced a stunting in their growth, unable to move beyond the infancy stages of organizing, even if they have been an accredited chapter for many years. These findings demonstrate that, like Bernstein's (1997) research attests, identity deployment of a straight identity must include a conceptualization of the effects of regional politics on successful strategies in a method similar to the political ecology models of Minkoff (1993, 1997).

My findings add a new dimension to other research on social movements that utilize the resource mobilization and political opportunity paradigms (Gamson 1975; McCarthy and Zald 1977; Meyer and Staggenborg 1996) by incorporating political ecology models into the theoretical conceptualization of organizational success. As I explained above, vocal straight allies are the primary resource sought in conservative areas. However, as my findings suggest, in more liberal areas, the primary resource that is sought through the deployment of a straight identity is not necessarily political legitimating, but monetary resources and social networks. The findings from chapters in the more liberal regions of the Untied States, rather than the conservative areas, seem to fit the findings of other research on social movements that utilize the resource mobilization and political opportunity paradigms.

SAGA chapters in liberal regions share a number of similar organizational trajectories and experiences due in part to the political environment. First, comporting with the findings of Minkoff (1997, 1999), chapters that operate within liberal political environments have a number of organizational allies, which suggest that the organizational density (as long as the organizations are not overwhelming in number or have too much overlap in shared goals) is a benefit to the lifespan of SAGA chapters. In addition, SAGA chapters in these areas do not have very many active countermovements to contend with and, therefore focus more attention and money on achieving broader goals, such as mobilizing LGBT and straight members, and cultural goals such as educating people on LGBT issues. These chapters tended to have larger budgets and paid staff members to operate the mundane aspects of social movement organizing, such as keeping tabs of memberships, sending out meeting reminders, and the like. The larger yearly budgets are derived primarily from donations from wealthy members and allies, corporations, and grants (rather than from membership dues as in the chapters from conservative areas).

SAGA chapters in the liberal political environments tended to focus on developing workshops with allied organizations. These workshops would educate teachers and high school youth on sexuality issues. In addition, SAGA chapters in these liberal areas would rely more on straight people for their social networks to secure financial and political resources, rather than as a source of political legitimacy. In other words, chapters in liberal political areas experienced steady growth, moving beyond the infancy stages of organizing, and becoming more professionalized over the years of accreditation.

Chapter Seven
Straight Ahead and Moving Forward

Let me conclude the book by repeating what I earlier claimed is assumed to be fairly obvious statements about the LGBT movement. First, the American culture and its social structure enforce and reinforce a set of heteronormative expectations by which people evaluate themselves and are evaluated against. The people who transgress these heteronormative boundaries (i.e., queer people, gay, lesbian, etc.) typically consider themselves as distinct (at least in terms of sexuality) from heterosexual people. And, lesbian and gay people expect the organizations that they created to reflect their shared identity by being comprised of people like them. Furthermore, the identity deployment strategies the organizations utilize are expected to reflect the identities of the LGBT constituents, as well as the fit the LGBT-slant of the organizational mission.

The LGBT organization Straight and Gay Alliance requires us to revise these assumptions because of their unique strategy of deploying a straight identity (albeit constructed around heteronormative notions of appropriate race, gender, and class) in order to secure the equal rights of queer youth in school districts across the United States. As I said earlier, many LGBT activists, including me, expect the movement to be "queer" like us, that all of the participants in our movement will understand our unique issues through personal experience, and that our movement strategies we reflect our shared history of gay liberation. I began this book discussing the many different interpretations of my title, "Are We Thinking Straight?" But, perhaps a better question might be, "Are They [Straight People] Thinking Queer?"

Here are selected definitions of the "queer" as noted in the Merriam-Webster Dictionary Online:

> . . . **1b**: Questionable, Suspicious **2a** : differing in some odd way from what is usual or normal . . . **2d** . . . Homosexual

The strategy of SAGA to deploy a straight identity is "queer" in that they differ in some odd way from what is normally found coming from LGBT organizations. But, we also find that the straight activists, although recognizing their heterosexual privilege and maintaining the identity boundary of "straight" and "queer," have begun to identify closely with the hurt and pain suffered by LGBT youth at the hands of ignorance. Although there is a lot of work still to be done on the flaws in the construction and deployment of a straight identity shaped by "-ist" assumptions, it remains to be a unique and effective strategy to maximize success in conservative and liberal areas in the United States.

Questions do remain, however. Have the straight people really become queer-identified in some way in order to develop this personal identification? And, if so, might the contemporary LGBT and queer movements find this to be a questionable or suspicious tactic? Can we, as activists of all sexualities in an LGBT organization, think straight queerly? As evidenced from over sixty hours of interviews with SAGA activists that provided the basis of this book, I argue that SAGA has accomplished this unusual task to withstand a number of the criticisms from all sides of the identity politics debates. It may be that SAGA has located a (straight) pot of gold at the end of the (queer) rainbow. And, with some hard work, it can create a diverse representation of activists working toward the goal of school safety for LGBT youth. But, as Casey Lina from SAGA Victoria warned us about increasing diversity in organization, "The process is fairly easy. That's not to say the work is easy. . . . It's really hard."

Further areas of research should consider other LGBT organizations in the same locations as SAGA chapters as well, and explore whether or not activists agree that the identity deployment strategies are the ideal. Community-based organizations would find this particularly useful, as it would provide empirical support to many of their feelings about how to maximize success with limited monetary resources and in hostile environments. Bringing them into the research process may be even more fruitful, as it would create a more "public sociology" (Baiocchi 2005; Burawoy 2005a) through a more active engagement with the public at large "not to control them but to expand their powers of self-determination" (Burawoy 2005b: 323).

IDENTITY COALITIONS AND IDENTITY DEPLOYMENT THEORY

This book explored the identity deployment strategies of the LGBT social movement organization Straight and Gay Alliance (SAGA). In this research endeavor, I addressed two specific research questions: First, why would an LGBT organization use a straight identity as one tool by which to effectively achieve their political goals? Second, would the local politics of particular regions of the United States affect the deployment of a straight identity? In order to answer these questions, I utilized the identity deployment theory as posited by Mary Bernstein (1997).

Bernstein's (1997) comparative historical research on identity strategies in LGBT movements builds upon resource mobilization, political opportunity, and new social movement theories to develop a theory called "identity deployment." She found that lesbians and gays strategically deploy two identities: "identity for critique," meaning activists confronted the "values, categories, and practices of the dominant culture" (Bernstein 1997: 537) or "identity for education," connoting that they suppressed their differences from the mainstream values and practices of the dominant culture to gain political legitimacy. Likewise, in certain historical time periods and geographical sociopolitical environments, LGBT activists have utilized a "mixed model" approach to identity deployment.

Although SAGA organizations deployed a straight identity, which is constructed around particular heteronormative gender, race, and class assumptions, the activists often stated that they take a "moderate" approach in their identity deployment strategies. Sticking to this model, their organizational success relied on the necessity to deploy a *straight*, rather than an LGBT, identity in order to gain political success. This deployment strategy was systematically built into the organization from its inception, and has remained constant over time. This is similar to the term "mixed model" as defined by Bernstein, which holds that the identity strategies incorporate both the identity for education and identity for critique deployments.

There is an additional major difference between the identity strategies of SAGA and what Bernstein theorizes in her research: I found that LGBT SAGA activists strategically deploy the sexual identity *different* from themselves, that being the identity of those *outside* of their identity boundary. In other words, SAGA strategically deploys a *straight* identity, rather than a queer identity, in order to achieve its political goals. Even though SAGA operates within the broader LGBT movement, and deploys a straight identity as a movement strategy, the sexual identity boundaries of the activists remain clear. These findings comport with the studies done by Joshua Gamson (1995, 1997a, 1997b) on the issue of identity boundary maintenance in queer movement organizations, whose goals often explicitly sought to eradicate identity boundaries. Similarly, these organizations and identity categories did not "self-destruct" because they ended up re-creating new boundaries of "us" and "them" in the movement by excluding some as queer and not others. As I learned from my research for this book, theorists utilizing identity deployment theory should consider these identity boundary negotiations in their models, noting that strategies do not always include the predominant identity of movement actors.

Related to this concept of identity labels is the important reconceptualization of the term "ally" as defined by social scientists in order to explain the unique circumstances of SAGA, as well as a shared LGBT culture. SAGA members maintain the sexual identity boundaries within the organization by calling the straight members "allies." Colloquially, LGBT people typically conflate the terms "straight" and "ally," or use the term "ally" to mean "straight" people who support LGBT people and many of their causes. In other words, all allies are straight, but not all straight people are allies. LGBT people colloquially consider straight people "allies" because they, by definition, can never become a part of a "queer" identity. Straight people then take on this identity definition while simultaneously existing within an LGBT organization as a member. In this instance, the social scientific term "ally" requires a reconceptualization because it suggests that in SAGA's case, "allies" can be both a member of the organization furthering LGBT interests and goals, but also a supporter of LGBT causes and not necessarily become members of the organization.

Another theoretical consideration of identity deployment involves the special circumstances of SAGA as having a federated structure that operates on both the national and grassroots levels under the same organizational name. In my research, I found that the identity deployment strategies vary somewhat due to the distinct political environments within certain regions of the United States. Activists in SAGA rely more on a straight identity for political validation in more conservative political areas of the United States. In this instance, when deployed strategically, straight allies can bring legitimacy to the message in conservative political environments, while also uniting networks of people and organizations that have typically been adversarial to the LGBT movement. And, although activists in more liberal areas continue to deploy a straight identity as well, they rely less on this as a form of political legitimacy and more on gaining broader access into "straight" social networks as a fundraising tool.

Almost like bookends to the project, the activists in my third (Adam Lieberman from El Reto) and my second-to-last interview (Xavier Lucas from Davis City) made a remarkable comment that requires further exploration. Their concern about deploying a straight identity is that, in some instances, it could replicate gender stereotypes. Their primary concern was that if SAGA chapters were comprised mostly of gay white men and straight white women, then many people would conclude that the straight women were just "fag hags," a colloquial term in the gay community that refers to straight women whose friends are almost exclusively comprised of gay men. "Fag hags," in this stereotype, are typically unattractive, perhaps even obese, and infrequently date straight men because most of their leisure time is spent in the company of gay men.

Perhaps there are differences between deploying a straight *male* identity versus a straight *female* identity, particularly because the straight male identity may provide even *more* political legitimacy as their participation would not run the risk of being reduced to a "fag hag" stereotype. This is a fair foundation to a research question because there is no monolithic "straight" identity, much as there is no one "Asian" identity or "woman" identity, and so on. So, if SAGA activists generally believe that including visible and vocal straight people in the organization is a good strategy, then perhaps straight activists might consider *different* straight identities to deploy depending on the particular circumstances. If there is a relationship between the performance of gender and sexuality, (Butler 1991; Esterberg 1996; Ingraham 1994), and if gender shapes sexual identity concepts (Schwartz and Rutter 1998), then might SAGA deploy *gendered* sexuality performances as a type of identity strategy? And, if so, what might be the benefits or costs to these strategies? Given my research findings as presented in this book, it merits further research to explore these new and interesting questions of identity deployment strategies.

BATTLING FOR THE SPIRIT OF AMERICA: REVISITING THE CULTURE WAR DEBATES

An interesting finding from this research endeavor did not directly arise from my research questions, or even from any direct questioning from my interview schedule. Throughout the interviews with SAGA activists, a number of them spoke that the reasons for being involved in the organization arose from them seeing a sense of injustice, as well as their interpretation that action to protect LGBT youth was a moral necessity. Furthermore, some activists spoke openly about their Judeo-Christian beliefs as being an impetus for their involvement in a lesbian and gay organization. These findings, although too small of a sample to draw broad generalizations to all LGBT organizations, provide tantalizing evidence that the current debates of diametrically-opposed framing strategies in a "culture war" may require some revisions. In this book I argued that culture war theories might be missing the nuances in the interweaving of moral and injustice frames that arise when straight people join LGBT organizations.

As I argued earlier in the book, framing analysis helps explain the process by which SAGA activists utilize identity deployment in achieving their political goals at the national and local levels of organizing, as well as in distinct sociopolitical environments. In addition, the literature on framing debates enlightens our understanding of a "culture war," which posits that liberal people today generally speak in secular terms as they seek to expand equal rights, while conservative people challenge these gains by trying to revert society to a Christian moral one through the limitation of personal freedoms. What are typically presented today as two opposing frames of the social issues used by the sides of the culture war, the data I found suggested that these frames were not necessarily oppositional but, at least in SAGA's case, delicately interwoven.

One of the more powerful examples I found was in Joshua David's admission that, as one of the leaders of SAGA on the national level, he sees his greatest strength as an effective evangelist, which he also notes is also his greatest weakness because of the challenges he experiences when confronted by LGBT people who may mock his personal religiosity. As one of the original founders of SAGA, it became clear in my research that he might have unintentionally shaped the organizational culture to reflect this moral symbolism when he framed the debate of organizational success in absolutist terms: "God is on our side." Although quick to specify that this is, as a gay Christian, his personal belief and not SAGA's, the comments from a number of other activists demonstrate that framing the issue of LGBT youth safety in both Christian moral and secular injustice is not as oppositional as one would expect, such as in the abortion debate (see Rohlinger 2002). This intriguing finding also merits further exploration, as it can have lasting positive and negative effects on not only the LGBT movement, but other movements that may consider utilizing this framing as a strategy as well.

Likewise, further research on movement/countermovement interactions under the "culture war" rubric should consider the ways in which activists on both sides of the debates intertwine the injustice and moral frames of the movements. As we saw with SAGA, it could be unique to particular circumstances of an organization's message, strategy, or even leadership charisma. However, the findings are interesting enough to merit further exploration of organizations like SAGA whose goals are to bridge identity differences in order to achieve their goals. I suspect that with further research like mine, the distinct boundaries in the framing of the "culture war" debate by both sides will be less distinct than has been theorized.

THE STRENGTHS AND WEAKNESSES OF DEPLOYING STRAIGHT IDENTITIES

I completed my book research during a remarkable time for LGBT people in the United States. My partner Abelardo González called me on my mobile phone while I was teaching my Introduction to Sociology course at the University of Texas during the early morning of the 2003 summer semester. After calling a quick break in the lecture, I went outside the classroom knowing that, if he called during lecture, the news he would bring was important. With a heart-skipping excitement in his voice, he asked me, "Did you hear?! Did you hear?! We're free!" On that date, June 26, 2003, in a 6–3 decision of the case *Lawrence v. Texas*, the United States Supreme Court ruled the Texas sodomy law as applied was unconstitutional (Greenhouse 2003). Justice Anthony M. Kennedy went even further; in a 5–4 decision, he spoke for the majority stating that all sodomy laws are unconstitutional and thereby overturned the 1986 *Bowers v. Hardwick* decision (Greenhouse 2003). Immediately, our tears flowed like mountain streams in the spring after a long, cold, and snowy winter. "Yes, Abel," I responded, "You are right. We are finally free!"

At the time of this writing, Canada legalized same-sex marriage. Likewise, the Massachusetts Supreme Court ruled that prohibiting same-sex marriage was unconstitutional according to the constitution of the Commonwealth of Massachusetts. And, much to the dismay of "State's Rights" supporters, Republican George W. Bush, continues to coerce Congress into passing a constitutional amendment prohibiting the federal and states' recognition of same-sex marriages performed by other states or countries, despite his party's platform on protecting states' rights. Although the future of LGBT rights remains hazy in our peculiar political climate, as Bob Dylan sung forty years ago, "For the times they are a-changin.'"

The 2003 Supreme Court case *Lawrence v. Texas* provides an interesting backdrop to the practical applications of the sociological theories and research findings that were presented in this book. Almost sixteen years to the day from the 5–4 Supreme Court ruling of *Bowers v. Hardwick,* the more conservative-leaning court today sent shockwaves to fuel the culture war debates, as seen in Justice Antonin Scalia's dissent. However, the majority of the Supreme Court today sent a resounding message to the public-at-large: same-sex sexual expressions cannot be found inherently illegal, opening the door to challenges to the Defense of Marriage Act. Was this remarkable shift in judicial thought within this brief timeframe due to the strengthening political work of queer people? Or, might straight allies have something to do with this remarkable reversal? I could not directly say if this is an either-or dichotomy, but as an activist who has rarely witnessed the influence of politicians that I lobbied, I find it difficult to fathom that straight allies did not have *some* influence on the outcome, whether directly or indirectly. Recently, I spoke with another queer activist about my research findings. She said, in response, "James Dobson from *Focus on the Family* might have over a million listeners to his radio program, but *Will and Grace* has over forty million watchers. By sheer numbers, it has to be that most of the viewers are straight!"

Like other LGBT-specific concerns, the same-sex marriage issue has sprouted on the community level, and successful legal challenges have rarely occurred on the national judicial level (Cain 2000; Rimmerman 2002). Using my research pragmatically, LGBT organizations may begin to consider following a federated structure as SAGA has in tackling this issue. To that end, being cognizant of the sociopolitical environments in the organizational identity deployment strategies is imperative to assure success on such a delicate issue.

From what I learned during my interviews with SAGA activists, I found that there are some potential challenges to the strategic deployment of straight people by an LGBT organization, particularly that the movement would self-destruct because of the inclusion of straight allies into an LGBT organization. However, I found that this potential pitfall did not occur. Activists found that straight people who speak *with* them and not *for* them will exert political influence and expand the resource and social networks of the organization because straight SAGA members are typically perceived by policymakers to be objective outsiders. However, their greatest strength of being an objective outsider to the LGBT identity was also considered to be their greatest weakness. The activists in SAGA continue to define sexual identity boundaries in the organization, which comports with Joshua Gamson's research on queer movements (J. Gamson 1995, 1997a, 1997b). I find that this boundary maintenance permits the strategic deployment of straight identity in order to achieve political goals. It also ensures that the organization or movement does not self-destruct because identity boundaries remain clearly defined in the organizational identity and the strategies used by the activists.

One issue in particular, though, may benefit from straight allies, regardless of the potential pitfall of including straight people into the organizational fold: Same-sex marriage. In this political environment, an overwhelming majority of state legislatures have passed "Defense of Marriage Acts" (DOMA), the Federal passage of its DOMA, as well as serious pressure to amend the constitution to ban recognition of same-sex marriages conducted by other states.

Straight allies may be a resource for this cause in liberal and conservative areas. If LGBT same-sex marriage activist organizations deploy a straight identity in a similar manner as is currently done by SAGA, the opposition to the amendment may erode. Optimistically, perhaps even some support may begin to blossom. After all, the attitudes of straight people toward homosexuals are more favorable with increased meaningful interpersonal contact with lesbians and gay men (Herek and Capitiano 1996). Straight allies in conservative areas could put a human face on the issue and, with their easier access into those social networks, may assist even further than anticipated. Likewise, in more liberal areas, straight allies could shore up their support in a similar manner and bring in more financial resources as well as we have witnessed with SAGA.

One concern with following this model in the same-sex marriage debate is the inherent contradictions might limit, rather than broaden, the definition of a family. By presenting "family" in a heteronormative monogamous two-coupled model, stable extended kinship or other relationships may find themselves on the defensive within the LGBT movement and with the hearts and minds of the broader society as well. The LGBT movement is a tenuous coalition of identities with competing interests assembled under one movement rubric (Bernstein 2002). If same-sex marriage that mimics an "acceptable" heteronormative model is the only family arrangement recognized by the public and state, then other broader arrangements such as domestic partnerships might be eliminated to the detriment of those groups who cannot or do not want to get "married" in the traditional sense. Groups affected by the eradication of broader family definitions could be elderly couples as well. At the time of this writing, in California, any two people in a committed relationship where one partner is age 62 can register as domestic partners, along with same-sex partners of any age, in order to receive many of the statewide benefits of married couples (McPherson 2005). Eliminating this option may inadvertently force families into a "choice" they do not wish or unwilling to make just to receive medical care, insurance, and other legal rights granted by the state.

For over ten years, the LGBT organization SAGA has found success with deploying a straight identity in order to secure the rights of LGBT youth to discuss their concerns openly. Although there are a number of potential downfalls to utilizing a straight identity for political success, there are also many positives. We must pay close attention to ensuring open dialogues about changing the ways in which this type of identity deployment is structured around heteronormative notions of appropriate gender, race, and class. And then, perhaps "queerly" thinking "straight" about LGBT issues would just do the trick.

Appendix A

DEMOGRAPHIC DATA (GRASSROOTS)

1. What is your gender identity (e.g., female)?

2. What is your age?

3. What is your racial and/or ethnic identity?

4. What is your sexual identity (e.g., gay male)?

5. What is your relationship status (e.g., partnered to female)?

6. In what range is your current yearly household income (Check one)?

    ☐ Under $10,000 ☐ $10,000–$25,000 ☐ $25,001–$40,000
    ☐ $40,001–$55,000 ☐ $55,001–$70,000 ☐ $70,001–$85,000
    ☐ $85,001–$100,000 ☐ Over $100,000

7. What is your current occupation title?

8. What is your position title in SAGA?

9. What is the highest degree you have attained?

10. Your parent's (e.g., mother) occupation:

    If retired/deceased, what was your parent's occupation before retirement?

11. Your parent's highest education level:

12. Your other parent's (e.g., father) occupation:

    If retired/deceased, what was your other parent's occupation before retirement?

13. Your other parent's highest education level:

14. Where would you consider yourself politically (Check one)

    ☐ Not political at all   ☐ Strong Liberal   ☐ Liberal
    ☐ Lean Liberal   ☐ Lean Conservative   ☐ Conservative
    ☐ Strong Conservative

15. What is the primary political party that you are registered or affiliated (Check one)?

    ☐ Democrat   ☐ Republican   ☐ Libertarian   ☐ Green
    ☐ Independent

    Other: _____

16. When was SAGA first founded *in this city* and by whom?

17. When did you become a board member of SAGA?

18. How many board members does SAGA *in your city* have presently?

    a. Out of these board members, about how many do you know are:

    Lesbians? Of lesbians, how many are racial/ethnic minorities?

    Gay men? Of gay men, how many are racial/ethnic minorities?

    Bisexuals? Of bisexuals, how many are racial/ethnic minorities?

    Transgenders: Of transgenders, how many are racial/ethnic minorities?

    Heterosexuals: Of heterosexuals, how many are racial/ethnic minorities?

    b. How does this representation compare to the maximum number of board members that SAGA *in your city* has had since you've been a member?

19. What other organizations were you a member of before your involvement in SAGA, or are currently a member?

20. Does SAGA *in your city* ally itself with other organizations? If so, which ones?

Appendix B

DEMOGRAPHIC DATA (NATIONAL)

1. What is your gender identity (e.g., female)?

2. What is your age?

3. What is your racial and/or ethnic identity?

4. What is your sexual identity (e.g., gay male)?

5. What is your relationship status (e.g., partnered to female)?

6. In what range is your current yearly household income (Check one)?

    ☐ Under $10,000   ☐ $10,000–$25,000   ☐ $25,001–$40,000
    ☐ $40,001–$55,000 ☐ $55,001–$70,000   ☐ $70,001–$85,000
    ☐ $85,001–$100,000 ☐ Over $100,000

7. What is your current occupation title?

8. What is your position title in SAGA?

9. What is the highest degree you have attained?

10. Your parent's (e.g., mother) occupation:

    If retired/deceased, what was your parent's occupation before retirement?

11. Your parent's highest education level:

12. Your other parent's (e.g., father) occupation:

    If retired/deceased, what was your other parent's occupation before retirement?

13. Your other parent's highest education level:

14. Where would you consider yourself politically (Check one)

    ☐ Not political at all ☐ Strong Liberal ☐ Liberal
    ☐ Lean Liberal ☐ Lean Conservative ☐ Conservative
    ☐ Strong Conservative

15. What is the primary political party that you are registered or affiliated (Check one)?

    ☐ Democrat ☐ Republican ☐ Libertarian ☐ Green
    ☐ Independent

    Other: _____

16. When did you become a staff member of SAGA?

17. What other organizations were you a member of before your involvement in SAGA, or are currently a member?

18. Does SAGA *in your city* ally itself with other organizations? If so, which ones?

Appendix C

SEMI-STRUCTURED IN-DEPTH INTERVIEW SCHEDULE (GRASSROOTS)

I. Social Movement Experience

1. What first brought you to [city]? Why did you first join SAGA [City] as a member? What is it like to be a board member of SAGA?

2. Can you tell me about a time when SAGA [City] was [successful/unsuccessful] in accomplishing its mission? If you had to do it all over again, what would you do?

3. Are there kinds of LGBT visibility that don't help SAGA achieve its goals? Are there people in the LGBT community who, when they publicly vocalize their ideas, don't help SAGA achieve its goals?

4. What kind of relationship does SAGA have with policymakers? Does anyone on the board have a better relationship with them than other board members?

II. Identities in the Organization

1. How well do feel board members communicate with each other?

2. What are the committees in your organization? In your experience, is there a pattern to who is on particular committees?

3. What are the strengths that you bring to the board of SAGA? What are the weaknesses that you bring to the board?

4. What are the strengths/weaknesses that straight people bring to SAGA? Are there particular strengths/weaknesses that you think gay men/lesbians bring to SAGA?

5. [*If straight*] How do you feel about being straight but speaking out for the LGBT community as a board member of SAGA? [*If gay*] What are your thoughts about straight people in SAGA speaking out for the LGBT community?

6. How do you think your own identity influences that of the organization?

7. Some people say that many of the issues LGBT organizations address are mostly male-defined, white, and middle-class issues. What do you think about this comment? Do you think SAGA differs from this model?

III. *Thoughts of the Future*

1. What is an activist? Do you consider yourself an activist? As an activist, where do you see yourself in ten years?

2. Where do you see SAGA in ten years? What keeps you involved in SAGA?

3. Is there any question you think I should ask participants that I forgot to ask?

4. What did you feel was the most difficult or controversial question I asked?

5. Is there anything you would like to ask me?

Appendix D

SEMI-STRUCTURED IN-DEPTH INTERVIEW SCHEDULE (NATIONAL)

I. *Social Movement Experience*

1. Why did you first join SAGA? What is it like to be a board member of SAGA?

2. When you think of the local levels of the organization, do any moments come to mind when an organization was [successful/ unsuccessful] in achieving the mission of SAGA? Why do you think they were [successful/unsuccessful]?

3. Can you tell me about a time when SAGA national was [successful/ unsuccessful] in accomplishing its mission on the national level?

4. What kind of relationship does SAGA have with policymakers? Do you notice if any people on the staff have a better relationship with them than other staff?

5. How well do you see SAGA National bridge together local volunteer-run chapters with the National organization? What does SAGA National do when organizations diverge too far from the mission [because of local issues]?

II. *Identities in the Organization*

1. How do chapters communicate with the National board? What type of board structure do you see is the ideal for local chapters of SAGA to achieve their mission?

2. What are the strengths/weaknesses that you bring to SAGA? What are the strengths/weaknesses that straight people bring to SAGA?

3. [*If straight*] How do you feel about being straight but speaking out for the LGBT community as a board member of SAGA? [*If gay*] How do you feel about straight people in SAGA speaking out for the LGBT community?

4. Some people say that many of the issues LGBT organizations address are mostly male-defined, white, and middle-class issues. What do you think about this comment?

5. Are there kinds of LGBT visibility that don't help SAGA achieve its goals?

Thoughts of the Future

1. What is an activist? Do you consider yourself an activist? As an activist, where do you see yourself in ten years?

2. Where do you see SAGA in ten years? What keeps you involved in SAGA?

3. Is there any question you think I should ask participants that I forgot to ask?

4. What did you feel was the most difficult or controversial question I asked?

5. Is there anything you would like to ask me?

Notes

NOTES TO CHAPTER ONE

1. A pseudonym.
2. http://www.merriam-webster.com; Accessed July 16, 2004.
3. A pseudonym.
4. At the time of writing, this chapter does not exist.

NOTES TO CHAPTER TWO

1. This is the pseudonym used by Arlene Stein in her book *The Stranger Next Door* (2001).
2. This particular chapter is not included in this study.
3. Like other LGBT social movement organizations, such as Human Rights Campaign, in SAGA celebrities also exist as "honorary" board members with little decision-making power on the trajectory of the organization. The celebrities are reduced to a fundraising tool; in economic terms, they are the "brand name" to bring visibility to SAGA. Because of the difficult access in speaking with the celebrity "honorary" board members, I could only conjecture on how they consider their role in assisting SAGA in achieving its mission. I leave this question for a further study.
4. In this book, I define a social movement industry as a broad aggregation of social movement organizations that interact within a common social movement category that share similar goals. For convenience sake, we can think of the "women's liberation movement" or "civil rights movement" as examples of social movement industries.
5. Interview with Joshua David of SAGA National, June 5, 2003
6. All names from this research project, including those of activists, are assigned pseudonyms unless otherwise noted.
7. Due to the time constraints from my impending deadline and continuous teaching load throughout every semester, including the summer months, I was compelled to hire transcriptionists at the end of the summer of 2003. They transcribed duplicate copies for ten of the thirty interviews. However,

upon their completion, I listened carefully to each tape with the transcription in front of me to correct the few omissions or typos, and to add audible reactions of my study participants.

8. I believe that this process of approximating the concentration of lesbian and gay people is reasonable, but I acknowledge that there are unfortunate methodological flaws. First, I assume that unmarried same-sex partner households reside in similar percentages as other unpartnered lesbian and gay people. It is less likely, but still possible, that the households themselves were coded incorrectly, as in the 1990 census, to change the sex of the unmarried partner (Census 2004). Also, transgenders are most likely invisible in this census data because one may consider the gender of a transgendered person to be the one listed as one's sex at birth, and not the reassigned or identified gender. This may be misinterpreted on the census data to be a heterosexual couple. Likewise, bisexuals are invisible within the data since they may be considered a heterosexual married couple as well if they are currently living with an opposite-sex partner.

NOTES TO CHAPTER THREE

1. Interestingly, Taylor Lynde is referring to Casey Lina (who identifies as a "bi-dyke") and *not* Gloria Wentworth (who identifies as heterosexual).
2. In Chapter Six, I argue that political environments have an effect on organizational strategy in deploying straight identities, as well as affecting the likelihood of organizational success or failure.

NOTES TO CHAPTER FOUR

1. The majority of this information, except where noted, was gathered through archival analysis of each chapter's accreditation files on record at SAGA National. The names of the papers are changed in order to comply with IRB regulations, and are not available for viewing without written permission from SAGA National.
2. Very few activists spoke about the needs assessment surveys. Those that did, however, complained that only a handful of public and private schools would complete them. Some activists justified it, saying that resources are so tight in school districts that there may not be enough resources to complete it. Others cited the sociopolitical environment in the school systems as reasons for the non-disclosure. Still others believed that because there was no legal requirement, school districts did not feel compelled to complete in when other, more pressing legal issues were first on the priority list. I found no measurable or notable sociopolitical environmental effect in predicting whether activists from a particular region would cite a particular justification for the noncompliance of school districts with the survey.
3. Out of thirty interviews, I only asked one person directly, Xavier Lucas from SAGA Davis City (a liberal city in the South), about how they see the role of religion in the LGBT movement.

References

Adam, Barry. 1987. *The Rise of a Gay and Lesbian Movement*. Boston: Twayne Publishers.
Amenta, Edwin and Michael P. Young. 1999. "Democratic States and Social Movements: Theoretical Arguments and Hypotheses." *Social Problems* 46:153–168.
Baiocchi, Gianpaolo. 2005. "Interrogating Connections: From Public Criticisms to Critical Publics in Burawoy's Public Sociology." *Critical Sociology* 31: 339–351.
Bernstein, Mary. 1997. "Celebration and Suppression: The Strategic Uses of Identity by the Lesbian and Gay Movement." *American Journal of Sociology* 103:531–565.
—— 2002. "The Contradictions of Gay Ethnicity: Forging Identity in Vermont." in *Social Movements: Identity Culture and the State*, edited by D. S. Meyer, N. Whittier, and B. Robnett. New York: Oxford University Press.
——. 2003. "Nothing Ventured, Nothing Gained?: Conceptualizing Social movement 'Success' in the Lesbian and Gay Movement." *Sociological Perspectives* 46:353–379.
——. 2005. "Identity Politics." *Annual Review of Sociology*.
Best, Steven and Douglas Kellner. 1998. "Postmodern Politics and the Battle for the Future." *New Political Science* 20:283–299.
Bloul, Rachel A. D. 1999. "Beyond Ethnic Identity: Resisting Exclusionary Identification." *Social Identities* 5:7–30.
Brockett, Charles D. 1991. "The Structure of Political Opportunities and Peasant Mobilization in Central America." *Comparative Politics* 23:253–274.
Bruner, Jerome S. 1990. *Acts of Meaning*. Cambridge, MA: Harvard University.
Buechler, Steven M. 1990. *Women's Movements in the United States: Woman Suffrage, Equal Rights, and Beyond*. New Brunswick, NJ: Rutgers University.
Burawoy, Michael. 2005a. "2004 Presidential Address: For Public Sociology." *American Sociological Review* 70: 4–28.
——. 2005b. "The Critical Turn to Public Sociology." *Critical Sociology* 3: 313–326.
Burstein, Paul, Rachel Einhower, and Jocelyn Hollander. 1995. "The Success of Political Movements: A Bargaining Perspective." in *The Politics of Social*

Protest, edited by J. C. Jenkins and B. Klandermans. Minneapolis: University of Minnesota.
Butler, Judith. 1991. *Gender Trouble*. New York: Routledge.
Cain, Patricia. 2000. *Rainbow Rights: The Role of Lawyers and Courts in the Lesbian and Gay Civil Rights Movement*. Boulder, CO: Westview Press.
Cantú, Lionel, Jr. 1999. "Border Crossings: Mexican Men and the Sexuality of Migration." Dissertation Thesis, Sociology, University of California at Santa Cruz, Santa Cruz, CA.
Census, United States. 2000. "American FactFinder, Summary File 3." United States Census Bureau.
———. 2004. "Technical Note on Same-Sex Unmarried Partner Data From the 1990 and 2000 Censuses." vol. 2004.
Charmaz, Kathy. 1983. "The Grounded Theory Method: An Explication and Interpretation." Pp. 109–126 in *Contemporary Field Research*, edited by R. M. Emerson. Boston: Little, Brown, and Co.
Chasin, Alexandra. 2000. *Selling Out: The Gay and Lesbian Movement Goes to Market*. New York: St. Martin's Press.
Chauncey, George, Jr. 1989. "Christian Brotherhood or Sexual Perversion?: Homosexual Identities and the Construction of Sexual Boundaries in the World War I Era." Pp. 294–317 in *Hidden From History: Reclaiming the Gay and Lesbian Past*, edited by M. Duberman, M. Vicinus, and G. Chauncey, Jr. New York: New American Library.
———. 1994. *Gay New York*. New York: Basic Books.
Clemens, Elisabeth S. 1993. "Organizational Repertoires and Institutional Change: Women's Groups and the Transformation of U.S. Politics, 1890–1920." *American Journal of Sociology* 98:755–798.
Cohen, Jean L. 1996. "Mobilization, Politics and Civil Society: Alain Touraine and Social Movements." Pp. 173–204 in *Alain Touraine, Consensus and Controversy*, edited by J. Clark and M. Diani. Washington, D.C.: Falmer Press.
Collins, Patricia Hill. 1990. *Black Feminist Thought*. London: HarperCollins Academic.
Cortese, Daniel K. and Julie A. Dowling. 2003. "You Call This the Ghetto?: Gay Urban Space in Dallas, Texas." Paper presented at *American Sociological Association*, Atlanta, Georgia.
Craft, James A. 1990. "The Community as a Source of Union Power." *Journal of Labor Research* 11:145–160.
D'Emilio, John. 1992. *Making Trouble: Essays on Gay History, Politics, and the University*. New York: Routledge.
della Porta, Donatella and Mario Diani. 1999. *Social Movements*. Malden, MA: Blackwell.
Drummond, Elizabeth. 2001. "On the Borders of the Nation: Jews and the German-Polish National Conflict in Poznania, 1886–1914." *Nationalities Papers* 29:459–475.
Duyvendak, Jan Willem and Marco G. Giugni. 1995. "Social Movement Types and Policy Domains." in *New Social Movements in Western Europe: A Comparative Analysis*, edited by H. Kreisi, R. Koopmans, J. W. Duyvendak, and M. G. Giugni. Minneapolis: University of Minnesota.

Emerson, Robert M., Rachel I. Fretz, and Linda L. Shaw. 1995. *Writing Ethnographic Fieldnotes*. Chicago: University of Chicago Press.
Epstein, Steven. 1994. "A Queer Encounter: Sociology and the Study of Sexuality." *Sociological Theory* 12:188–202.
Espiritu, Yen E. 1992. *Asian American Pan-Ethnicity: Bridging Institutions and Identities*. Philadelphia: Temple University.
———. 1994. "The Intersection of Race, Ethnicity, and Class: The Multiple Identities of Second Generation Filipinos." *Identities* 1:249–273.
Esterberg, Kristin. 1996. ""A Certain Swagger When I Walk: Performing Lesbian Identity."" in *Queer Theory/Sociology*, edited by S. Seidman. Malden, MA: Blackwell.
Evans, Sara. 1979. *Personal Politics: The Roots of Women's Liberation in the Civil Rights Movement and the New Left*. New York: Vintage Books.
Eyal, Gil. 2000. "Antipolitics and the Spirit of Capitalism: Dissidents, Monetarists, and the Czech Transition to Capitalism." *Theory and Society* 29:49–92.
Ezzy, Douglas. 2002. *Qualitative Analysis: Practice and Innovation*. New York: Routledge.
Foucault, Michel. 1978. *The History of Sexuality: Volume I*. New York: Random House.
Gagnon, John H. and William Simon. 1973. *Sexual Conduct: The Social Sources of Human Sexuality*. Chicago: Aldine.
Gamson, Joshua. 1995. "Must Identity Movements Self-Destruct?: A Queer Dilemma." *Social Problems* 42:390–407.
———. 1997a. "Messages of Exclusion: Gender, Movements, and Symbolic Boundaries." *Gender and Society* 11:178–199.
———. 1997b. "Organizational Shaping of Collective Identity." Pp. 526–543 in *A Queer World*, edited by M. Duberman. New York: New York University.
Gamson, William A. 1975. *The Strategy of Social Protest*. Homewood, IL: Dorsey Press.
———. 1997. "Constructing Social Protest." Pp. 228–244 in *Social Movements: Perspectives and Issues*, edited by S. M. Buechler and F. K. Cylke, Jr. Mountain View, CA: Mayfield.
Goffman, Erving. 1974. *Frame Analysis: An Essay on the Organization of Experience*. Cambridge, MA: Harvard University.
González-López, Gloria. 2000. "Beyond the Bed Sheets, Beyond the Borders: Mexican Immigrant Women and their Sex Lives." Sociology, University of Southern California, Los Angeles.
Gould, Deborah. 2001. "Rock the Boat, Don't Rock the Boat, Baby: Ambivalence and the Emergence of Militant AIDS Activism." Pp. 135–157 in *Passionate Politics: Emotions and Social Movements*, edited by J. Goodwin, J. M. Jasper, and F. Polletta. Chicago: University of Chicago.
Gould, Roger V. 1993. "Trade Cohesion, Class Unity, and Urban Insurrection: Artisanal Activism in the Paris Commune." *American Journal of Sociology* 98:721–754.
Greenhouse, Linda. 2003. "Justices, 6–3, Legalize Gay Sexual Conduct in Sweeping Reversal of Court's '86 Ruling." in *New York Times*. New York.
Herdt, Gilbert. 1997. *Same Sex, Different Cultures*. Boulder, CO: Westview Press.

Herek, Gregory M. and John P. Capitiano. 1996. ""Some of My Best Friends": Intergroup Contact, Concealable Stigma, and Heterosexuals' Attitudes Toward Gay Men and Lesbians." *Personality and Social Psychology Bulletin* 22:412–424.

Herman, Didi. 2000. "The Gay Agenda is the Devil's Agenda: The Christian Right's Vision and the Role of the State." Pp. 139–160 in *The Politics of Gay Rights*, edited by C. A. Rimmerman, K. D. Wald, and C. Wilcox. Chicago: University of Chicago.

Hunter, James D. 1994. *Before the Shooting Begins: Searching for Democracy in America's Culture War*. New York: Free Press.

Ingraham, Chrys. 1994. "The Heterosexual Imaginary: Feminist Sociology and Theories of Gender." *Sociological Theory* 12:203–219.

Jenkins, J. Craig and David Jacobs. 2003. "Political Opportunities and African-American Protest, 1948–1997." *American Journal of Sociology* 109:277–303.

Johnson, Hank, Enrique Larana, and Joseph R. Gusfield. 1997. "Identities, Grievances, and New Social Movements." Pp. 274–295 in *Social Movements: Perspectives and Issues*, edited by S. M. Buechler and F. K. Cylke, Jr. Mountain View, CA: Mayfield.

Kane, Anne E. 1997. "Theorizing Meaning Construction in Social Movements: Symbolic Structures and Interpretation during the Irish Land War, 1879–1882." *Sociological Theory* 15:249–276.

———. 2001. "Finding Emotion in Social Movement Processes: Irish Land Movement Metaphors and Narratives." Pp. 251–266 in *Passionate Politics: Emotions and Social Movements*, edited by J. Goodwin, J. M. Jasper, and F. Polletta. Chicago: University of Chicago.

Katz, Jonathan. 1997. ""Homosexual" and "Heterosexual": Questioning the Terms." in *A Queer World*, edited by M. Duberman. New York: New York University.

Kimmel, Michael S. 1996. *Manhood in America*. New York: The Free Press.

Kinsey, Alfred C., Wardell B. Pomeroy, and Clyde E. Martin. 1948. *Sexual Behavior in the Human Male*. Philadelphia: W. B. Saunders.

Kowalchuk, Lisa. 2003. "Peasant Struggle, Political Opportunities, and the Unfinished Agrarian Reform in El Salvador." *Canadian Journal of Sociology* 28:309–340.

Lee, Camille. 2002. "The Impact of Belonging to a High School Gay/Straight Alliance." *The High School Journal* 85:13–26.

Linneman, Thomas. 2003. *Weathering Change*. New York: New York University.

Mansbridge, Jane J. 1986. *Why We Lost the ERA*. Chicago: University of Chicago.

McAdam, Doug. 1982. *Political Process and the Development of Black Insurgency*. Chicago: University of Chicago.

———. 1988. *Freedom Summer*. New York: Oxford University.

McAdam, Doug, Sidney Tarrow, and Charles Tilly. 2001. *Dynamics of Contention*. New York: Cambridge University Press.

McCarthy, John D. and Mayer N. Zald. 1977. "Resource Mobilization and Social Movements: A Partial Theory." *American Journal of Sociology* 82:1212–1241.

McDonald, Kevin. 2002. "From Solidarity to Fluidarity: Social Movements beyond 'Collective Identity'—The Case of Globalization Conflicts." *Social Movement Studies* 1:109–128.
McPherson, Bruce. 2005. California Secretary of State, Bruce McPherson. "Domestic Partner Registry." http://www.ss.ca.gov/dpregistry. Accessed on August 26, 2005.
Melucci, Alberto. 1989. *Nomads of the Present*. London, UK: Huchinson Radius.
Meyer, David S. and Joshua Gamson. 1995. "The Challenge of Cultural Elites: Celebrities and Social Movements." *Sociological Inquiry* 65:181–206.
Meyer, David S. and Suzanne Staggenborg. 1996. "Movements, Countermovements, and the Structure of Political Opportunity." *American Journal of Sociology* 101:1628–1660.
Minkoff, Debra. 1993. "The Organization of Survival: Women's and Racial-Ethnic Voluntarist and Activist Organizations, 1955–1985." *Social Forces* 71:887–908.
———. 1997. "The Sequencing of Social Movements." *American Sociological Review* 62:779–799.
———. 1999. "Bending with the Wind: Strategic Change and Adaptation by Women's and Racial Minority Organizations." *American Journal of Sociology* 104:1666–1703.
Moraga, Cherríe. 1983. "La Güera." Pp. 27–34 in *This Bridge Called My Back: Radical Writings by Women of Color*, edited by C. Moraga and G. Anzaldúa. New York: Kitchen Table Press.
Morone, James A. 2003. *Hellfire Nation: The Politics of Sin in American History*. New Haven: Yale University.
Morris, Aldon. 1984. *The Origins of the Civil Rights Movement: Black Communities Organizing for Change*. New York: Free Press.
Morrow, James D. 1991. "Alliances and Asymmetry: An Alternative to the Capability Aggregation Model of Alliances." *American Journal of Political Science* 35:904–933.
Mottl, Tahi L. 1997. "The Analysis of Countermovements." Pp. 408–423 in *Social Movements: Perspectives and Issues*, edited by S. M. Buechler and F. K. Cylke, Jr. Mountain View, CA: Mayfield.
Nagel, Joane. 2000. "Ethnicity and Sexuality." *Annual Review of Sociology* 26:107–133.
Naples, Nancy A. 2003. *Feminism and Method: Ethnography, Discourse Analysis, and Activist Research*. New York: Routledge.
Otis, Eileen M. 2001. "The Reach and Limits of Asian Pan-Ethnic Identity: The Dynamics of Gender, Race, and Class in a Community-Based Organization." *Qualitative Sociology* 24:349–379.
Phelan, Shane. 1993. "(Be)Coming Out: Lesbian Identity and Politics." *Signs* 18:765–790.
Pichardo, Nelson A. 1997. "New Social Movements: A Critical Review." *Annual Review of Sociology* 23:411–430.
Piven, Frances and Richard Cloward. 1977. *Poor People's Movements*. New York: Pantheon.

Plumb, Marj. 2000. "Advocating for Lesbian Health in the Clinton Years." Pp. 361–381 in *Creating Change: Sexuality, Public Policy, and Civil Rights,* edited by J. D'Emilio, W. B. Turner, and U. Vaid. New York: St. Martin's Press.

Plummer, Ken. 1995. *Telling Sexual Stories: Power, Change, and Social Worlds.* New York: Routledge.

Polletta, Francesca and James M. Jasper. 2001. "Collective Identity and Social Movements." *Annual Review of Sociology* 27:283–305.

Raeburn, Nicole C. 2000. "The Rise of Lesbian, Gay, and Bisexual Rights in the Workplace." Dissertation Thesis, Sociology, The Ohio State University, Columbus, OH.

Richardson, Laurel, Verta A. Taylor, and Nancy Whittier. 2001. "Feminist Frontiers." New York: McGraw-Hill.

Rimmerman, Craig A. 2002. *From Identity to Politics: The Lesbian and Gay Movements in the United States.* Philadelphia: Temple University.

Rohlinger, Deana A. 2002. "Framing the Abortion Debate: Organizational Resources, Media Strategies, and Movement-Countermovement Dynamics." *Sociological Quarterly* 43:479–507.

Rom, Mark Carl. 2000. "Gays and AIDS: Democratizing Disease?" Pp. 139–160 in *The Politics of Gay Rights,* edited by C. A. Rimmerman, K. D. Wald, and C. Wilcox. Chicago: University of Chicago.

Rust, Paula C. 1995. *Bisexuality and the Challenge to Lesbian Politics: Sex, Loyalty, and Revolution.* New York: New York University.

Ryan, Charlotte. 1991. *Prime Time Activism.* Boston: South End Press.

SAGA Memorandum. 1997. "Memorandum: Your Chapter Affiliation Status." SAGA El Reto County.

Schroedel, Jean Reith and Pamela Fiber. 2000. "Lesbian and Gay Policy Priorities: Commonality and Difference." Pp. 97–118 in *The Politics of Gay Rights,* edited by C. A. Rimmerman, K. D. Wald, and C. Wilcox. Chicago: University of Chicago.

Schwartz, Pepper and Virginia Rutter. 1998. *The Gender of Sexuality.* Thousand Oaks: Pine Forge Press.

Scott, Ellen K. 1998. "Creating Partnerships for Change: Alliances and Betrayals in the Racial Politics of Two Feminist Organizations." *Gender and Society* 12:400–423.

Sedgwick, Eve Kosofsky. 1993. "Epistemology of the Closet." in *The Lesbian and Gay Studies Reader,* edited by H. Abelove, M. Barale, and D. Halperin. New York: Routledge.

Seidman, Steven. 1993. "Identity and Politics in a 'Postmodern' Gay Culture: Some Historical and Conceptual Notes." Pp. 105–142 in *Fear of a Queer Planet: Queer Politics and Social Theory,* edited by M. Warner. Minneapolis: University of Minnesota.

Sherrill, Kenneth. 1996. "The Political Power of Lesbians, Gays, and Bisexuals." *PS: Political Science and Politics* 29:469–473.

Snow, David A. and Robert D. Benford. 1992. "Master Frames and Cycles of Protest." Pp. 133–155 in *Frontiers in Social Movement Theory,* edited by A. Morris and C. M. Mueller. New Haven, CT: Yale University.

Snow, David A., E. Burke Rochford, Jr., Steven K. Worden, and Robert D. Benford. 1986. "Frame Alignment Processes, Micromobilization, and Movement Participation." *American Sociological Review* 51:464–481.
Staggenborg, Suzanne. 1995. "Can Feminist Organizations Be Effective?" Pp. 339–355 in *Feminist Organizations: Harvest of the New Women's Movement*, edited by M. M. Ferree and P. Y. Martin. Philadelphia: Temple University.
Stein, Arlene. 2001. *The Stranger Next Door*. Boston: Beacon Press.
Swidler, Ann. 1986. "Culture in Action: Symbols and Strategies." *American Sociological Review* 51:273–286.
Tarrow, Sidney. 1998. *Power in Movement: Social Movements and Contentious Politics*. New York: Cambridge University.
Taylor, Verta A. and Nancy Whittier. 1992. "Collective Identity in Social Movement Communities." Pp. 104–129 in *Frontiers in Social Movement Theory*, edited by A. Morris and C. M. Mueller. New Haven: Yale University.
Touraine, Alain. 1981. *The Voice and the Eye*. Cambridge, UK: Cambridge University Press.
Vaid, Urvashi. 1995. *Virtual Equality: The Mainstreaming of Gay and Lesbian Liberation*. New York: Anchor Book.
Valocchi, Steve. 1999. "The class-inflected nature of gay identity." *Social Problems* 46:207.
Vicinus, Martha. 1992. ""They wonder to which sex I belong": The Historical Roots of the Modern Lesbian Identity." *Feminist Studies* 18:467–498.
Whittier, Nancy. 1995. *Feminist Generations: The Persistence of the Radical Women's Movement*. Philadelphia: Temple University Press.
Wilhite, Allen and John Theilmann. 1986. "Unions, Corporations, and Political Campaign Contributions: The 1982 House Elections." *Journal of Labor Research* 7:175–185.
Young, Michael P. 2001. "A Revolution of the Soul: Transformative Experiences and Immediate Abolition." Pp. 99–114 in *Passionate Politics: Emotions and Social Movements*, edited by J. Goodwin, J. M. Jasper, and F. Polletta. Chicago: University of Chicago.
———. 2002. "Confessional Protest: The Religious Birth of U.S. National Social Movements." *American Sociological Review* 67: 660–688.

Index

A

Abortion debate
   culture war, 24
Accreditation
   SAGA National, 88
Activists. *See also* Lesbian, gay, bisexual, and transgender (LGBT), activists; Straight activists; Straight and Gay Alliance (SAGA), activists
   ambivalent, 138
   bisexual, 69
   gay, 2, 154
   lesbian, 154
Adler, Greg, 12, 78
   Boy Scouts, 151
   LGBT activists, 111
   religious affiliation, 109
   straight identity, 108
Affirmative action policy, 76
African American Civil Rights Movement, 71, 104
   white gay males, 72
Alaska, 37
Alliances
   LGBT organization, 15
   NOW, 26
   SAGA, 156
Allies
   Judeo-Christian- going SAGA, 22
   LGBT movement, 125
   political science research, 17
Ally
   LGBT definition, 176
   political definition, 16
   sociological definition, 16

Aloo, Edit
   SAGA National, 134
Ambivalent activists
   SAGA, 138
American social movement studies, 18
Anderson, Marc
   SAGA former cochairman, 165
Anti-discrimination policies
   LGBT, 146
Anti-gay agenda promotion
   LGBT rights, 146
Anti-gay issues
   public schools, 105
Anti-gay legislation, 159
Anti-gay rights proposition
   Oregon, 21
Anti-initiatives
   LGBT, 147
Arizona, 37

B

Bernstein, Mary, 3, 19
   different identities, 139
   identity deployment, 32
Bi-dykes, 132, 194
Bigotry
   public school systems, 162
Bisexual activists
   SAGA National, 69
Bisexual rights movement, 132
Bisexuals
   exclusion, 7
   invisibility, 194
Black movements
   LGBT, 72
Board members

203

honorary
  SAGA, 193
Bowers v. Harkwick, 179
Boy Scouts, 151

C
California, 37
Campus Crusade for Christ, 109
Candor, Amanda
  conservative political environment, 141
  frustrated SAGA members, 145
Cantu, Lionel, 11
Catholicism, 96
Celebrities
  LGBT, 118
  SAGA, 26
Census data
  invisibility, 194
Chadwick, Pete, 152
Charmaz, Kathy, 42
Chicken and egg problem
  SAGA, 66
Chinese
  pan-ethnic movements, 28
Chrissi Williams, 93
Christian moral symbolism, 97–112
Church communities
  LGBT, 110
Civil Rights Movement, 112, 193
  African American, 71, 104
Class
  LGBT movement, 75
  SAGA activists, 61
  sexual diversity, 70
Coalitions
  identity deployment theory, 174–177
Collective identities
  definition, 27
  LGBT movements, 27–32
  political opportunity theories, 27
  resource mobilization, 27
College students
  LGBT, 92
Colorado
  SAGA, 36
Community activism
  SAGA, 94
Compassionate pulls
  United States, 81
Concerned Women for America (CWA), 21, 25
Conservative political environments, 143–163

SAGA, 143
Counter movement dynamics
  culture war, 110
Courageous pushes
  United States, 81
Critique strategy, 20
Culture war, 13, 87, 102, 110
  abortion debate, 24
  counter movement dynamics, 110
  debates, 177–178
  equal rights expansion, 178
  framing identity deployment strategy, 23–27
  movement-countermovement interactions, 178
CWA. *See* Concerned Women for America (CWA)

D
Daniels, Grant, 79
  LGBT activist, 122
  religious issues, 107
  SAGA mission, 135
David, Joshua, 9, 13, 80–81, 92, 98
  evangelical ability, 99
  LGBT activists, 111
  safe school movements, 100
  SAGA interview, 138
  SAGA leader, 87, 97
  SAGA National, 111
Debates
  culture war, 177–178
Deep South
  SAGA, 39
Defense of Marriage Acts (DOMA), 180
Democratic National Convention, 48
Democrats, 48
Demographic data
  grassroots, 183–185
  national, 185–188
Discrimination
  LGBT people, 169
  public school systems, 160
Diversity
  SAGA National, 69
DOMA. *See* Defense of Marriage Acts (DOMA)

E
Eberhardt, Judy, 12, 88, 99
  LGBT community, 134
  religion issue, 104

SAGA board member, 134
SAGA co-chairman, 167
straight SAGA activists, 130
Education
LGBT, 171
SAGA, 33
Eggert, Melissa, 49
Catholicism, 96
SAGA, 95
Equal rights expansion
culture war, 178
Essex relationship
LGBT liaison, 168
Ethnicity
identity, 28
sexuality, 29
Evangelism
LGBT, 98
Exclusion
bisexuals, 7

F
Fag hags, 43
stereotype, 177
False dichotomy
sexuality, 123
Federal tax exemption status
SAGA National, 88
Female identities
vs. male identity, 177
Fine, Cameron, 60
SAGA National, 73
straight identity social privilege, 132
Fleischer, C.J., 50
gay youth, 141
legal challenges, 142
Framing analysis, 23
components, 23
identity deployment, 178
SAGA, 113
Framing identity deployment strategy
culture war, 23–27
Framing theories, 25
Freeman, Paul, 152
public school systems, 124
straight activist, 104, 130
straight policy maker issues, 119
Frustrated SAGA members, 145

G
Gamson, Joshua, 4, 26
queer movement, 180

Gay activists, 2
LGBT rights, 154
Gay and Lesbian Association of Teachers (GLAT), 8
name changes, 9
Gay identities
objective relationship, 121
Gay issues
public school systems, 150
Gay liberalization movement, 75
Gay males
African American Civil Rights Movements, 72
SAGA, 43
Gay movement, 7
Gay politicians, 149
LGBT issues, 151
Gay Pride parade, 103
Gay rights organization
SAGA, 95
Gay-straight alliances, 126
student-run, 22
Gay teachers
public school systems, 160
Gay white male issue
SAGA, 58–78
Gay youth, 141
legal challenges, 142
Gender
fluid, 134
LGBT movement, 75
participant demographics
SAGA board members, 46
SAGA activists, 61
SAGA National Board of Directors, 59
SAGA National Staff Members, 59
sexual diversity, 70
sexuality deployment
SAGA, 177
Geographical allies differences
SAGA, 18
Geographical area
research project, 144
GLAT. *See* Gay and Lesbian Association of Teachers (GLAT)
Graphic material distribution
LGBT activists, 148

H
Harrington, Dixon
straight identities
SAGA, 128

Hell Fire Nation, 112
Heterosexism thermometer
   SAGA, 130
Heterosexist oppression
   LGBT people, 133
Heterosexuality, 1
   relationship, 29
   Western culture, 1
Heterosexual parents, 136
Heterosexual privilege
   SAGA, 84, 135
High school students
   LGBT, 170
Homosexuality
   LGBT movement, 96
   social assumptions, 7
Honorary board members
   SAGA, 193
HRC. *See* Human Rights Campaign (HRC)
Huerta, Ruth, 87
   frustrated SAGA members, 145
   liberalism, 146
Human Rights Campaign (HRC), 22, 88, 95, 193

I

Identities. *See also* Collective identities; Sexual identities; Straight identities
   ethnic options, 28
   female *vs.* male identity, 177
   gay, 121
   LGBT, 4
   queer, 6, 136
   rational-actor dynamic, 30
Identity deployment, 19, 32
   framing analysis, 178
   mixed model, 20
   political environments, 141–172
Identity deployment theory
   coalitions, 174–177
Identity paradigms
   LGBT movements, 87
Identity strategy
   combined efforts, 80
   historical research
      LGBT movements, 175
Ignorance
   public school systems, 162
Impression management strategy
   public school systems, 140
Income levels
   participant demographics, 48
In-depth interviews
   grassroots, 189–190
   national, 191–192
Indian
   pan-ethnic movements, 28
Injustice frames
   SAGA, 113
Institutional Review Board (IRB), 35
   restrictions, 143
Intercommunication meetings
   SAGA, 53
Interviews
   in-depth
      grassroots, 189–190
      national, 191–192
IRB. *See* Institutional Review Board (IRB)
Irish Land War, 106

J

Judeo-Christian- going allies
   SAGA, 22
Judeo-Christian regions
   SAGA, 87

K

Kane, Anne, 106
King Jr., Martin Luther, 104

L

Latinos
   SAGA, 155
Lawrence v. Texas, 179
Legal challenges
   gay youth, 142
Legislation
   anti-gay, 159
Lesbian, gay, bisexual, and transgender (LGBT), 2
   activists, 111, 122, 170
      graphic material distribution, 148
      issues, 69
      SAGA, 123
      straight allies, 122
      straight policy makers, 119
   ally relationship, 176
   anti-discrimination policies, 146
   anti-initiatives, 147
   black movements, 72
   church communities, 110
   college students, 92
   community, 16, 134

Index

cultural goals, 166
definition
    ally, 176
evangelism, 98
high school students, 170
issues, 72
    celebrity status, 118
    education, 171
    gay politicians, 151
    lesbian politicians, 151
    member mobilization, 142
    politics, 118
    queer thinking, 181
    SAGA safety, 153
    statewide level, 159
    straight identity education, 171
    straight thinking, 181
liaison
    Essex relationship, 168
lobbyist organization, 147
mainstream, 96, 98, 128
movement
    allies' population, 125
    Christianity, 113
    class, 75
    collective identities, 27–32
    gender, 75
    homosexuality issues, 96
    identity paradigms, 87
    identity strategy historical research, 175
    male middle class issues, 62
    race, 75
    religion, 194
    SAGA, 61
    SAGA activists, 30
    straight allies, 105
    straight identity strengths, 131
    United States, 5
organization
    alliances, 15, 148
    Christian morality, 97
    mission, 173
    racial histories, 71
    racial issues, 71
    SAGA, 173
    SAGA chapters research, 174
    straight identities, 13
    straight identity weaknesses within, 133
people
    discrimination, 169
    heterosexist oppression, 133
    political behavior studies, 117
    straight world, 129
political success, 175
queer identity, 6
queer movements, 174
resource tool
    straight social networks, 176
rights
    anti-gay agenda promotion, 146
    gay activists, 154
    lesbian activists, 154
    security, 115
    social changes, 142
safe-schools movement
    parental strengths, 126
SAGA activists, 3
same-sex marriage, 180
    straight allies, 181
social issues, 98, 157
social movements, 80
    goals, 15
    SAGA activists, 131
    sociological debates, 15
    Tierra Blanca school district, 153
straight activists, 80
straight ally security, 170
straight culture, 129
straight identities, 49, 164
straight people, 4, 81
straight relationship, 176
students
    controversial issues, 163
    mental health, 161
    public school system conservatism, 163
us *versus* them, 139
youth, 2
Lesbian activists
    LGBT rights, 154
Lesbian issues
    public school systems, 150
Lesbian movement, 7
Lesbian politicians
    LGBT issues, 151
Lesbian youth, 142
LGBT. *See* Lesbian, gay, bisexual, and transgender (LGBT)
Liberalism, 146
    political environments, 163–170
Liberal political environments
    SAGA chapters, 164

Liberal regions
    SAGA, 163, 171
Lieberman, Adam, 24
    LGBT issues, 115
    religious issues, 108
    safe schools movement, 107
    SAGA chairmen, 149
    SAGA chapter chairman, 115
    SAGA co-chairman, 106
Lina, Casey, 73, 194
    SAGA liberalism, 156
Linneman, Thomas, 101
Lobbyist
    LGBT, 147
Local politics
    SAGA, 166
Local school districts
    SAGA, 170
Lopez, Gloria, 40
Lopez, Gonzalez, 35
Lucas, Xavier, 81, 194
    culture war, 110
    frustrated SAGA members, 145
    LGBT activists, 111
    straight identity motivation, 120
    straight identity strengths, 117
Lynde, Taylor, 91, 92, 109, 194
    anti-gay legislation, 159
    political monetary influence, 158
    public school systems, 124
    SAGA, 68
    SAGA co-chairman, 155

M
Mainstream
    LGBT, 96, 98, 128
Male-dominant culture
    SAGA, 76
Male identities
    versus female identities, 177
Male middle class issues
    LGBT movements, 62
McCarthy, John, 17
McIntyre, Trey, 49, 70
    demographic questionnaire response, 136
    public school system alienation, 161
Meetings
    intercommunication
        SAGA, 53
Member mobilization
    LGBT issues, 142
Men having sex with men (MSM), 11

Mental health
    LGBT students, 161
Merriam-Webster Dictionary Online, 3, 173
Meyer, David, 26
Meyers, Anson
    SAGA, 120
    SAGA activist, 134
Microsoft Excel, 40, 42
Microsoft Word, 40
Midwest
    SAGA, 39
Minkoff, Debra, 5
Minority membership
    SAGA, 68
Mistrust
    SAGA National, 51
Monroe, James, 112
Moral frames
    SAGA, 113
Moral symbolism
    Christian
        LGBT organizations, 97
        SAGA, 97–112
Movement-counter movement interactions
    culture war, 178
MSM. *See* Men having sex with men (MSM)
Murphy's Law, 50

N
NAACP. *See* National Association for the Advancement of Colored People (NAACP)
National Association for the Advancement of Colored People (NAACP), 6, 21, 33
National Gay and Lesbian Task Force (NGLTF), 88, 95
National Organization for Women (NOW), 21, 24, 88
    alliances, 26
Needs assessment surveys, 194
Nevada, 37
New Mexico, 37
NGLTF. *See* National Gay and Lesbian Task Force (NGLTF)
NOW. *See* National Organization for Women (NOW)

O
Objective relationship
    gay identity, 121
    straight identity, 121

Index

O'Donnell, Chase, 63
  SAGA straight identity, 137
Oregon, 37
  anti-gay rights proposition, 21
Otis, Eileen, 29

P

Pan-ethnic movements
  Chinese, 28
  Indian, 28
  United States, 28
  Vietnamese, 28
Parents. *See also* Straight parents
  heterosexual, 136
  influence, 125
  strengths
    LGBT safe-schools movement, 126
Participant demographics
  income levels, 48
  political ideology, 49
  political party affiliation, 48
  race, 47
  SAGA board members, 46
Pasquarelli, Vincent, 62
  former SAGA co-chairmen, 149
  public school systems, 150
Petrov, Justin, 64
  parental influence, 125
  Saga local school districts, 170
  SAGA straight identity, 137
  social movement history, 118
Plummer, Ken, 35
Political behavior studies
  LGBT people, 117
Political environments
  conservative, 143–163
    Candor, Amanda, 141
    SAGA, 143
  identity deployment, 141–172
  liberalism, 163–170
  SAGA, 147
Political ideology
  participant demographics, 49
Political influence, 158
  SAGA activists, 120
  straight identity, 144
  straight parents, 124–127
Political opportunities, 19, 171
Political opportunity theories
  collective identity, 27
Political party affiliation
  participant demographics, 48
Political science research
  allies, 17
Political sociology studies
  SAGA, 113
Political success
  LGBT, 175
  straight identity, 175
Politicians
  gay, 149
Politics
  LGBT issues, 118
Power structure
  SAGA activists, 61
Private school systems, 158
Proactive stands
  SAGA, 66, 78
Public schools, 121, 124, 150, 158, 169
  anti-gay issues, 105
  bigotry, 162
  discrimination, 160
  gay issues, 150
  gay teachers, 160
  ignorance, 162
  impression management strategy, 140
  lesbian issues, 150
  SAGA members, 150
  sexual identity, 122
  sociopolitical environment, 194
  straight identities importance, 127
  straight parents
    activists relationship, 127
  system alienation, 161
  system changes, 142
  system conservatism, 163

Q

Quakers, 81
Quasi-religous activism
  SAGA, 100
Queer
  classifications, 173
  identities, 6, 136
  movement, 174, 180
  straight identity, 174

R

Race
  LGBT, 71, 75
  participant demographics, 47
  SAGA, 59, 60, 61, 67, 68
  sexual diversity, 70
Rational-actor dynamic

identity construction, 30
Reaccreditation
　SAGA National, 89, 147
Recruitment
　SAGA, 94
Red States, 144
Relationship
　heterosexuality, 29
Religion, 102, 104, 107–109
　Christian moral symbolism, 97–112
　sexuality, 102
　symbolism, 106, 109
Religious Right movement, 30, 98
Republican allies
　SAGA, 154
Republican National Convention, 112
Research
　cooperation, 50
　geographical area, 144
　interview responses, 116
　methodology, 32–40
　mobilization
　　United States, 171
　participants
　　sexual identity, 47
　sample population, 105–106
Resource mobilization theory, 17, 19
　collective identity, 27
　SAGA, 18
Roberts, Pat, 25
Roberts, Reid
　public school systems, 169
　sexual identity problems, 132
Robertson, Pat, 112
Ross, Adam, 83
Ross, Anson, 50

S

Safe school movement, 100, 101, 107
SAGA. *See* Straight and Gay Alliance
　　(SAGA)
Same sex marriage
　concerns, 181
　contradictions, 181
　LGBT, 180
Security
　LGBT rights, 115
Seven-step method, 41
Sexual diversity
　class, 70
　gender, 70
　race, 70

Sexual identities, 29, 132
　public education, 122
　research participants, 47
　SAGA, 78, 120
　woman, 6
Sexuality
　deployment
　　gender, 177
　ethnicity, 29
　false dichotomy, 123
　identities, 29
　perceptions, 119
　religious arguments, 102
　SAGA activists, 61
　SAGA chapters, 172
　SAGA National Board of Directors, 59
　SAGA National Staff Members, 59
Sexuality participant demographics
　SAGA board members, 46
Sexuality perceptions, 119
Sexual orientation
　term, 148
Shepherd, Cybil, 83
Sheppard, Brooks, 73
　private school systems, 158
　public school systems, 158
　straight activists role, 120
Social activism
　SAGA, 14
Social assumptions
　homosexuality, 7
Social changes
　LGBT rights, 142
Social issues
　LGBT, 98
Social movements, 118
　American, 18
　defined, 193
　LGBT, 80
　SAGA, 113
Social network establishments
　SAGA chapters, 172
Sociological debates
　LGBT social movements, 15
Sotheby, Don, 54, 121
St. James, Sebastian, 129
Starbucks, 38
Stein, Arlene, 101, 157, 193
Stereotype
　fag hag, 177
Straight
　definition, 3

identity, 4
  LGBT definition, 176
Straight activists, 104, 120, 130
  LGBT, 80
  SAGA, 82
Straight allies
  definition, 16
  LGBT activists, 122
  LGBT movement, 105
  LGBT same-sex marriage activist organizations, 181
  SAGA, 84
Straight ally security
  LGBT, 170
Straight and Gay Alliance (SAGA), 2, 62, 68, 81, 95, 120
  accessing unavailable social networks, 129
  activists, 61, 116, 134
    ambivalent, 138
    chapters' future, 35
    class, 61
    demographics, 43–50
    gender, 61
    LGBT, 3, 30, 131
    political influence, 120
    power structure, 61
    race, 61
    research interview responses, 116
    sexuality, 61, 119
    straight identities, 79, 131–137, 131–138, 139
  alliance development, 156
  board members, 46, 59, 134
  case studies, 77
  celebrities, 26
  chairmen, 149
  chapters, 10
    budgets, 170
    chairman, 115
    liberal political environments, 164
    liberal regions, 171
    research, 174
    self assessment, 89
    sexuality issues, 172
    social network establishments, 172
    workshop development, 172
  chicken and egg problem, 66
  Christian moral symbolism, 97–112
  co-chairman, 106, 155, 167
  Colorado, 36
  community activism, 94

conservative political environments, 143
crucial benefits, 135
data collection, 34–40
Deep South, 39
educational organization, 95
education organization, 33
exclusionary tactics, 62
experiences, 171
fieldwork, 34
flexibility, 101
former cochairman, 165
founder, 97
framing analysis, 113
frustrated members, 145
gay males, 43
gay rights organization, 95
gay white male issue, 58–78
gender sexuality deployment, 177
geographical allies differences, 18
GLAT, 8
  name changes, 9
Group Exemption, 89
heterosexism thermometer, 130
heterosexual privilege, 84, 135
including straight identities importance, 128
influential perceptions, 65
injustice frames, 113
intercommunication meetings, 53
interview, 138
Judeo-Christian- going allies, 22
Judeo-Christian regions, 87
Latinos, 155
LGBT, 61, 123, 173
liberalism, 156
liberal regions, 163
local goal achievement, 178
local politics, 166
local school districts, 170
male-dominant culture, 76
members' strategic decisions, 113
middle-class white male issues, 63
Midwest, 39
minority membership, 68
mission, 135
mission objectives, 87–114, 90–97
moral frames, 113
National Board of Directors, 59
national goal achievement, 178
national leadership, 36
National Staff Members
  gender, 59

race, 59
  sexuality, 59
objectives, 122
organizational changes, 84
organizational culture, 101
organizational diversity, 54
organizational mission, 62
organizational popularity, 68
organizational strategy, 30
organizational structure, 10, 52
origin, 8–10, 88
parent organization, 88
political environment strategies, 147
political sociology studies, 113
proactive stands, 66, 78
public school systems, 142, 150
quasi-religous activism, 100
race, 60, 67, 68
recruitment, 94
religion, 106, 108
Republican allies, 154
research, 33, 50, 105–106
resource mobilization theory, 18
safety, 153
sample demographics, 44–45
sampling, 34
self-labeling, 96
setbacks, 100
sexual identities, 78, 119, 120
social activism, 14
social justice involvement, 157
social movement studies, 113
sociopolitical environments, 21
straight allies, 84
straight identity, 116–131, 181
straight males, 43
straight strategy, 9, 115–140
straight vocal allies, 138
straight women activists, 82
suburban focus, 65
synagogue-going allies, 22
teacher focused group, 93
tragedies, 171
trickle down method, 92
United States, 39
universal message, 127–131
us *versus* them, 139
white males, 83, 108
youth focused group, 93
Straight and Gay Alliance (SAGA) National, 43, 73, 111, 134
  bisexual activists, 69
  demographic data, 32
  diversity, 69
  federal tax exemption status, 88
  mistrust, 51
  organizational diversity, 58
  reaccreditation, 89, 147
  steering committee, 91
Straight culture
  LGBT, 129
Straight identities, 4, 5, 11, 108
  deployment, 116
    strengths, 179–181
    weaknesses, 179–181
  LGBT, 13, 49
    education, 171
    mobilization, 164
    strengths, 131
    weaknesses, 133
  motivation, 120
  objective relationship, 121
  political influence, 144, 175
  public school systems, 127
  queer, 174
  SAGA, 125, 128, 137
    activists, 79, 131–138
    credibility, 123
    political influence, 139
    role, 122
    strengths, 116–131
    weaknesses, 138
  social privilege
    Fine, Cameron, 132
  strengths, 117
Straight males
  SAGA, 43
Straight parents
  political influence, 124–127
  public school systems
    activists relationship, 127
Straight people
  LGBT, 4, 81
  SAGA, 9
Straight policy makers, 119
Straight relationship
  LGBT, 176
Straight social networks
  LGBT resource tool, 176
  St. James, Sebastian, 129
Straight strategy
  SAGA, 115–140
Straight thinking
  LGBT issues, 181

Straight vocal allies
  SAGA, 138
Straight world
  LGBT people, 129
Stranger Next Door, 193
Strengths
  straight identity deployment, 179–181
Student-run gay/straight alliances, 22
Suburban focus
  SAGA, 65
Synagogue-going allies
  SAGA, 22

T
Tax exemption status
  SAGA National, 88
Taylor Lynde Scholarship, 54
Teachers
  focused group, 93
  gay, 160
The Stranger Next Door, 51
Tierra Blanca school district
  LGBT social movement, 153
Timbertown, Oregon, 157
Tragedies
  SAGA, 171
Transgenders
  invisibility, 194
Trickle down method
  SAGA, 92

U
Underground Railroad, 81
United States
  compassionate pulls, 81
  courageous pushes, 81
  LGBT movement, 5
  pan-ethnic movements, 28
  political opportunities, 171
  regional map, 37
  research mobilization, 171

SAGA, 39
  movement objectives, 122
  straight identity, 5
Universal message
  SAGA, 127–131
Unmarried same-sex partner households, 194

V
Vietnamese
  pan-ethnic movements, 28

W
Washington, 37
Weaknesses
  SAGA straight identity, 138
  straight identity deployment, 179–181
Welcoming
  definition, 107
Wentworth, Gloria, 51, 104, 109, 194
  SAGA, 62, 157
Western culture
  heterosexuality, 1
White gay males
  African American Civil Rights Movements, 72
White male population
  SAGA, 108
White professional males
  SAGA, 83
Williams, Chrissy, 73, 155
Woman
  social identity category, 6
Women's liberation movement, 193

Y
Youth focused group
  SAGA, 93

Z
Zald, Mayer, 17